Rebel Rising

REBEL
WILSON

HarperCollins*Publishers*

Some names and identifying characteristics have been
changed and some dialogue has been re-created.

HarperCollins*Publishers*
1 London Bridge Street
London SE1 9GF

www.harpercollins.co.uk

HarperCollins*Publishers*
Macken House, 39/40 Mayor Street Upper
Dublin 1, D01 C9W8, Ireland

First published in the US by Simon & Schuster 2024
First published in the UK by HarperCollins*Publishers* 2024

1 3 5 7 9 10 8 6 4 2

Interior design by Lewelin Polanco

Plate-section images courtesy of the author, unless indicated otherwise;
plate 16 courtesy of Jenna Henderson and Andrew Ferraz/
White Rabbit Photo Boutique

A catalogue record of this book is available from the British Library

HB ISBN 978-0-00-868412-9
PB ISBN 978-0-00-868413-6

Printed and bound in the UK using 100% renewable
electricity at CPI Group (UK) Ltd

This book contains FSC™ certified paper and other controlled
sources to ensure responsible forest management.

For more information visit: www.harpercollins.co.uk/green

To everyone who is a nonconformist.

To everyone who thought they weren't lovable or good enough.

To everyone who tries to improve themselves and their lives.

To everyone who has contributed to my life, starting of course with my amazing mother.

To the younger me, who went through it all and kept diaries and notes that I'd written, thinking that one day I might be able to use it.

To R & R.

REBEL XOXO

Contents

ONE

The Drive

I'm driving to Beverly Hills in my matte-black Mercedes-Benz G-wagon, which I should add has extra tint on the windows. Illegal tint, apparently? But it looks cool. I'm wearing shiny DITA sunglasses, an expensive, lightweight Japanese brand that I heard was also a favorite of Brad Pitt's. They ARE lightweight. I don't like feeling a ton of pressure on my nose bridge. I'm sensitive, in almost all ways. "At least my nose is my nose," I think. And that's a rarity in Beverly Hills. I guess I'm a rarity too, a big girl from Sydney's suburbs who came to LA a decade earlier with just one suitcase and a doona (that's Australian for "duvet"). Stupidly, one-quarter of that suitcase was filled with a box of Caramello Koala chocolates—but we'll get to my emotional eating later.

I wind down my window as I emerge from the canyon, cross Sunset and drive down Beverly. It's one of those famous palm-tree-lined streets that pouting influencers love. My fine blond tortured hair blows around in my attempt to air-dry it. I have what's called "working girl" hair—constantly colored and styled because of my work as an actress. At least I have hair—some Hollywood actresses don't. Some of them legit have bald patches from all the styling. I just try to let my hair go feral on days like today—when I'm not working—which means I wash it and do absolutely no styling. It's an attempt to try to strengthen it. Some days when my hair's feral it can miraculously look like it belongs to a mermaid beach princess, with gorgeous soft curls . . . other days it can look like I've been lost out in the bush for weeks. Full feral. Today, it's in between these two extremes.

I'm thirty-nine years old and weigh a beautimous 225 pounds (102 kilos). People say I have "such a pretty face" when I meet them in person, or "You're not as big as I thought you were." Is this a compliment? Who cares. I am a big girl. I'm proud of it. I've made millions of dollars playing the fat funny girl. I'm an international movie star. I've won things—cool shit like MTV Movie Awards. The four Golden Popcorn awards sit in a trophy case I have at my second home in Los Angeles. Because yes, I have two. One house, up in the Hollywood Hills, is where I actually live, with a view of my beloved Hollywood sign. Sometimes I get coyotes and the occasional stalker, both of which freak me the fuck out, but apart from that it's peaceful. It's like a Snow White house—hummingbirds fly around the bird feeder, bunnies come out at sunset in the backyard, a giant deer once appeared randomly just outside my bedroom. Squirrels run across the roof in the morning, and I can hear them while I'm in bed. Some nights you can see the fireworks from Universal Studios' Harry Potter castle.

My other house is in West Hollywood, and I call it "the office house." It stores all my movie posters and memorabilia. I'm not that "up myself" that I have that stuff in my real house. It's all in my office house. The picture of me working with Channing Tatum in an MTV promo sketch (right before he touched my boobs, which I had craftily written into the script and told him to do if he wanted to . . . obviously this was a highlight of my career). The picture of me working with Ben Stiller on *Night at the Museum: Secret of the Tomb*. (I froze my tits off working with him all night, in the middle of winter, but it's awesome to work with legends . . . and when you can get them to crack a smile in a scene, even better!) My original Bellas performing outfit from *Pitch Perfect*, the navy skirt suit and necktie that made us look a bit like singing airline stewardesses (no further boob comments to add). My cheerleading outfit from *Senior Year* that made me feel like

I could do the splits . . . I still can't. My stunt double Meredith can, though. Ahhh, the memories! Wigs from when I performed live at the Hollywood Bowl in Disney concerts. A camera slate from *Cats* signed by Dame Judi Dench, James Corden, Sir Ian McKellen, Idris Elba, Taylor Swift, etc. My Academy membership—yes, I'm a member of the Academy, bitches, and get to vote for the Oscars now. I feel like a success. Especially when I'm in my office house.

I drive past Rodeo Drive with all the posh shops—shops I've never actually shopped in—mainly because I could never, ever fit into any of their clothes. I can buy the handbags, pointless silk scarves—never the clothes, though. I normally wear cheaper plus-size brands that are sold online, to save myself the indignity of having to try on something in a store. I'm a US size 16–18, which is the average size of an American woman. MOST women in America are considered plus-size, but in Hollywood, where I live, less than 1 percent of us are bigger girls. There are only a few of us. Melissa McCarthy, Gabourey Sidibe, Queen Latifah, Chrissy Metz (I know I'm forgetting some, but seriously, there are not many). We're like a rare sighting, the leopards of the LA Private Game Park.

Also, some actresses would get offended if I called them plus-size in this book, so I have to be careful with what I say. This is why, I think, Adele hates me. There was a moment when she was bigger, and some people would confuse us for one another. I'd be in England and people would come up and say, "Oh, I love your new album." I legit signed an autograph once as Adele at Claridge's because the people truly thought I was her and wouldn't leave me alone until I did. I am assuming, because to be fair I've never asked her (she always quickly turns away from me at the few events where I've seen her, as if my fatness might rub off on her if I were near her for more than thirty seconds), that she didn't like being compared to "Fat Amy." Whereas I was flattered by the comparison; Adele's fucking awesome.

I drive past my agency, WME—William Morris Endeavor—on Wilshire, the biggest talent agency in the WORLD. They signed me on my second day in America a decade ago because they "didn't have anyone like" me on their books. The combo of being plus-size, Australian and a multi-hyphenate (actress-writer-producer) was unique. But I'll get to that story later too.

My GPS tells me to turn right, and I pull into the parking structure. I've had instructions to come through a side door because I'm a VIP celebrity. So I drive to a specific floor and meet a special nurse who's holding the exit door open for me while scrolling on her phone. I pay extra for this treatment.

I don't want anyone to notice me being at this clinic, because today, it's personal. I don't want the paps to follow me. They normally get me in my leggings just going for a walk by myself. That's the usual shot that quickly pops up on the *Daily Mail*. If I'm doing something super scandalous or private, I make sure to ditch them through my expert Jason Bourne driving techniques. I can ditch those motherfuckers if I want to ditch them. But today, luckily, I don't have to.

I enter the side door of the floor that houses a high-end reproductive center. It's not as flashy as you might think. It's still more medical than Beverly Hills chic. (Only the following year will they build a luxury office floor especially for VIPs.)

I get a quick glimpse of some other ladies in a main waiting room as I'm ushered into a private room by my special nurse. I see them filling out their forms—some of them with partners, some by themselves. I fill out my forms in the private room—it's just me. NAME: Rebel Wilson.

One of the girls from *Pitch Perfect* told me about this place. We were all having dinner at my house, just us girls, and among the racy sex stories that we all like to share, she had thrown this personal tidbit into the mix. She'd had a good experience freezing her eggs and said it was a smart thing to do. "It gives you options," she said. "Was it painful?" I asked. "A bit," she said. Then we all got back to laughing about pegging. (And no, I won't tell you which Bella is into pegging . . . you can just imagine that for yourself.)

I sit there . . . waiting by myself. Do I want a free water from the nearby mini fridge? My bogan instincts say yes—"bogan" is Australian slang akin to "white trash." I always take free shit. That's why I have an extra house to put it all in.

I sit there thinking. For most of my life, I didn't want kids. I saw what my mum went through having us four—I have two sisters and a brother—and she was basically a servant to us. We sucked on her life-force every time we yelled "Muuuuuuuum!" and then demanded something banal, like "Where's my shirt?!" She did all the cooking, the cleaning and the washing and had to earn money on top of that. She'd breed beagle puppies in our kitchen or pimp out stud dogs in our garage for matings at $500 a pop. (Yes, that was a super-weird thing to walk in on as a child! Adults standing around two dogs mating whilst you're just there looking for your skateboard after school. "Ugh!" I'd say as I walked in on this mysterious dog-sex gathering. You can't UNSEE two dogs having sex in your garage whilst a woman called Glenda checks that the dog has ejaculated.)

Mum got married young at twenty-one and had me, her first child, at twenty-four. Every time I look at her varicose-veined legs, her scars from breast and skin cancer, her reconstructed knees, I see that my mum is a warrior woman—a dedicated, loving mother who gave her all to her children. And it shows. She used to look a bit like Bette Midler, with plump, youthful skin. She used to sing, dance ballet and play guitar. But not after she had us. She gave us kids so much of herself that she lost parts of herself in return. I didn't want to be like that, a sacrificing martyr always carrying a heavy laundry basket of responsibilities up the stairs. No time for herself. No time to shine. Sometimes she says that she probably should've married the long-haired Julian, her cooler boyfriend who rode a motorcycle, but instead she settled for my dad. Settled young. Had kids young. Self-sacrificed like so many women of that generation were trained to do.

Mum told me, "Get out into the world and chase your dreams. Don't settle down too early like I did." There was that . . . and then there was going to a Christian all-girls high school. "Don't have sex, girls . . . it'll limit your possibilities." I specifically remember a teacher saying once, "Even if you call a boy on the telephone, you'll get pregnant and be trapped."

So, I didn't get trapped. I wasn't the school slut who got pregnant and was "asked to leave" the school in disgrace. (We watched from the classroom window as she was escorted off the school grounds with her parents. Where was she going? Some pregnancy shame home? We never saw her again.) I wasn't like some of my cousins who got pregnant at fifteen and sixteen and who were living small lives in rural Australia. I was living my dreams out in the world like Mum had told me to do. I was living a HUGE LIFE in Los Angeles. A bigger life.

I was just driving my sick G-wagon through Beverly Hills this morning. And now I'm off to make a baby.

TWO

The Fertility Doctor

So here I am, waiting to see a well-respected fertility doctor. On the outside my life is a fucking Lizzo song—"It's bad bitch o'clock, yeah, it's thick thirty!" On the inside, well, who cares what's happening on the inside. Emotions, ewwwwwww. I save them for the "very sad, handwritten book" that is my diary (which you'll be hearing excerpts from soon enough! Stay tuned!). But I am starting to feel this biological clock tick inside me. I can't ignore it. I am rapidly approaching the big 4-0, and it's like I am the bloody crocodile in *Peter Pan*. Tick, tick, tick. (Oh, and yes, just to let you know, reader, I will be referencing ten billion movies in this book . . . so maybe as a drinking game, take a sip every time you read one . . . or eat a chip, I don't know . . . I'm just imagining you on a sexy beach right now reading this with a margarita, or bag of chips, in hand.)

I'd never quite thought about my ovaries—apart from when I was twenty-one and was diagnosed with PCOS (polycystic ovarian syndrome). The doctor just put me on birth control pills and neither of us ever spoke about it again. Like my uncle's craziness at Christmas, "better NOT to talk about it."

But now it was like my little cyst-y ovaries were yearning. "Rebel!!! Don't you wanna have kids? It's the smart thing to do." Shit. I am smart. That one got my attention.

Sometimes it was like my ovaries were yelling at me, muffled of course by my FUPA, but I could still hear them: "Hello! Can you hear us down here? We're your ovaries. Activate us!"

My Year of Love, this little experiment I was doing for my fortieth year, was feeling like a failure, so I didn't have a partner. But now I did really want to become a mother. Every time I'd see a baby my heart would feel warm—like the gooey inside of a chocolate molten lava cake. "Awwwwww," I'd think to myself, "how cute." I'd look at mothers breezily sipping coffees in cafés with their beautiful babies: Oh, look, there's a mum now pushing her newborn down the street in a stroller whilst taking a business call—she looks good. Has she had a blowout? Like she's not a vapid shell of a human being who trudges around like the "house-elf" in a twelve-year-old stained nightgown . . . what is this? She's conducting important business AND has a baby. Wow. And then look over there, some cute kids at the park playing. I power-walk by them alone . . . in leggings, followed by a pap, naturally. Can I go into the park? No, better not. That park is for KIDS and PARENTS. That's a club I'm not a part of despite my VIP status. I have created so many things in my life artistically, created a career and a name for myself, but having a baby . . . well, this is the ultimate—this is creating LIFE.

Ummmmm . . . where is this fertility doctor? I've almost finished my free bottle of water and am about to move on to the free candies in the bowl by the window. I am paying an extra $5,000 for this VIP experience, so I may as well.

What am I going to be like when I'm "old Rebel"—like when I'm in my eighties or nineties (hopefully still acting up a storm like Betty White)? If I don't have a family, will I be even lonelier than I am now? Not that I'm sad or anything, I'm crushing life, as I've mentioned. I post a fun picture of myself on Instagram and get two thousand likes instantly. There, that's not lonely.

I think I am becoming slightly less selfish at thirty-nine years old. Before, the thought of putting someone else first seemed alien to me; now it isn't so much.

Yes, it's true, reader, the entertainment industry breeds egomaniacs—and you have to be some level of egocentric to survive. Because in my business YOU are your product. I am my face, my tortured hair, my overweight physique, my brain, my personality. You have to care about YOU. It's YOU that has to perform. So my life, my journey, has been primarily about me.

But meeting the Tennis Player in my Year of Love (and yes, we'll get to that story too . . . sorry, I know I'm a tease) taught me that I could put someone else's needs ahead of my own. I was ready to give up on my own career to follow them around the world. Because of love. It shocked me that I could put someone else first. I was changing—I was different. I have so much love to give. I am READY. Ready to have a baby.

Bang! The special nurse suddenly opens the door and takes the clipboard with my forms. "Ready?" she says.

"Ready," I think.

I get ushered down a corridor and into the fertility doctor's office. Oooooh, it's got a nice view of Beverly Hills below. From up here the people down below look like little Chanel-wearing ants.

On the desk, there are some plastic models of female reproductive organs. There are framed certificates of qualifications on the walls. Photos of babies that he helped conceive, I think. This guy is the real deal. I mean he's kept me waiting for almost thirty minutes and I'm a celebrity VIP.

And then the doctor walks in—he's about sixty, with wiry white hair and wearing a white lab coat. He gives me a "Doc from *Back to the Future*" vibe. I guess he is on the cutting edge of technology. IVF and egg freezing isn't new, but the technology has rapidly advanced in the past few years. Lots of people are doing it. Lots of people have used this guy.

"So. Why are you here?" he asks dryly as he sits down at his desk opposite me. I pause.

Well, I'm not going to tell him everything, am I? That, in like a 30 percent effort way, I attempted to get pregnant in the past year.

That I was going on quite a few dates and occasionally sleeping with guys unprotected in the event that maybe magic might happen. Do I say that?

Okay, before I continue, it wasn't like I was one of those crazy women who approach forty and then try to bonk any random dude to get their jizz and have a baby. I wasn't tricking anyone. I guess I just wasn't scared of being "trapped" anymore. I was open to getting pregnant. It just hadn't happened. I see that the doctor is getting annoyed as I'm mulling all these things in my head. He must think I'm an idiot—most people who see me in movies do. He's a super-busy guy. He has plastic models of female reproductive parts to point to.

"Um," I finally say. "My friend used you to freeze her eggs . . . and I think I want to do that . . . too. As well."

I am not exactly communicating well, though. I feel nervous. Like this might be a bad idea—because maybe if I was meant to get pregnant, God would have let it happen naturally with one of those guys. I did think I was pregnant once when I was very casually dating this guy I nicknamed "the Criminal" and my period was late. One of the *Pitch Perfect* girls ordered a pregnancy test from a delivery app whilst we were doing press at a hotel . . . I peed on it during a break but it was negative. Not meant to be.

I'm a single woman. I don't have a partner. Maybe I shouldn't be doing this?

"I just wanted to ask you some questions about it."

"How old are you?" he says, again dryly. He's clearly NOT a *Pitch Perfect* fan. You can tell when you're talking to someone and they KNOW who you are. This guy doesn't give a shit. He sees actresses in here all the time. He's probably looked up half of the vaginas in Hollywood.

"Thirty-nine," I say.

"Well, you might still have eggs. We'd have to check. That's the first point of call."

Oh, shit—I didn't think of the possibility that I might not even have any eggs.

I am taken to another ultrasound room down the hall to examine my lady parts. Fifty-nine-dollar Eloquii pants off. Legs up in the stirrups. A huge amount of gel goes onto an ultrasound wand that gets put up my vagina. I elect for the female nurse to do this, but the male doctor is standing right there looking up at the screen. I see my ovaries, left side, then right side. They're like two small floating potatoes in the darkness of my insides.

"Yes, you still have follicles," the doctor says. "Phew," I think. For a second, I thought my journey would be over before it'd even begun. They do a blood test to check my anti-Mullerian hormone level, which I'll get back in a few days. The AMH level shows how many eggs a woman has left. It's like a fertility countdown.

I'm told to put on my clothes and then marched back to the doctor's office. Someone's just put a lubed wand up my vagina, but it all seems very natural and normal to these folks. They do this every day. But to me it's weird. Invasive. Emotional. I'm sensitive, as I've said.

"You'll probably still have eggs until you're about forty-two or forty-three. Although I have seen women now into their late forties successfully harvest eggs and have children from those eggs."

Then he looks me up and down. My youthful chubby face, my thick arms and thighs, my stomach, which I think is flattered by the black high-waisted leggings. He has a kind of look of disdain on his face as he clinically says, "You'd have a much better chance if you were healthy."

WHOA. That hit me like running into the sharp corner of a kitchen counter in the middle of the night (whilst searching for ice cream). It hit me right in the gut. I'm not healthy?

Clearly, I know I'm a big girl. I'm "Fat Amy," and I'm proud of it. I know I'm about 225 pounds (102 kilos). Even though I know logically that makes me "medically obese," that hasn't stopped me from doing anything in my life.

When I was filming Pitch Perfect, I looked around at the girls one day—and we're all very different body types, all gorgeous and beautiful in our own unique ways—and I vividly remember thinking: "If we had to do a small triathlon right now—like a bit of a swim, a bike and a run—I wouldn't be coming last." I was very physically active. I had energy. I went to the gym. I was strong. I had fat but I also had muscles. I did aerial silks in *Pitch Perfect 2*, which is like total Cirque du Soleil shit.

I don't have any MAJOR health problems. What is this doctor talking about? I'm not healthy!? I am a beacon of body positivity to so many people, Doc. Young people. "Beauty at any size." "Confidence at any size." People should believe that, right? I presented at the MTV VMAs in a parody of a Victoria's Secret supermodel outfit—and instead of PINK written on my butt I put THINK—because young girls should see that! Young girls should think about how society's trying to force them to be small—because it's in society's benefit to keep you tiny. It's why cult leaders like to restrict women's calorie intake. It's to CONTROL them! But I'm not controlled. I am REBEL WILSON. I am loving and embracing myself despite society saying that my weight is well above normal. Despite people saying "how brave" I am for merely existing in Hollywood, which always confuses me. I am the size of the average American woman, and I am representing. But now this *Back to the Future*–esque stranger is basically telling me, "Stop kidding yourself."

I was so upset. This isn't a bad review that I can brush off—this criticism hits home. But I'm not going to tell this guy what I really think. I'm too polite. I say, "Thank you. I have a lot to think about," as I feel a bit of excess gel on my vagina flaps. I'm now so uncomfortable, but my people-pleasing personality causes me to smile and just get out of there quickly. (Through the VIP celebrity side door.)

I bolt to my G-wagon. "I'm NOT a healthy person? Ha!" I've always thought it's healthier to be overnourished than malnourished, right? All those anorexic Hollywood bitches are going to get osteoporosis—whereas with the tub of ice cream I'm eating every night, I'm safe from that. "I'm not THAT unhealthy!"

I drive home, not singing to the radio like earlier in the day. I'm stuck in classic LA traffic, contemplating. When I'm stopped at a light, I look at myself HARD in the visor mirror. I have some mascara smudged under my eye and I lick my finger to rub it off. But this doctor's comments I can't just rub off. Why?

Because even though body positivity, self-confidence—all that stuff—is so super important, if I'm going to be really honest with myself, I know this doctor is telling the truth. I know deep down I'm engaging in unhealthy eating habits. I know that I am carrying excess weight that eventually could lead to serious disease. I know that my father died of a heart attack a few years earlier, with complications due to diabetes. I know that I'm often in pain after a long day's work—my legs, my feet, my lower back. I know that I have a ton of inflammation in my body because of the toxic foods I consume every day.

I know that at thirty-nine years old, I've trashed my body with junk food, I guess because deep down I think of myself as trash. Sure, sometimes I feel like I'm a success. Some days I feel like I've "made it" or I've "done good." But a lot of the time I feel I'm not worthy. Not worthy of a proper relationship. Not worthy of love. I'm not worth caring about, not by myself or by others.

Why am I so confident in some areas—how could I come to America with basically nothing but the smell of my own confidence—but still have such low self-worth that I hurt myself with food every day?

In screenwriting terms, this consultation with the male fertility doctor was the "inciting incident" for changing my life for real. (That, and, well, I thought maybe the Tennis Player would like me if I was slimmer . . . because don't us bigger girls always think that if somebody doesn't like us it's because of our weight?)

I'd have a much better chance of having a precious baby if I were healthier. It's like I CAN'T LOSE WEIGHT for myself. I tried so many times in the past and it hasn't worked. I'd try for a few weeks and successfully lose like ten pounds or so, and then it would always come back—sometimes with interest. It has to be for a future little Rebel. If I get healthier, I'll increase my chances of harvesting healthy eggs. Which could lead to a baby.

Still in traffic. Sunset's really not moving. Not like my mind, which is racing.

I feel like there's an emotional war going on inside me. On the one hand I'm a proud fat female. I've used my weight to my advantage. I've turned lemons into lemon cheesecake. On the other hand, I'm ashamed of my eating behaviors. I feel guilty. I feel unlovable. Luckily nobody lives with me, so they can't see what I do at night.

I emotionally eat. I overeat. I'm addicted to sugar. Somebody's upset with me during the day, they don't even have to say anything—I can just tell by their look. I feel shit. So now I wanna eat shit. I sit in front of the TV and shovel in a pint of Ben & Jerry's ice cream and half a bag of salty chips for some crunchy texture. (That "look" could've just been a lazy eye, by the way . . . but I don't rationalize it . . . I eat.)

"But, Rebel, do you want to end up like your father? Dead! And do you want a child?"

"Yes. Yes, I do."

I have to act now.

I call my main agent, Tabatha at WME, from the car. "I'm going to get healthier," I say.

Silence. Is she muting me whilst yelling something at her assistant? Then she speaks: "But, Rebs, why would you want to change? You're doing sssooo great as you are." Her voice always sounds like she has a little evil smile on her face, like she's softly suggesting but then will ruin me if I don't do exactly what she says. It's as if she knows that for me, as a human being, it's probably good to lose my excess weight (she did rep Jonah Hill and probably had a similar conversation with him at some point). But as my agent, when I'm her cash cow, it wouldn't be good to mess up everything we're building. She knows she has power over me. She's a smart, important Hollywood agent and I am just this girl who came from Australia knowing nobody. I was so grateful when she started representing me that the power balance was thrown off. Technically she was supposed to work for me, but it never felt like that.

Tabatha, who makes a commission on every bit of work I do, wanted me to keep all the success going. I'd recently had my best year ever, earning twenty million US dollars for *Pitch Perfect 3*, *Isn't It Romantic*, and *The Hustle* combined. (Did you just take three sips or eat three chips? . . . Ha-ha!) The agency liked me fat because they got hundreds of thousands of dollars in commission for each film where I played the fat funny girl, making self-deprecating jokes. They never thought about my mental or long-term physical health. They never thought about my fertility. It's called show business. Not "I'm going to care about you as a human being" business. As I slowly nudge my car down Sunset Boulevard, I look at all these huge billboards promoting the latest movies and shows. My face has been on some of those billboards, and I loved it.

It feels like I'm now being forced to decide—continue to have a career OR get healthier and have a family. Although she's being cleverly diplomatic, Tabatha has indicated that losing weight wouldn't be good for my career . . . that I'd lose my multimillion-dollar pigeonhole. But why is this now the fucking decision?? Career or family?? Well, "because you've put yourself in this predicament, Rebel." Ahhh, there it is—my supercritical interior voice. The voice that's even harsher than Tabatha's, that tells me I'm never good enough. The voice that tells me I've been too slow to find love. The voice that tells me off for eating too many desserts and forces me to get up early the next day and hit the gym. I hate that voice. Is this why I have low self-worth?

I'm the one who has been so fucking dedicated to my career for the past twenty years. I'm now the idiot who, at thirty-nine, is just starting the process of trying to have a baby. I'm the one who is single and alone. This is all because of me and my mistakes.

I call my mum in Australia to ask what she thinks. She's obviously into me having a child—she even says she'll retire so she can help. She thinks I should 100 percent freeze my eggs. This is like the best news she's heard from me in a while. "That's great, darling!"

I'm startled as a cop car blares his sirens at me. I pull over to the side of the road. There's a homeless camp on the sidewalk, so I pull a few meters farther up. For both of our sakes. The cop says that my windows are illegally tinted and writes me a ticket. I say, "I'm sorry, Officer, I didn't know." I did know, though. It's the second time I've been pulled over for this. Just like I knew that weighing 225 pounds (102 kilos) on my five-foot-four-inch frame is bad. I still ate the cupcakes and ordered the box of twelve when one would've been enough. But it's not that bad having dark-tinted windows, is it, Officer?

Who am I hurting?

THREE

Young Rebel

People are always like, "What were you like as a child? I bet you were HILARIOUS!"

"Ummm . . . no. Not really," I say, and then watch the excitement die a bit in their fangirl eyes. "Sorry . . . do you mind if I just . . . Sorry, I'm just going to move past you and into the bathroom." I maneuver around them awkwardly to get into the stall. I lock the door. I hope they're not still looking at me. I peek through the little gap between the door and the doorframe. Why is there always that gap of a few millimeters? Yep, they're still staring. I love having millions of fans, don't get me wrong, but not when I'm about to take a slosh.

They're now debating whether or not to ask me for a photo when I come out of the stall. "You ask her!" "No, you!" . . . "She's much prettier in real life." . . . "What movie was she in again?" "Stephanie!!!! You know . . . The singing one!!!"

The truth is, I was a very shy, introverted child. That is the beginning of this story. Rewinding four decades, and here's the origin flashback for you:

Born prematurely. Born small. Born to my parents, Sue and Warwick, in the Sydney suburb of Balmain, where my great-great-grandfather (on my mother's side) Dr. Robert Stopford settled after arriving from England (via New Zealand). A well-respected doctor and politician, he was beloved in the area because he would treat poor people for free. At his funeral in 1926, thousands of people lined the streets to send him off.

My mother wanted to call me Rebel, after Rebel Bissaker, the little girl who so brilliantly sang a song by the Carpenters at my parents' wedding. But my father disagreed and didn't allow her to put that on my birth certificate. "What kind of a name is Rebel? They'll never let her into Tara with that name!"

Even then, he had planned to send his children to the same Christian private schools he'd attended, so on my birth certificate, I was given the pretty average-sounding name Melanie Elizabeth Bownds. Mum didn't stand up to Dad that day, nor for almost seventeen subsequent years, but she would always pull me aside and say, "Rebel is the name I called you."

We lived in an old house that my parents had bought for fifty-two thousand Australian dollars. Balmain was not the cool, upmarket community it is today. (#BalmainLiving . . . we pride ourselves on eating a $25 avocado toast at a café's outdoor table on Darling Street, wearing designer athleisure. Cue the parade of Cavoodles.) When I was born, it was a humble suburb for the working class. Then one day, as I was just a little bub lying there in my crib, one of my mother's beagles was found dead. This was devastating to her and highly unusual. My mother was always devoted to her dogs, so whenever one died it was as if one of her own children had passed away. You see, dogs were a VERY BIG THING in my family. They were the (occasionally flea-ridden) STARS OF THE SHOW!

My great-grandmother on my mum's side had brought beagles over from England back in the day and started the Beagle Club of New South Wales. Beagles were everywhere in my family. We had a beagle door knocker, framed beagle photos, beagle tea towels, and dog-showing ribbons and trophies everywhere. And if you were to forget the importance of the beagles, here's our family Christmas card with a professional photo of Mum displaying the latest prizewinning beagle on the front.

So, the house where I was born had areas where the paint was chipping off the walls. And like a lot of old houses in the area, that paint contained lead. After the vet's autopsy, my parents figured out that the dog must've woofed up the paint chips, causing severe lead poisoning, which led to its tragic death. Beagles do have a naughty habit of hoovering anything in sight. My parents then took me to get tested as my bedroom had the most peeling on the walls. As it turned out, I had also eaten the dodgy paint chips as a baby. Yep, I was ingesting harmful things I shouldn't have from the moment I was born. I had lead poisoning too!

My parents immediately sold the house and moved out to a "healthier" suburb in northwestern Sydney called Castle Hill. It was still quite rural then but growing due to urban sprawl. It was full of families wanting a nice place to raise their kids about an hour outside of Sydney, and luckily, a mega mall called Castle Towers would eventually be built, with everything we'd ever need to live and prosper . . . like a cinema, food courts, and shops that sold shiny cheap leggings.

I was part of a government study on lead poisoning until about the age of six, which I vaguely remember because I'd get a toy each time the doctor came to visit every six months. I guess they were testing my cognitive abilities. My reflexes. On his last visit, I remember the doctor hitting my knee with what looked like a miniature hammer. Of course, my leg moved—he's hitting me with a miniature hammer! "I think she's fine . . . Yeah, she'll be right," said the doctor in a classic Australian way. He stopped coming round after that. But I wasn't exactly fine. I can recall very few early memories. Is this because of the lead poisoning or am I just a late bloomer in general? My earliest memory is probably this weird one:

I'm maybe four or five, and I'm holding the reins to this giant chestnut racehorse named Ginger, a.k.a. Ginge. The adults, including my father, have gone away to talk. We're on a farm owned by my grandma Nanny—my father's mother—up near Cessnock. Ginge gets spooked by something and rears up in the air. And from my perspective, it looks like this horse is going to come down right on top of me and crush me. I'm so scared of this powerful beast. I think I'm going to die.

My dad runs over and quiets the horse, making "tut tut" noises like he knows how to talk to horses. He doesn't. He worked at the National Australia Bank but was fired under mysterious circumstances. When my dad was eighteen, his life changed drastically when his father was apparently murdered. Well, that's what my dad said. My grandfather Robert Edward Bownds had fought bravely in the Australian Army (Second AIF) for five years during the Second World War. After the war he worked for the Customs Service. He was found dead on the same night that he'd called my grandma Nanny saying, "I've just cracked a big case. I'm coming home to celebrate!" His car was later discovered on the side of the road. Although he was the only person in the car, his bloodied body was found in the passenger seat. My dad then struggled with his final year of high school, only to drop out of college, where he had hoped to graduate with a business degree. He was smart, but with the turmoil of his dad's death, he never fulfilled his potential.

My dad calms down the horse—"Tut tut tut tut. Easy! Easy!"—and looks at me. "Do you like that horse?" And I'm like, "Yeah." (You'll notice one of my bad habits is saying the word "yeah" a lot, like my brain is processing and I just spit it out to give me some time to think.) I should've said, "No, I hate this horse because it just almost trampled me, and why the hell are we out at this farm with these weird dodgy men!" But I'm not good at standing up for myself. I'm just a small, quiet girl who needs her Cabbage Patch Kid to sleep. So, I just say, "Yeah."

"Well, that's your horse," Dad says.

Turns out Ginger was in my name, in some kind of dubious tax-avoidance scheme. It was one of many racehorses that my father owned a "share" in—usually it was something like a one-tenth or one-twentieth share. We'd never be able to own horses outright. And maybe my father's share was cheaper in this case because he was using my name for the tax deduction? These are the kinds of sketchy things that a man who used to work at a bank but was fired under mysterious circumstances would know.

My family was a bit bogan in that way. In the 1980s, pretty much all bogans had mullet haircuts and zero fashion sense, and we wore Ugg boots in all seasons. We lined up at Sizzler for all-you-can-eat buffets with the keenness of a beagle at a dog bowl, waiting for that gelatinous cylinder of Pal dog food to shimmy out of the can. All-you-can-eat meant excellent value! We loved value. We loved drive-throughs, primarily McDonald's and KFC. We loved an overchlorinated water park. And while my mother and her side of the family came from classier roots (apparently on that side we're related to an archbishop of Canterbury), there were family members on my dad's side who had dodgy traits. Basically, you can tell that we have some kind of convict blood running through our veins. I wouldn't be surprised if I went on one of those genealogy TV shows and found out one of my relatives back in the day stole a loaf of bread and was transported to Australia as punishment. (I do have that undeniable love of carbs!)

At Christmas, other families would camp out for hours in the city for the Carols by Candlelight, an Australian Christmas tradition, with their nice picnic blankets and prepared meals. My family would rock up thirty minutes before with one bag of chips that we'd fight over. We'd "do a dodgy" and work our way up to a good position in the front. I'd sneak into a good spot looking innocent, like I'd been there all along but just went to the toilet for a bit, and slowly each family member would join. I'd subtly inch back another family's nice picnic blanket to carve out our patch of grass. Mum would've been happy to sit in the back and not make a fuss, but the rest of us were looking for an upgrade.

My grandma Nanny also taught me to snag food from the all-you-can-eat buffets. "See, what you do is, you wrap it up like this in a serviette and pop it in your handbag when the guy's not looking! Go for the mangoes, 'cause they're real expensive!" I didn't even like mangoes, but I nabbed them from the Sizzler buffet for Nanny. We were also all experts at sneaking into movies when we'd only bought one ticket. We'd call it "the daily double." See one movie and then sneak right into another!

My dad would take me to the racetrack quite a lot as a kid, sometimes with my sister Liberty, who was two years younger. Occasionally, we'd escape the ferals in the regular section and have members tickets if one of the horses Dad co-owned was racing. The Members' Stand at Rosehill Racecourse was great because you could order mini sausage rolls and orange juice in champagne glasses. To us, this was mega fancy! One of Dad's favorite horses was called King Tourmaline. My dad wanted to become king of the track, to be a big hotshot, wealthy and respected, but the reality was that he wore a cheap suit and was never a big player. He never had a share in a horse that ran in the Melbourne Cup. He wasn't SOMEONE. No one looked at my father in admiration. Except for me. I'd look up at him as I snuck behind him into the Members' Stand when there weren't enough badges. We did the sneak. Dad would smile at me. Proud.

I became quite good at betting on the horses—reading the form guide, looking at the odds, placing bets. There I was, a seven-year-old with a bogan spiky fringed haircut (short on top, long in the back) and wearing my one outfit that was nice enough for the Members', mini sausage roll in one hand, while with the other I was giving the bookie $6 to place on number five, race three, "three dollars each way." This is when I was becoming quite good with numbers. Maybe the lead was finally draining from my system, but I could look at the odds and stats of the horses and work out a neat little betting system. One time I won a trifecta worth $800. My uncle Alan tells me that my dad took $795 and only gave me $5. "There you go," he said sweetly as he pocketed the rest. I was happy with the $5, though. I used it to buy Fruit Pastilles, the fanciest sweet they had at the cigarette shop under the stands.

I had definitely been developing since I first started school. When they had tested all the kids in my kindergarten class at Castle Hill Primary School, I was in the bottom percentile. I wasn't stupid. I think it just took a bit of time for my brain to develop. But now I was showing flashes of . . . intelligence. I credit Mrs. Apps, a nice teacher I had in year four who was kind and creative, as well as my mother, who, apart from the dog stuff, was also a public school teacher—mainly kindergarten. Like all the smart women of her generation, Mum was encouraged with a government scholarship to go into teaching. She would read to me every night—mainly Roald Dahl books—and would help me with my homework.

Mrs. Apps noticed that I'd rather sit inside the classroom than play with the other kids during lunch. "Why don't you go outside and play?" she said. I looked out the window at my classmates playing handball and jumping rope. I didn't really have any friends. I was too shy. I didn't really relate to other kids much. I think I was borderline for some sort of social disorder but things like that weren't picked up when I was a kid—not in Australia.

Even though I had my sister Liberty, I would rather have played by myself with all my stuffed animals. My toys were my prized possessions—some Cabbage Patch Kids (thanks, Santa, you bloody legend! That's why I believed in you until I was eleven), one Pound Puppy, and some random no-brand toys that I'd won at carnivals or had been given to me. One was a pink hippo that had a measuring tape around the largest diameter of its big belly, as if to say, "Uh-oh, fat hippo . . . you've eaten too much and now you need to be measured." (Sign of things to come?)

I would spend hours in my bedroom just having imaginary conversations with my toys. I did open up to those rare few people I really got to know, like our family friends the Bells, who lived next door from the day we moved to Castle Hill. Their dad worked in AMERICA and later they owned a Jaguar with a phone in it. They were rich (well, compared to us) and they HAD IT ALL. I was blessed to have them as my godparents. On Christmas Day, we'd usually go over to their house and see all their presents proudly displayed on their neatly made beds. Part of me wished I had been born into their family. They didn't have smelly beagles everywhere, they had MADE BEDS, they ate carefully cut-up fruit as a snack in clean individual plastic bowls. To me, the Bell family was as golden as their children's blond hair.

Our family would fight over a whole packet of Tim Tam cookies, which would be gone only minutes after hitting the cupboard. You had to be quick in our house or you missed out.

"What happened to the all the chips?" Dad would say.

"The vultures got them!" Mum would report back. If you weren't ferreting out the good shit (junk food) and scarfing it within ten seconds, someone else in the family would take it. Mum would sometimes hide a block of Cadbury chocolate for herself in a high-up kitchen cupboard, but us beagles would sniff it out. What other joy in life was there? Money was tight because Dad didn't really work and gambled. Food was joy. Playing with the Bells was joy. We'd play Monopoly—the games would last for days on end. I'd always win. We'd skateboard and ride our bikes to the park. I'd make up a "Mini Olympics"—always with events that I was good at, like how many times you could spin a Hula-Hoop around your outstretched wrist without letting it fall. On some lucky nights we'd have a bonfire and set off some fireworks in the backyard. One time a firework malfunctioned and flew straight into Alissa Bell's gorgeous blond hair. The dads quickly snuffed it out. "She'll be right," they said as a chunk of her charred golden hair fell to the ground. Soon after, fireworks were banned in Sydney for being "too dangerous."

With the Bells I could be myself—inventive, fun, cheeky—but at school, I was too scared to even talk to new people. "Go on," Mrs. Apps kindly encouraged me. "Why don't you go out there? You can't stay inside all lunch." She talked to a bucktoothed little girl named Joanne, I guess saying a nicer version of "Can you play with this nigel?" ("Nigel" is Australian slang for someone who's unpopular or has no friends.) She was bargaining with this little girl to get her to be nice to me, I'm sure of it. What was she bribing her with? A frozen yogurt from the canteen? They were like gold at my primary school, especially on a hot day. She gestured for me to come outside with the others. Mrs. Apps, with her flowing auburn hair, pale skin and red lipstick (totally a Julianne Moore vibe), urged me into the playground.

I walked to the entrance of the classroom, where all our school bags were on hooks. It was only a few steps to the door but my heart was racing. "I can't do it! But this nice teacher can't have me sitting in the classroom for the whole day either!" I was sure she wanted a break. I wanted to play with other kids, not just my god-sisters, the Bells. I tried to step outside and then . . .

I fainted.

Well, I didn't really faint. The thought of having to go outside and interact with other kids terrified me. So instead, I fake fainted.

Mrs. Apps came running in. I gave an Oscar-winning performance of being really out of it. My parents were called. Mum came and picked me up, so I had to carry on my charade for several hours. Did I have epilepsy? What was wrong with me? I don't think anyone took it too seriously, though: "She'll be right" was said several times.

Later that year I broke my left arm in a three-legged race at the school Athletics Carnival. It was such a bad break that the bone was sticking out of the skin. "You'll be right," the teachers said as I lay on the grass waiting for the ambulance. Sadly, I'd fallen right before the end of the hundred-meter track, so the whole school had to wait for the ambulance before the carnival could continue.

Under Mrs. Apps's tutelage, I won third prize in a creative writing competition about bike safety. This was the first time I showed any real skills in English. Plus, I got my mulleted head in the newspaper! There I was, proudly showing off the pink Stackhat bike helmet I had won. First and second place won an actual bike, and they were older kids from the sixth grade. But surprise, surprise, I had won. Maybe I wasn't a dum-dum after all?

I started to go toe-to-toe with the smartest kid in my grade, Scott Farquhar. (Side note: he later became a tech genius, cofounding a company called Atlassian, and is now one of the richest men in Australia.) Math came easy to me now, almost like I knew how to do it before the teacher taught me. Most kids found math difficult. But then, they found it easy to be out in the playground and make friends. I felt like the personification of Opposites Day. I wasn't like other, normal kids.

The day after the fake faint, I decide that I'm not going to sit in the classroom anymore for the whole of lunch. I must have a plan. So, I take my pink lunch box and walk out of the classroom . . . and I go . . . to the girls' bathroom. I sit inside the cubicle and have my lunch there. Through the slim gap in the doorframe, I occasionally see another little girl washing her hands or picking her nose. I eat my plain cheese sandwich. I take a bite and hit plastic with my teeth! "Muuuuuuum!!!" She forgot to unwrap the slice of processed cheese!

Nobody notices that I am spending the one-hour lunch break in the toilets. I'm like my father at the track—basically invisible. I'm not exceptional at sport, I'm not a "cute kid." I'm from an average Australian family, living in an average Australian suburb, with an average-sounding name. I tried hard to "bring it" in my yearly Jazzercise concert with the Bells, but I was back row, to the far left, wearing a neon scrunchie that shone brighter than I did. No one was looking at me. (And by the way, I don't think Mum put me in Jazzercize because she thought I was a dancer—she did it because she didn't want me to be overweight. Jazzercise was a dance form of aerobics that was super big in the eighties.)

But the one thing I am—if not special—is smart and strategic. So right there, with that gross girls' toilet smell hanging around my head, I start making my plan to be a normal girl who has normal friends. That way, despite what I know is true on the inside, I'll fool them all. Mum will think I'm a typical girl. I could get invited to other kids' birthday parties at McDonald's, which is of course my favorite restaurant. My order is: a Junior Burger, fries, a Coke, and a chocolate sundae (with a Cadbury Flake in it). One time I ordered the apple pie, and it burned the roof of my mouth when I bit into it—so I've been full Team Sundae since then.

I walk out into the playground and find bucktoothed Joanne. There

she is half-shading her freckled face from the strong Aussie sun with
her lunch box lid. I walk up to her, and I don't quite know what I'm saying, but I notice I'm putting on a weird accent—like what I do when
I'm playing with my toys. I often put on a "voice." It's not me, it's like
a character that I'm playing. This voice is my primitive version of an
American accent that I've heard on cartoons. I hit my R's HARD and
drop in cool American words I know, like "Disneyland" and "ketchup."
Cool words I heard the Bell girls use. It seems to work. Joanne wants
to be my friend . . . and then so do others. Like the movie sneak or
stealing the mangoes from the buffet, once you get one, it's easier to
get more.

As the school term continues, we play games at lunch that I make
up with marbles and footy cards under the shade of the huge gum
trees . . . and half of us get chicken pox. But I've done it. I've made
friends. The birthday parties at McDonald's are great . . . pass the free
chocolate sundae, Joanne! "Yeah, of course I'll eat yours if you're not
going to have it." If only she knew how weird I am on the inside. How
different I am. But I'll never tell her. I'll never tell her that my parents
fight and my dad gets really angry. Especially when he loses money at
the racetrack. I don't even tell the Bells that.

"What did you do on the weekend, Mel?" says new little friend
number three.

"Well, I had a really rad time," I say in my third-rate American accent. "I went to the beach with my dad and we went in the surf, and it
was like, COWABUNGA, DUDE!"

FOUR

Petcetera Etc.

One day my dad comes home towing a huge yellow caravan (or, as you might say in America, trailer). It's pulled by a Land Cruiser and is the size of a large metal shipping container but on wheels. "Kids, get out here and look at this. THIS is our new business!" he says. Now Dad has a plan to make money: this yellow caravan named Petcetera Etc. We'll tow it around to different dog shows every weekend and sell dog products out of it. Mum loves this idea because there's nothing in the world she LOVES more than dog shows . . . I have a feeling this whole thing is in fact Mum's idea (I mean, a dog-centered business, which means we'll spend even MORE time at dog shows!), but she's letting him have this moment.

"Aren't you excited?" says Dad, gleaming.

". . . Yeah," I say.

In truth, I never felt that comfortable around the dogs. I sneezed constantly and had red eyes and a bit of a headache. I'd feel pressure right between my eyes. (Of course, as an adult I finally did a test revealing I am indeed allergic to dogs and cats, but no one thought to test me at the time . . . allergies, like political correctness and equality, weren't a thing back in those days. This is Sydney in 1987. So, suck it up, you galah!)

I kept my discomfort around dogs a secret. Why? Because our family had a proud dog-showing legacy. Our dogs had agents and sometimes did commercials or appeared on TV—shows like *Burke's Backyard*, a lifestyle and gardening series that was very popular. (Side note: Don Burke famously dissed our beagles once within earshot of my grandmother Gar and to this day she holds a grudge. Don was later Me Too'd for allegedly being a dick, so my grandma was totally right. Don't mess with our family's beagles—they are champions!)

Now the era of Petcetera Etc. has started. I'm seven years old, and I want our family to smell success . . . rather than the loathsome wet-dog smell that permeates my bathtub after Mum washes the dogs in there before a big show. Come on, family, come on, come on! Let's be like the Bells, whose dad works for Herbalife in America—he's an entrepreneurial success! Let's all dress in power prints and back-tease our hair and succeed as a family. Sounds good, right? Petcetera Etc. would combine my father's business skills with my mother's excellent reputation and network in the dog-showing world. This was going to be so cool . . . and maybe, if we sold enough dog products, we'd save up enough money to go on a family cruise! The ultimate in eighties bogan vacations (one family friend had been on one and had only found one poop on the waterslide)!

The whole family would get up before sunrise on weekends and head out to a dog show. Mum, Dad, my sister Liberty and me. We'd pull up to the showground and set up the caravan, placing little bits of wood under the wheels for stability. Pop out the awning and hammer it in using these big old Thor-like hammers. I could barely lift one; they were that heavy. We'd sell things like dog leads, dog beds, grooming brushes and dog treats. Well, my parents sold the products and spoke to the customers; we girls helped out but mainly stayed quiet in the back of the caravan.

My favorite product was called Dog Chocs—carob chocolate buttons in little tins that were suitable for dogs. When I was bored, I would sneak some from the back and eat them. I was pretty fucking bored, so I seemed to do this a lot. I did LOVE the Mason Pearson brushes that we sold because these were in fact the best hairbrushes on the planet (designed for humans but sold by us to dog lovers who treated their pups as if they were). The Mason Pearson brushes had lush bristles and were the fanciest things I'd ever seen. One year I got one for Christmas from the stock because it had a damaged box and was ecstatic!

But before I sell you this dog product dream success story, please remember that we were essentially one baby step above being carnies. Often the carnivals were held at the same locations as the dog shows. Dog showing was considered slightly more elevated, but we weren't that much better than the toothless men running those poorly maintained rides. It's just that . . . we had teeth—aaaaaand when we were in our "dog-showing outfits," we wore blazers with hefty shoulder pads and thought we were classier. But the dog shows in Australia were not like the ones that you might see on TV, like Crufts or Westminster. There were some rich people, sure, but mainly it was everyday people who obsessed over their dogs and would devote ALL their weekends to them.

Most of the time, the dog shows were held at regional or rural showgrounds across New South Wales with shoddy public toilets and flat grassy areas that were turned into dog show rings. I had to listen to the competitors' nonstop bitching about how biased the judges were and how their bitch should've won. If you've seen that movie *Best in Show*, well, that was exactly what my childhood was like. To me that film is not a comedy, it's a scarily real documentary.

I was inspired, though, by my parents' entrepreneurship. They were creating something for themselves! A business. Still shy, I didn't really want to interact with customers, but I realized that my arms were long enough that I could dig around the giant rubbish bins at the dog shows and collect the aluminum cans. Then I could recycle them and make a few dollars cash for each trash bag full of cans. I'd reach into the bin, pull out a discarded can of Fanta, pour out any excess onto the grass and stomp the can with my little sneakered foot. I was paid by weight, so it made sense to crush the cans so I could fit more per bag. The more people at a show, the more discarded cans. Some days "bin juice" would run down my arms, attracting bees and flies. Gross-er-roo. But I was on a mission to make my own money. (When I see homeless people now in LA collecting plastic bottles and cans out of the trash, I think: "Yeah, I've 'bin' there.") Liberty watched as she twirled incessantly on the metal railing nearby like a sugared-up gymnast. She didn't have the same moneymaking spirit that I had. Being the second born, maybe she didn't feel the same responsibility I felt? For now, she just liked to hang upside down. Whereas I was already like a dog running around in the capitalist ring.

Recycling cans was my first real go at making money. Well, apart from two years earlier when I cut circles out of the center of the newspaper and then tried to sell them as "aprons" on the side of the road for five cents each. As the little girl who was given two pairs of shoes per year—one for school, one for sport—I always knew I needed money. I knew that I wasn't going to be handed things in life—I was going to have to get up early and work and be entrepreneurial.

I think Mum was disappointed that I didn't share her love for dogs. She wanted me to follow in her footsteps, in my grandma Gar's and great-grandmother Dotty's footsteps, and show dogs. She wanted me to feel that glory of winning a Best in Show and collecting the grand prize of a plastic picnic set (yes, often the prizes were shit considering the effort people put into dog shows). I wanted to make Mum happy, I loved her so much, so I wiped off the bin juice and told her, "Okay, if you want me to, I'll go in Junior Handlers." What else was I going to do? Sit in the hot car for the rest of the day?

Junior Handlers is basically the kids' competition at dog shows, usually held during the lunch breaks. Think *Toddlers & Tiaras* but instead of crowns, there are canines. There's a seven-to-eleven-year-old age category and then a twelve-to-seventeen-year-old one. Mum says that if I win enough local shows, I could qualify and make it all the way to the BIGGEST show of the year, the Sydney Royal Easter Show. (It used to be held at the Sydney Showground, Moore Park, which today is the home of Disney Studios. Right where we used to park our yellow Pet-cetera Etc. caravan is where huge movies like *The Matrix* and *Moulin Rouge* were later filmed. I filmed a movie there called *A Few Best Men* where the legend Olivia Newton-John played my mother! And currently I am shooting *The Deb* there, the first movie I am directing . . . but back in the day it was where we sold dog products all day to the masses.)

After school the next week, Mum gives me some lessons on the grass in our front yard. You must learn how to stack your dog (standing it still, presenting it to the judge) and then also how to do a series of moves like "running around the ring," "doing a triangle" and "out and back," and the trickiest of all: "the T shape." This is so the judge can see how the dog moves. What's difficult is that whilst you're moving you must always keep the dog between you and the judge. You can never block the judge's view of the dog with your body. That's what a champion handler does. Because it's ALL about the dog . . . except it's also sometimes about your cute face and outfit and the big eyes you make toward the judges.

"Do it again!" Mum would say as I dragged one of our beagles around the front lawn whilst it was much more interested in trying to smell some other animal's pee. Mum was a perfectionist at times. Maybe it was from all her intense ballet training when she was younger. Not that you'd look at her now and think "excellent ballet dancer." She just looked like most eighties mums, with mousse in her curly hair and sporting a parachute tracksuit. I was glad Mum was spending so much time with me, though, and happy to go along with her plan for my Junior Handlers greatness!

"Keep her head up!" Mum would say in her schoolteacher voice as I was stacking the beagle in front of her.

"I'm trying to!" I'd reply. Beagles are hard to control. They are free-spirited.

I tried showing the beagles, but it never quite worked out, so I gravitated toward a breed called bichon frise. They are hypoallergenic (surprise, surprise, I felt much better around them!) and Mum was friends with a nice lady who had amazing bichons to show. They look like fluffy stuffed animals, like the ones I liked to play with, and would wear cute bows on the tuft on the front of their heads.

So, I'm eight going on nine years old now, and today I'm at Castle Hill Showground, bichon on a leash by my side. I'm sporting a little Melanie Griffith–in–*Working Girl* number—a white blazer with shoulder pads, a tight pencil skirt and my tennis shoes. I am ready to wow the judges. Even though I'm still bashful, I'm developing a very competitive side to my personality, so when it comes time to WIN, I can get over my timidity for a bit and deliver. Winning is important and I want to make Mum, a pillar of the Sydney dog-showing world, proud. I grab my bichon and run round the ring whilst Mum looks on lovingly from the sidelines. "That's my daughter," she says proudly. "And by the way, I don't think that basenji bitch should've won the Hound Group. Rigged." Another loser from earlier in the day nods to Mum in solidarity.

"Out and back," the judge says to me. In real life he's probably a bakery assistant who's going through a divorce, but today he's an important judge in a suit. I nod and take off with my bichon. "Thank God he didn't give me the T shape!" I think. I then kneel on the soggy pissed-on grass to stack my dog, constantly giving "eyes" to the judge. He makes us all run around the ring again (good cardio!). There's a boy with an Afghan, which looks hilarious because the dog is three times his size. You can't even see him behind all that hair. There's a girl with a ridgeback who's older than me and gives off a vibe like she's just come off a shift at the outback slaughterhouse. My bichon is cute as hell and has been lacquered with so much hairspray that no one better put a naked flame anywhere near us.

We stack our dogs again in a line. I look at the judge. "Give it to me," I project with my eyes. My posture is suddenly flawless as I hold the leash and stand absolutely still, my dog perfectly posed—front legs, back legs, tail fluffed. It's junior-handling perfection. Girl and dog working together as a team for junior-handling domination. The judge pauses. This is a big decision. Today's winner will receive the grand prize of $5 and automatically qualify for the Royal. I literally feel my nose getting sunburnt from the strong Sydney sun as I stand there, waiting for the judge's decision. Dog show judges milk this moment—the anticipatory minute right before the winner is announced.

He points to the boy with the Afghan. "First!" The boy smiles—I don't know, actually, I can't see him, just the top of his moppy head, but his mother shrieks in excitement from the ringside. "This is fucking rigged," I think. "Second!" He points to me. Well, whatever. Of course, you're going to give it to the only boy in the ring—there were hardly any boys in Junior Handlers, so I guess this was another attempt to encourage one. Why were boys always encouraged and girls were just . . . girls? We only got encouraged to be quiet. Third goes to slaughterhouse girl. At least I beat her. We do our victory lap in our order of placement around the ring and then exit. Adults halfheartedly clap and then get back to their boxed wines.

I receive an envelope with $2 in prize money. Mum hugs me. "We'll need to work harder if you're going to get to the Royal," she says, not satisfied. I huff off, give the dog back to its lovely owner and go and collect some more cans from the rubbish bins. I watch my parents sell dog products for the rest of the afternoon. Sometimes the only place to rest is in a dog crate.

"Why couldn't I be doing something cooler with my life?" I think as I run my little fingers across the bars of the crate. It's like I'm imprisoned by my own life. "I wish I was something cooler, like a professional tennis player," I think.

I loved playing tennis. I'd just started having proper lessons, and my uncle Alan, who had been a really good player, was now a tennis coach. He might've even gone pro if it hadn't been for a freak, tragic accident when he was eleven years old. His coach accidentally hit him in the eye and he lost 90 percent of his vision. My uncle Alan's THE BEST. He tells classic jokes like "Where do bees go to the toilet? . . . The BP." Or "What's blue and shaped like a bucket?" "What?" I say. "A blue bucket!"

Mum didn't think I could be a tennis player, though. "You'll never be tall enough!" she'd say. She certainly didn't want to drive me to tennis tournaments, which were also on the weekends, when all the dog shows took place. That's what Dad told me. Mum wanted me to follow in her footsteps. But I didn't want any part of this, despite the amazing success of Nangunyah Beagles, the prefix (kennel name) started by my grandmother Gar and my mother, which produced more than seventy-five champion dogs. I tried to make her happy, though. Apart from when she was showing dogs, she didn't seem that happy. She didn't seem that happy with my father . . . I'd started to notice that he was constantly criticizing her and putting her down. Telling her that she couldn't work outside the business (she quit her public school teaching job), that she spent too much time with us kids and not him, that she spent too much time with the dogs and not him, or that she confided in her mother too much. With him, Mum couldn't win. But she could win in the ring at the dog shows. And that would make her smile.

Often, whenever we stopped to get petrol, Mum would buy a bag of lollies (Australian for "candies") for us to share. That's the other time we'd see her smile—walking back to the car waving a bag of lollies as if to say, "Don't worry, girls, everything will be all right, look what I have for us!" Sometimes even after we'd driven home, Mum would just sit by herself in the car parked outside. "What is she doing out there, just sitting in the car by herself?" I'd think. I guess it was the only time she could truly be alone and have a moment of quiet.

One weekend we get home from a dog show and everyone is exhausted. It's been one of those really hot Sydney summer days, where it's like 95 degrees Fahrenheit (35 in Celsius) and that muggy heat lingers at night. Dad parks our giant yellow caravan in front of our house and tells us all to get inside. Turns out Petcetera Etc. is a hard business. Driving to the various dog shows, the setup, standing on your feet wearing a bum bag (or "fanny pack" in the US) and selling all day—plus the dog showing on top of all that—it's a lot. We all smell like dogs and sweat.

I'm arguing with my sister Liberty, who is naturally skinnier and more sociable than I am—both of which annoy me. I'm an introvert and like to do my own thing, whereas she always wants to hang around me. This also annoys me. My sister is sweet, though, she's always smiling through her jagged baby teeth—always wanting to be part of things. So now we BOTH have big blunt fringes like the Olsen twins from *Full House*. So annoying. Mum recently had the brain wave to try to help us get along better by making us share a bedroom. Great idea, Mum! NOT! I loved my imaginary playtime in my bedroom BY MYSELF. "Sharing" with Libby is a nightmare.

So, naturally, I put a line straight down the middle of the bedroom and told Libby, "This is my side. That's your side. You are NEVER to come onto my side of the room EVER!" The problem for my sister was that the door to the bedroom was on my side of the room, so whenever Libby wanted to enter, she'd have to make a running leap to get to her side without setting foot in my area. Exactly like Mum, she did ballet and was weirdly good at leaping.

But tonight, we're all too hot and tired to care about my rules. I say to Liberty, "Let's get the face washers from the bathroom and wet them so we can wet our faces and cool ourselves down." Liberty agrees to my genius plan. She even improves on it by pouring cold water from the fridge on the washcloths. It's too hot for bedsheets, so we take them off and cool ourselves down with the dripping-wet face washers. Then I get a brain wave: "Why don't we just wet the whole mattress? We'll be soooo much cooler." Liberty goes along with this, because I'm the smarter, older one and of course she wants to do it if I think it's a good idea. We wet my mattress and lie in the dampness, finally cooling down and grinning as we stare up at the glow-in-the-dark stars that I've put on my side of the ceiling. We're very, very pleased with our new cooling invention.

Dad comes in. "What the hell are you two doing?!"

"Nothing," we both say.

He touches the mattress and feels it's damp. I think he believes we've wet the bed or something. "What have you two done?"

"Nothing!" I say.

But in a split second he goes from being our dad to becoming a red-faced angry giant. It's like veins suddenly pop out of his face, and his head is a veiny balloon that's about to burst. "That's it! I'm sick of you!" he says. He brings his palm up to his cheek and, with the full force of a strong, stocky adult man, hits me as I'm lying there on the wet mattress. Whack. Whack. Whack. He hits my sister too. But I'm the oldest, I'm supposed to be responsible, so I get it the hardest. Then after about thirty seconds of terror, he leaves. We're left with red marks on our arms and legs where we've tried to defend ourselves against the blows. I look at my sister and we don't say anything, but we communicate with our eyes. Our dad loves us, but we were just too naughty this time. We went really overboard trying to cool ourselves. We deserve this. At least our dad didn't use a belt like our friend Shane's dad, who left him with worse bruises. Our red patches will definitely go down by morning.

I remove the line dividing our bedroom. There's no reason now to fight with my sister.

In the car the next morning, as we're heading to yet another dog show, we stop at the petrol station. Liberty and I watch through the back window to see whether Mum will come out with a treat. The electric sliding doors open, and she walks out. We can't see her hands. We can't see anything sticking out of her handbag. Dad, who's driving, tells her to hurry up, and Mum gets in the car. We drive off and after a few seconds Mum surreptitiously passes us a bag of Allen's jelly snakes (Allen's is the most popular candy brand in Australia). We sit in the backseat and chew them . . . trying not to crackle the packet too much and attract Dad's attention. Minutes later Mum discreetly stretches her hand back to us. Libby places two jelly snakes in Mum's hand. We can sacrifice two. Mum closes her fist and sneaks the jelly snakes into her mouth so my father can't see what she's doing.

We never talk about what happened the night before.

We arrive at the dog show, and I try to win the Junior Handlers for Mum and help with the business for Dad. He seems fine now. He grins at an iconic dog shower who always dresses in all purple as they purchase a dog bed, and he pockets the $10 cash in his bum bag. "Have a good day!" he says nicely. The red-faced giant only came in flashes, only in private—when it was just the family at home. When we were out and about at the dog shows, he was the high-flying businessman who eagerly sold pooper scoopers. But I guess at home he was angry. He could be fine for days at a time, sometimes weeks. But the anger would always bubble up. Anger that his father was murdered when he was eighteen. Anger that he hadn't completed college and gotten a better job. Anger that no one knew his name. Anger that now, with the arrival of my brother, he had three children to support and the stress of that weighed heavily on him.

The roving weekend Petcetera Etc. and the mail-order business we started out of our garage were a success for our family. Mum and Dad worked tirelessly to make it so. They could now afford Tara, the private Christian high school that I was destined to go to from birth. Well, maybe, if Dad didn't gamble all the profits.

We did eventually book a holiday on *Fairstar*, "the Funship"—a massive cruise boat that left Sydney and sailed to nearby Pacific Islands like Vanuatu, New Caledonia and Fiji. It was a treat because we'd all been so good . . . well, except for my brother, who was now like a little Tasmanian Devil with his ADD toddler antics. But he was a blond-haired boy, so he got away with it and it was just deemed "cute." We traveled with Shane's family and we each had a cabin on the second bottom level of the boat with two sets of bunk beds and a small porthole window that was mainly covered by ocean because we were so far below. But to us this was heaven. It was endless all-you-can-eat buffets, and there was a kids club, and I got to run around Champagne Island and collect coconuts. No bin juice there! It was paradise. We'd worked hard and now could enjoy the rewards.

We loved the *Fairstar* so much that we went a second time when my youngest sister, Anna, was a baby. There's a professional picture taken of us on the gangplank as we are about to board. There we all are. A father, a mother, three daughters and one spunky son. We all smile and look like a happy family. This is where selling pooper scoopers can get you!

FIVE

Sweet Tooth

I've always had a sweet tooth. I love lollies, I love chocolate, I love ice cream. I love anything sugary and sweet. The first prayer I ever remember saying was to ask God to let me win the Easter raffle at the dog show, where the prize was a giant basket of chocolate eggs. I prayed all weekend, desperate to win.

"Dear God, if you really exist, then you must give me a sign. You have to make me win the raffle this weekend. And if I don't win then I'm not even joking, I'm going to worship a different god . . . like one from Japan." (Dad had enrolled me in Japanese lessons that year because apparently the ability to speak an Asian language was going to be highly sought-after in the future business world.)

And then: HOLY JESUS, I did win the raffle! I bloody won it! "Arigato!" The smile on my face was bigger than my whole head, and I took the huge basket to a quiet corner and started eating the whole thing, egg by egg. I don't have an off switch when it comes to sweets. It's never too much, it's never too sweet.

"Thank you, God Jesus! I knew you were real, and I was totally kidding about that Japanese god 'Shinobu-son.' I will never doubt you ever again."

About two hundred people entered that raffle, so it was pretty miraculous. I am generally lucky, though. One time I won a giant block of

Cadbury chocolate that was the height of a tween in a massive game of
Heads or Tails with five hundred players. Two years in a row, I won a
trip for my whole class to visit the World's Greatest Chocolate Factory
(that was its name . . . I'm sure there were other chocolate factories
that were indeed greater). We all got large bags of free chocolate offcuts to take home. I also won a Sega Master System in a newspaper
competition, and I played it so much in a year that even to this day, I
find it hard to straighten my thumbs. When I was new to Hollywood, I
even won two business-class flights to Australia at a pre-Oscars party.
Thank you, Lord God!

By the time I was ten years old, there were other kids at the dog
shows collecting cans, copying my idea to make money. But then I had
an amazing brain wave—what if I start my own side business, next to
Petcetera Etc., selling lollies!

I go to the Australian equivalent of Costco, which is called Camp-
bells Cash & Carry, and I select large boxes of bulk candies. I set up
at the dog shows, commandeering a dog-grooming table and doing my
best bubble writing on a cardboard sign that says "LOLLY SHOP."
Now, with my own bum bag strapped around my waist, I have my own
float so I can give customers change. This is my first business. And I
sell, sell, sell.

My biggest sellers are white and milk chocolate frogs, which go for
ten cents each. But I also sell Allen's lollies (Allen's is the most popular candy brand in Australia), Chupa Chups and a few other things.
My storeroom is the corner of my bedroom (in the space that used to
be Liberty's half; luckily Mum moved her back into her own room, as
we are now getting along). Do I sneakily wake up at night and eat the
lollies? Yes. I call it "eating into my own profits."

"You have to employ your sister," Mum turns to me and says one day.

"No way!! Whyyyyyyy!?!" I'm living the dream. And it's truly a sweet
one. I'm making about $100 (AUD) on a good day, plus I have access
to all the lollies that I want. "I don't want to employ Libby, she's annoying!" I say. But I need Petcetera Etc. for my venture, so I need to make

a deal. On busy days, I employ my sister and share some of the profits with her . . . like $5 max. Let's not go crazy!

My little business is doing so well that the adult food vendors, the guys who have the pancake and toasted-sandwich food trucks, start to complain that I'm not paying rent. They go from "Oh, wow, this young girl is so enterprising" to "We want her gone." I overhear them arguing with my parents. It's my first taste of others' jealousy over my success. It's weird that they see me as such a threat. But as a child, I can't afford to pay rent for ground space, so I feel forced to shut down the business. I do have a lot of spending money for the *Fairstar* cruise, though . . . I'm what you'd call a "cashed-up bogan." I buy toys, I buy postcards, I buy . . . more lollies.

Life is going pretty okay. I've made a new best friend—a boy named Michael who moved into the house behind ours. His family fled the Middle East and came to Australia to begin a new life. Michael is really sporty. We play tennis together, we play handball in the street, we go ten-pin bowling and roller-skate in his garage whilst we listen to his Michael Jackson cassette. We're in the same grade at primary school. Because he's so good at sports, he's popular and has social currency. He's my first crush, but I'm too innocent to even realize it. I just know he's my best friend and I love hanging out with him.

I tell my mum that I don't want to catch the bus to school anymore, that I'd rather walk the few miles because it would be better for my fitness. In truth, it's about going to the candy shop before class to buy sweets for the day with the remaining profits from my now-shuttered shop. The stash in my bedroom is gone, eaten of course, so I now need a new supply of sugar. Each morning I walk into the milk bar (the Australian equivalent of a general store) on Castle Hill's main street and spend a few dollars buying a huge bag of mixed lollies. Then I sit at the back of my fifth-grade classroom slowly eating them throughout the morning. It's comfort. It's warmth. My teacher is showing us the times tables, but that is easy for me. I don't need to listen. I'm just in total sugar heaven. Yummy, yummy, yum-yum.

I do this for a couple of weeks and then suddenly, the teacher busts me. She catches me digging into this giant bag I have tucked between my belly and the desk. She gives me a horrified look. "What are you doing, Melanie?!" It's clear what I'm doing. I'm eating lollies behind my desk. "Why are you doing that? That's not right," she barks.

I've still got half a red jelly frog in my mouth that I am trying to chew. The teacher grabs the bag and gives me a disgusted look and I feel really embarrassed. She sends me to detention at lunchtime, where I must write "I will not eat lollies in class" one hundred times on the chalkboard.

But everyone ate sweets, I thought. It was a really great way to make yourself feel better when you were sad or anxious. It numbed those feelings. We had sugar at birthday parties and Christmas. When we'd go out for afternoon tea after school, my grandma Gar gave me treats like donuts or a caramel slice—a cookie bar with a biscuit base, soft caramel filling and chocolate topping. Those are some of my most treasured times with my grandma: afternoon tea treats. My other grandma, Nanny, taught me how to make pancakes from a very young age. It was the first "meal" I learned to cook.

"What are those little black things in the flour, Nanny?" I said as I stirred the pancake mixture.

"Oh, don't worry about that. They're weevils. They'll die in the pan."

I was growing out of my stuffed toy collection by this point. Now I had Michael, my cute next-door neighbor, as my best friend and lollies as my other friends and confidants. I just wouldn't eat lollies in class anymore. I'd eat them in secret.

Forget about Dad's angry outbursts. Forget about his stressing over whether he could afford to send me to private high school (which was only a year away now, as high school typically begins at age eleven or twelve in Australia). Forget that he says that if I don't go to a private high school, I won't have any chance of succeeding in my life. Forget about all that. Eat the lollies. Feel that sweetness. Feel the comfort.

I think I have one of those brains where eating sugar is like taking a hit of cocaine. My face lights up when I eat it. Many people have told me that my eyes literally sparkle! (My production company, which has now produced stage shows, TV series and three big Hollywood films to date, is called . . . Camp Sugar.)

This "not taking the bus" initiative was my first attempt to rationalize bad eating habits. I'd say: "Well, I walked all the way to school, a few kilometers, so therefore I've earned my bag of sweets for the day." Later, when I was at my heaviest as an adult, about 253 pounds (115 kilos), the bargain would be: "Well, I've worked hard all day and/or I have gone to the gym today, so therefore I've earned that whole block of chocolate or tub of ice cream at night." (The reality is, though, you can't out-train a bad diet.) I was making bargains with myself, from as early as ten years old, where I was the clear loser, but I kept making those dodgy deals day after day.

Later that term we had a fête where students would do various things to raise money for the school. I did a "guess the number of lollies in the jar" competition. Mum bought the lollies (Sherbies, Fantales, Jaffas . . . allllll the good shit!) and I counted each and every one meticulously as they went into a large glass jar. I, of course, told Liberty that the exact number was 897. I made her line up with the other kids, and surprise, surprise, she guessed the right number. Liberty brought the huge jar home as the winner. Those poor Castle Hill Primary School suckers who held the jar and tried to win with their ten-cent guesses never had a chance.

Mum looked us up and down like a CIA agent. She was now suspicious. I had obviously struck a secret deal with Liberty to share the spoils when we got home. But we weren't about to admit that to Mum. What was she going to do? Call up the school and reveal our deception? Instead, Mum, after staring into our souls, said, "Well, are you going to give me some?" As we sat around our small circular dining table, our hands went one by one into the glass jar like hens' beaks at a battery farm feeding trough. The three of us were in this together. This was our form of female bonding. This was our "I love you."

SIX

Blue Bay

My paternal grandmother, Nanny, owned a small cottage about a ninety-minute drive north of Sydney, on a beach called Blue Bay. Now, I know what you're thinking: "Beach cottage? And didn't she also own a horse farm? That sounds bougie." Except that neither really was. The pancakes smelled fantastic but there were dead weevils inside. Back in those days property in Australia outside of the big cities could be found for cheap, and the areas where Nanny bought weren't sought-after at the time. I guess Nanny just did her best with what she had—a war widow's pension and money left from my grandfather's good job at customs. When she purchased Blue Bay, it had a big mortgage, which I later learned my parents helped to pay off. So even though she couldn't fully afford Blue Bay, this was her dream, to have a little cottage by the beach, where she could relax and enjoy a cheap bottle of wine or five.

As Nanny holds my little nine-year-old hand, I walk into the cottage, which smells mainly of expired face powder and sunscreen. There's a magazine poster of a Kim Wilde–esque eighties singer, in a sexy pose, stuck on the dining room wall with sticky tape—but not at eye level. It's attached just above the baseboard. "That's a weird place to stick a poster," I think.

Nanny, a strong, stocky woman in her late sixties with a pinned hairstyle straight out of World War II, tells me to get into my swimsuit and we'll go straight down to the beach. Nanny loves the beach. This is her escape. There she'll collect shells and bird feathers by the shore and swim in the ocean wearing a bucket hat. This weekend I was lucky enough to accompany her. We drove up in her little orange Datsun, which had holes in the floor, so you could see the road underneath your feet. "Free air-conditioning!" Nanny would say.

Sometimes she'd get lost after missing a turn and she'd wind down her window and talk to total strangers on the street. "Hello, gentlemen, I appear to have lost my way, how do I get back to the main road?" The road workers would point us in the right direction, and I'd marvel at Nanny's confidence. She just . . . talks to people? She's funny and always tells amusing stories, like the one about when she went to England as a little girl for a time and attended a very strict school. She got in trouble with the headmistress for not reading a Bible verse and said in front of the class, "But, miss! We don't have religion in Australia." Other stories scare the shit out of me . . . like the one where she says she went to India and saw dead children's bodies floating down the river. Nanny's a rebel; she has a mischievous twinkle in her eyes. Particularly when sneaking food from a buffet into her handbag. Apparently, she wanted to be an actor at one point and was in a local play when she was younger, but unlike all those horses she bet on, she never backed herself. She worked at the Peters Ice Cream factory but for the most part was a devoted wife and mother.

To get to the beach you have to walk down from the cottage through patches of overgrown beachy succulents, which are overtaking the whole path. You have to kind of whack them with your boogie board to get down there unscratched. But once you reach the bottom of the small hill and cross the road—there it is: Blue Bay. A classic Australian beach with soft yellow sand and beautiful blue water that changes colors depending on the time of year.

It's not that long of a beach, maybe half a mile (one kilometer), with rock pools on one end and a sandbar on the other dividing it from the next beach.

Some days the waves at Blue Bay were tame, and I would float in the water with Nanny and then get out and make sandcastles. I liked making cool "drip sandcastles," letting the water-and-sand mixture drip through my little hand. Other days the giant waves would churn me up like I was inside a washing machine, pounding my face into the sand and grazing my knees. Sometimes I thought I was going to die under those big waves. You'd hold your breath and wait for the calm, knowing that at some point you could come up for air. Everything would go dark, sometimes for a few seconds; other times it would be a lot longer before you eventually bobbed back up. Then you'd bolt to the shore with snot running out of your nose or turn back into the waves and brave more.

I could swim well—most Australians are pretty good swimmers. At six months old I was thrown into a pool and had to survive on primitive instincts (supervised of course). This is good training in case as a baby or toddler you were to accidentally fall into a body of water. You have an instinct to float or swim and you have to use that. I also took swimming lessons for many years. But I was nine, still a child, and there I was confronting the huge power of the Pacific Ocean.

Sometimes my cousins would come with us, and sometimes Liberty would join us, but often it was me and Nanny. One time Nanny pretended to be the Easter Bunny and hid eggs in the overgrown garden. I went searching for them like I was looking for a cure for cancer. I gathered every single egg and then walked gleefully back inside to find Nanny cooking pancakes—but strangely today she was adding orange cordial into the mixture.

"Why are you putting cordial in it, Nanny?" I asked.

"Sometimes you can be a bit different," Nanny said. There was that twinkle.

As the years passed, Nanny's driving got worse, and our family started going to Blue Bay without her. It became an escape for all of us.

Now I'm eleven and my parents have moved from Castle Hill to a house in a suburb called Kenthurst, which is farther out in the bush. The house isn't an upgrade, but it's on five acres, which makes Mum happy because it means more room for the dogs. The house also came with a free donkey, which our parents tried to use as a selling point. We quickly discover that the donkey is super annoying with its loud noises, so it's no wonder the previous owners simply left it.

I had to say goodbye to my best friend Michael. He wrote me a beautiful going-away card that had a sweet bird on the front. We'd spent every afternoon together for almost three years and then suddenly, poof, I never saw him again. (Hi, Michael, if you're reading this!)

But to ease the pain of moving and my transition into high school, my other grandma, Gar, generously decided to take Liberty and me to Disneyland. This was something that I'd long campaigned for after watching *Saturday Disney* religiously every weekend, which showed snippets of Disneyland in each episode. Nanny had also told me from a very young age that we were related to Walt Disney because our great-aunt Lillian had married him. Wow! I really, really wanted to go to Disneyland. I reminded my parents daily that once I turned twelve, I'd be considered an adult on airlines, so it was extremely cost-effective for them to take me now when I was still considered a child. Sadly, our whole family couldn't afford to go, so Gar took me and Lib. It was the best gift ever! (Gar is also the sweetest, best grandmother EVER! And back in the day she owned her own hair salon in a time when it was extremely rare for women to own their own businesses.)

It really was the happiest place on earth. We sat in the gutter to watch the colorful parade. I got autographs from some of the characters in a little book. I got legit scared in the Haunted Mansion and thought the ghosts were real. We then forced Gar to come with us on Space Mountain. "It's really fun, Gar, you'll like it!" She screamed and held on so tight she got bruises down both her forearms. We went to Universal Studios too, and Lib and I got selected out of the crowd to be in some *Star Trek*–type show. I loved seeing all the movie sets on the studio back lot tour. Hollywood seemed like some magical place— so different from Kenthurst, where there was just bush and snakes . . . and the annoying donkey, which I think disappeared to a glue factory?

We were so isolated living out at Kenthurst. But I guess with the birth of my youngest sister, Anna, we needed extra space. But the biggest news in my life was that I was now about to start at the private high school Tara Anglican School for Girls. I'd just gotten a handle on being a kid and now there was so much change. So much uncomfortable change. Things going on with my body, like the start of my period and growing boobs. I'd only heard about the menstrual cycle once at school, when the sixth-grade teachers gathered us girls into one classroom and told us that on our upcoming field trip, we had to be prepared, because some girls would drip blood from their vaginas. Apparently, I looked horrified. This was the first I'd ever heard about such a thing. Mrs. Crawford called me out in front of everyone and said, "You don't need to look so shocked, Melanie!" How could I not be fucking shocked? It's blood! Dripping out of YOU!!

When it happened to me, I was even more stunned. It was a monthly curse that was something extra I now had to navigate. Why does being a girl suck so hard? After one of my first very heavy periods, I hid a pair of bloodied underwear around the side of the house under some leaves. The sucky part about owning so many beagles, who have one of the world's best senses of smell, was that of course they discovered my soiled underwear. Eventually Mum worked out what was going on and taught me about pads and tampons. I didn't wanna talk about it with her as much as she probably didn't want to talk about it with me. My mother loved me dearly, I knew that—it's just that we didn't discuss deeply personal things back then. We certainly didn't discuss things about our bodies. We didn't discuss that Mum now slept downstairs in the small study whilst Dad slept upstairs in the bedroom. I think maybe she was trying to leave my father but couldn't see a way out, especially not now that she had four kids under twelve.

I decide that I am old enough to stay home by myself and don't need to go to dog shows anymore on the weekend. I don't want to be a professional dog shower. That is clearly not my destiny. Mum cries when I tell her this. (I did make it a few times to the Royal Easter

Show as a junior handler but never won.) She can try with Liberty if she wants, I tell her, totally passing the buck to my sister. (Liberty competes in dog shows for the next twenty years.)

On my first weekend alone at Kenthurst, I start my tween dream day toasting a crumpet and watching Saturday morning television. I go to put something in the rubbish bin under the sink and I see what looks like an electrical cord hanging down. I grab it to put it in the trash. And it moves! It's the tail of a gigantic bush rat! I scream! "Ahhhhhhhh!!!" The rat, the size of a small dog, lunges at me and I jump out of the way as it runs into the other room. I call my parents and ask them to come home. Dad now has a car phone that's the size of a brick. But that chunky yellow caravan isn't moving anywhere in a hurry. And my mum is like, "They're only up to the bassets," as they judge in alphabetical order. "The beagles haven't even been on yet."

I hide in my new bedroom, clutching the portable phone. I'm terrified of this giant rat, that it'll attack me. I call my parents again to plead with them to come home. "That's why you should've come with us to the show!" Mum says. "Ugh. We lost. We'll be home soon. Just stay in your room." I stay frozen in my room looking up at my magazine poster of Michael Jordan, which I sticky-taped to my wall. Everything American seems cool to me. Theme parks, the NBA, rap music. Australia just has giant statues of things, like the Big Banana and the Big Merino (a giant sheep statue) . . . it doesn't seem that good in comparison.

When my family finally comes home, they grab a collection of mops and brooms, like the villagers from *Beauty and the Beast*. My little brother spots the rat behind the sideboard. They beat it out of the house while I stand there terrified. How my four-year-old younger brother could attack it like it's a fun game of quidditch I don't know. Life was becoming scary.

I started school at Tara in Parramatta (which was over an hour away—normally two different buses, so I had to get up quite early, especially if I had sports training). I got shit from the other kids at Castle Hill Primary School for not attending the local public high school.

But, I mean, if given the opportunity, of course I was going to go to Tara. It had its own swimming and diving pools, tennis courts, and its own gymnasium where you could do things I'd never even heard of, like rhythmics. My dad had gone to the King's School, the fancy boys' school next door, and was adamant that we attend these schools as well. Put down the pilfered mangoes; we ferals were going to be well educated! But with the expense of the new Kenthurst house, and helping to pay off Blue Bay, Dad now had to get a second job at a petrol station to help pay for the expensive school uniforms and books that I needed. I felt a lot of pressure because of this. Dad was literally working day and night . . . working so that I could succeed . . . and have a brand-new navy-colored Tara uniform: a summer dress with blazer and hat. It was a big privilege to attend this school and my father was never going to let me forget it. While he was collecting people's money for gas, I was learning French and German and how to solder a piece of metal in a new class called Design and Technology. (It really was a well-rounded education.) I also made a cake server in that class, which I proudly brought home to show the family.

My first week at Tara was as tumultuous as the waves at Blue Bay. On day one of high school, it's like a tsunami of emotions. What's it going to be like? Will I make any friends? Is it cool to put all these *Beverly Hills, 90210* stickers on my folder?

I knew some of the girls at Tara from a Christian fellowship group Mum had put me in called Girls' Friendly Society (another one of Mum's missions to socialize me . . . and/or it was cheap babysitting at the church). Olivia was impressive: she could recite all the books of the Old Testament in order. Her friend Kiah was twelve going on twenty-three. Probably because she had an older sister who would teach her cool things. Turns out Olivia and Kiah from GFS were the coolest girls in our grade at Tara. The tides were in my favor. "You can sit with us," they told me as I was placing my *Beverly Hills, 90210* folder inside my new locker.

"Phew," I thought. "I knew it was cool to like that TV show."

Somehow, I was in the cool group—maybe high school was going to be okay? Maybe despite the bush rats, this posh life was for me. Maybe I was going to thrive at Tara. And then it came—week two of school, and Olivia and Kiah say, "We're going to smoke behind the gym, you coming?" Am I coming?? Oh my God, what do I say? First, I don't smoke. Half my family is asthmatic, and I actually hate smoking. I hate the smell of it. I look at their pretty Bible-reciting tween faces. I never saw them smoking at GFS! That was basically a sin, wasn't it? I can't do it—so naively I say, "I'm sorry, I don't smoke." That's when my high school life changes in an instant. The girls give me a bitchy look and walk away. "You're out of the group, then," they say as they leave me by the lockers. "Don't tell on us . . . or else."

I panic. Maybe I could join another group? I only have one other friend at Tara—Lucinda, who also attended Castle Hill Primary School. We sold her family a beagle. I look for her—but she's already sitting in a closed circle with a new group on the grass in the quadrangle. All the groups have formed—the cool group, the sporty girls, the nice pretty girls, the dorks, the country boarders, the uber-religious Christians. What on earth am I going to do? Should I have just smoked with Olivia and Kiah? No. I made my unpopular bed and now I'm lying in it.

I eat my lunch in the library. I will now have zero friends for the whole first year of high school . . . and it will suck. Maybe some groups will open up their circle, but I'll have to wait and see whether anybody wants me. Until then, I decide to basically just make myself invisible. Why? Because being invisible is better than being bullied.

"How was school today?" Mum would ask, excited to hear whether I had made new friends or experienced anything new. She really wanted to go to a private school when she was younger, but her grandmother who had some money only offered this to "boys in the family." "Fine," I'd say, and retreat up to my dark bedroom. I didn't want to bother her with my problems. She had enough on her plate.

When my dad suggested we go with him to Blue Bay during the school holidays, I was excited to go. The beach was far from the bush and far from lonely Tara. "I don't understand," Mum said. "You don't have any friends you'd like to invite?" "No, Mum," I said. I could see that she was disappointed. The CIA agent had figured out that I MUST have been unpopular and was now cross-examining me as to why. But that didn't help, and I shut down. I felt like she would have loved nothing more than for me to be more like Lucinda, who was blond and sporty and had no problem making friends.

But I didn't have ANY friends, because I still had an almost paralyzing shyness. It was like puberty and all the changes brought back the shyness and anxiety. It slithered into my mind like the bush snakes that would crawl onto our concrete back porch at night looking for warmth and a place to shed their skins.

At times, in primary school, I had been able to break out of my shell and make some new friends, but it took almost all my mental energy to push through. Plus, now I had other issues too—I had a snaggletooth! Yep, right in the front of my mouth where an adult tooth should've grown! I blame the lead poisoning. It looked awful and was right in the center of my face. I vowed to never smile. Puberty was probably one of my darkest times. I felt isolated out in the bush, and I was isolated inside my own mind. I was blue. Just so blue.

Even if I had had friends at Tara, I wouldn't have wanted them to see Nanny's beach house. Sure, it was a house close to the beach, but I'd figured out that the random posters were in fact covering holes in the walls—holes kicked in by either Nanny or her de facto partner Syd when they were drunk. Or maybe it was my crazy uncle Robert, my father's brother who, it appears to me, didn't get enough oxygen at birth and, in my opinion, did lots of mental stuff. Also, there was now a smell of urine coming from Nanny's room. Did she have an accident when she was last there? I wasn't sure—Nanny wasn't coming with us anymore to Blue Bay. Apparently, she might have had something called "dementia." My dad was now taking control of Blue Bay, so at least we could still enjoy the beach. But I wasn't going to let a Tara girl see that house and realize my family wasn't as well-off as what we tried to convey.

So, I did what every lonely tween girl did during her school holidays—I became a gangsta rapper. I was obsessed with a kid rap duo called Kris Kross. They played b-ball and wore baggy jeans backward . . . cool shit like that. They had ATTITUDE! CONFIDENCE! SWAGGER! I wanted to be like that.

Even though I was a white girl living in the bush, I really related to rap music. Rappers wanted money and prestige—I wanted that too. Rappers normally had a hard life—even though I clearly wasn't growing up in Compton, around guns and drugs, in my own mind things were tough. I had no friends, my parents were increasingly bickering and money was again tight. Tight because of MY expensive school fees, Dad said. One year for Christmas around this time I got shampoo and conditioner because we needed it. "Thanks, Santa!" I said, knowing this must have been a really bad month.

(My mother's going to hate the above paragraph, by the way. She HATES when I say anything negative about my childhood because she thinks that it paints her as a bad mother. For the record, my mother was and is an excellent mother who did the best she possibly could for her four children, and I love her very much.)

I wanted to spit verse. I just liked how rap music made me feel.

So, in the scorching heat of those long summer days at the Blue Bay cottage, when it was too dangerous to be out on the beach, I formed a rap group with my sister Liberty. I would've enlisted my brother, Ryan, because he looked very cool in his backward baseball cap, but he was too young. Instead, I tapped Libby, whose only performing experience was at the local ballet concerts. I devised our routines, basically Kris Kross songs mashed up with a bit of Will Smith. I was the main rapper, and my sister was the hype girl/backup dancer.

I read in the local coastal newspaper about a kids' talent contest being held at the Mingara Recreation Club, which was a typical Leagues Club where families came for cheap meals of chicken schnitzel and chips and men drank alcohol while their wives and mothers played the slot machines. For us, it was quite a classy place . . . but this is because we didn't go to nice restaurants. Dad could bet on sports and horses at the Mingara club, which is probably why I knew about this place.

"This is my chance," I think. "I could become a famous rapper and then people will notice me."

I practice hard with Liberty, bossing her around. I think I'm so "hard" when I rap. I learn all the words by studying the inserts of the cassette tapes. I'm actually not bad. My mother can't quite believe I want to enter this talent contest because she knows how painfully shy I am. She doesn't understand it. But the thing is, my desire for money and success outweighs my timidity just enough for me to be able to do this. Would my little heart beat out of my chest with nerves? Yes. Would this performance feel internally like I was going to die? Yes. But my desire to win, my desire to be somebody, is so strong that it compels me to do the hardest thing possible: to perform in public.

Mum decides to return to our house in the bush with the newest addition to the family, baby Anna, who is one year old—also she can't be away from the dogs for too long. Well, that's what she says as she leaves, and Dad takes us to the auditions. I'm twelve and Liberty's ten. There are other coastal kids there—mainly singers and dancers. No other kids are rapping, so at least we're original. I don't think anyone expected two small white girls from Sydney to perform rap music—but we do.

I think our group was called SISTERZ or something equally woeful—but we went out onto that makeshift stage and tried to crush. I rapped while Libby danced and added the occasional hype words at the end of lines. We wore the baggiest jeans we could find, backward of course, and baseball caps. I thought we were so fly. The judges must've thought so too, because even though we didn't win first, second or third in our heat, we won a "Highly Commended" award and advanced to the finals later in the school holidays. "Holy shit!" I thought—highly commended! That was it, we needed to get a record deal! I spent the rest of the afternoon at Blue Bay looking through the big telephone book called the Yellow Pages to try to find people to contact about a record deal. I found the addresses of companies and wrote them letters. I wrote a dope original song, which was to be our first single, called "When Skeletons Rule the Earth," and recorded it on blank cassettes to send out as a demo. I was just focused on being the flyest white chick out there, so good that they'd have to give me a multimillion-dollar record deal.

A week later, Dad drives us back to the Mingara club for the talent contest finals. There are more kids now, some pretty talented. One girl sings Whitney Houston. What talent contest would be complete without that? Several girls perform jazz dance solos. One boy is dressed in a suit, and I'm not sure what he does but he looks good. This competition is hard-core. Then Liberty and I hit the stage with the confidence of a whole NBA team about to take a championship. We have zero production value—we don't use a backing track, it's just me freestyling and doing my own beatboxing and occasional body percussion. But in my mind, we're like an MTV music video—onstage performing to thousands and hyping up the crowd with our sick lyrics. In reality, there are probably about a hundred bogans in the audience who find picking their nose more interesting than watching us. But I'm flying up here. My sister and I high-five at the end of the routine, just like we've rehearsed, and then, with hard-core looks on our faces, stand back-to-back in our final pose. Mic drop.

"Oh my God, are we going to win?! That was awesome!!" Libby and I crushed it. As we sit in the theater awaiting the results, I put on sunglasses . . . because that's what a cool rapper would do. The judge comes up onstage to announce the winners. We don't hear our names for third or second—maybe that's because we came first? Nope. We don't come first either. Damn, we can't even win a local talent contest after two weeks of rehearsing. We didn't even place. Dad tells us to get in the car. We take off our baseball caps. We have pretty un-gangsta hat hair underneath.

As we're driving back to Blue Bay, we pass the 7-Eleven on the main road. "Dad! Dad! Can we please stop and get a Slurpee!" We love Slurpees, on hot days especially, but on any day really. I love that special straw that's half little spoon, half straw. I love the Coke flavor. I also love the red flavor even though it sometimes makes me cough. That icy-sugary goodness is the perfect way to deal with our defeat. "I want a Slurpee," Libby says. "Please, Dad, can we stop and get a Slurpee? Please!"

Dad turns around from the driver's seat and grabs my leg as I sit in the back. Suddenly the red-faced giant is back. "Shut up! Shut up! You're not getting a Slurpee!" he spews from his clenched jaw. He shakes a bit, as if the fury overtakes him as it tries to escape his body.

"I just really felt like a Slurpee," I say sadly, more to myself than anything as we pass the entrance to the 7-Eleven.

"I'm going to choke you and kill you if you say one more thing, Melanie . . . I'm going to throttle you." He whips around violently like he might actually try to choke me, then and there. He's furious. It's like a switch has flipped. He's trying to grab me again but then the traffic starts to move, and he has to drive forward. The green light saves me. Otherwise, would he literally have tried to choke me?

I'm twelve years old, and worse than being deemed talentless, my own father threatens to kill me—over a Slurpee. The whole thing kind of ruined Slurpees for me. I never again wanted one with the same enthusiasm. I never dared ask Dad for one again, that's for sure. I just asked Mum.

If I had been gangsta, truly gangsta, I would've taken out my Glock and popped a cap in my dad's ass right about then. Bang! But I wasn't gangsta, was I? There was no gun. Australia doesn't really have guns . . . and even if there had been, I wouldn't have used it. All I could do was stay silent in the backseat for the five minutes it took to get back to the beach house. Just like my mum, I couldn't do anything against Dad's angry outbursts.

When we get back to the cottage, Liberty and I escape down to the beach. The blue water . . . the deep blue . . . my mind needs it. I like the sound of the waves. It's relaxing. My eyes sting in the water and snot comes out of my nose when a big wave dumps on me. But I always come back up for air. We girls might not be gangsta, but we are resilient.

Eventually I learn that vibrant, hilarious Nanny had been officially diagnosed with dementia brought on by alcoholism. That's why she can't get out to Blue Bay anymore. When she needs that deep blue water the most, she can't get to it. She can't escape. She's now really lost.

When we return home later that week, I try to take some "promotional shots" for our rap group on the most hard-core-looking bush rock I can find in our backyard. Our family friends visit—including Shane, the boy whose father beats him with a belt. I'm too distracted working on my imminent rap superstardom, but Mum notices that our new cat is slowly choking in the carport. Someone has tied a helium balloon tightly around its neck. It turns out it was Shane. Luckily Mum found the cat when she did. We never hang out with that family again.

SEVEN

Drama

I am starting my second year of high school and our teacher warns us that the eighth grade is when girls can be really mean to others. Something about hormones and our newfound teenager-ness can cause us to go crazy! There'll be "lots of drama." (I think a reality show about girls in a private school would be fascinating . . . like the junior version of *Real Housewives . . . Real Private School Girls of Sydney*.) We'll rebel against our parents, against society. We'll push boundaries to see how far we can go. That's what girls our age are supposed to do. Go a bit crazy. Do and say stupid things. Make mistakes.

But not me. I wasn't going to be involved in "drama." I was a good girl, petrified that if I wasn't my dad would yank me out of Tara. My job was to go to school and get excellent grades so that I could make something of myself. And if you didn't get that from my serious facial expression, or my serious low ponytail with a ribbon around it, well then . . . okay, I forgive you, because I was pretty much invisible at this point in my life.

My family had sold Petcetera Etc., and we now had a new business called Osco Pet Products, which imported and exported products, not just for dogs, but for all animals. This was a more expensive business than the basic yellow caravan, so it added more pressure on my family.

At school, I was still taking my lunch every day to the library. I was great at not being seen. You didn't want to stand out in a negative way because then you'd get bullied. I didn't want to be like Martha, who had been bullied so mercilessly the year before for having dandruff that she had to leave the school. Another girl jumped into the pool at our swimming carnival whilst still wearing a sanitary pad and it floated to the surface for the whole school to see. That was mega embarrassing, and she was bullied too. At least I was smart enough to go "under the radar," as they'd say on *Survivor*. Well, except for the time I accidentally shaved off half my eyebrows.

While I'm in the shower one morning I decide to "tidy up" my eyebrows with the new razor I was given by Mum to shave my legs. Suffice it to say that I cut off the entire end halves of my eyebrows in a way that really does scream, "I took a leg razor to my face." (Teenage Mistake Number 1.)

"Did you SHAVE your eyebrows?" one girl asks me.

"No," I quickly say, and hide for most of the day in the library.

Though one girl did try to bully me. Let's call her Mousy after her dull brown hair. Mousy was an observant little bitch and noticed one day that I was strangely lugging bricks in my school bag. I was carrying them to make my shoulders stronger for tennis. (My rap dreams had been dashed because no record label ever wrote back, so now I was determined to become a professional tennis player.)

During homeroom, Mousy put red ink on my chair so that when I stood up it looked like I had period-ed myself. Another day, she hid my books. I never reacted. I tied my blazer around my waist to hide the red stain. I calmly found my books where she had thrown them. On the inside I was upset, but I didn't give that rodent bitch any satisfaction whatsoever. I didn't cry. My face remained . . . still. Unmoved. A lot was going on in my mind, but you wouldn't know it from looking at me. I never looked happy or sad (again, couldn't smile at anyone because of the snaggletooth). I just looked . . . studious.

At the end of the seventh grade, I'd won a prize as one of the top five girls in my grade academically—which put me on the radar of the smart girls as a potential threat to their rankings. But apart from that, no one noticed me.

It was lonely. I was becoming a teenager and it totally sucked. I'd spend most nights in my bedroom doing homework. At least math came easily. I would skip ahead in the textbook and teach myself the new chapters. (When I was only fourteen, I won a special award for the highest standardized test score in the Australian Mathematics Competition and received a prize at our school assembly.)

One day an Irish girl in my grade named Orla comes up to me. She wears her school overcoat even though it's not that cold, but I think she wants to be a bit different from the rest of us. We have strict uniform rules but technically you are allowed to wear any of your school uniform pieces, so she's chosen to be the only girl wearing her heavy overcoat in March.

"Come meet us behind the language labs at lunch," Orla says, with kind of a cheeky smile. "We have something to tell you."

"Oh my God, what is happening?" I think. "Is this a mean teenage girl trap?" Once, Mousy told me a teacher wanted to meet me outside her classroom at lunch, and so I waited for her—only to realize fifty minutes later that Mousy was just playing a trick on me. Now here's Orla, dressed like a school shooter, summoning me.

I think about what to do—but I guess that my life couldn't really get more shit than it is. If they're going to beat me up or something, then maybe I could throw a brick at them from my schoolbag?

The lunch bell rings and I venture toward the language labs at the far corner of the large school grounds. I've never been behind them before. It seems that only the school maintenance men go back there, to dig up pipes when too many tampons are flushed. At least I wasn't summoned to the back of the science labs, because that's like some bizarre graveyard for the rats and frogs we have to dissect in biology class.

I walk around the corner, well and truly expecting something bad to happen—but instead I see a small group of girls from my grade sitting in an open circle. "Surprise!" they yell. "Ahhh! What's happening?"

I think. Then I notice each girl has brought a bag of candy or some kind of treat and has placed it in the center of the circle. Hang on—it's March 2; today is my thirteenth birthday, and this is a surprise birthday party . . . FOR ME! Orla gives me a big one-armed hug. "Happy birthday, Mel," she says warmly. My face wants to smile—but I don't because now, apart from the snaggletooth, I have a small metal chain cemented to some of my front teeth and connected to a random tooth stuck way back in the roof of my mouth. The aim of this contraption is to, over an eighteen-month period, slowly drag the random tooth into the correct gum position so that then I'd be able to get braces (which will be another eighteen months of hell). I would like to say this to all orthodontists: "What the actual fuck!"

It's like medieval torture occurring inside my own teenage mouth.

But I look at this new group of girls smiling at me . . . and I really want to smile. Wait . . . do I actually have friends now?

I don't quite know how it happened, but these girls had decided to invite me into their group with this surprise birthday lunch. Maybe it was because I was smart and in the top five of our class? Whatever it was, I was grateful. Of course, I accepted. There were different cliques at Tara, but the best way to describe my new friends was "the multicultural group." They were all either smart or creative. Happy, a.k.a. Haps, and her bestie Ann were both Egyptian, very smart and Coptic Orthodox, so from quite a strict religious background. There was Zahra, the skinny Indian Muslim girl who wore thick glasses and was so smart and a good runner. There was Orla, who was very into English and creative writing . . . and this month, into wearing her overcoat. And Amo, who was a tall Italian girl whose Catholic mother made all her clothes. They weren't the typical girls you'd expect to find at a private school. They weren't from extremely wealthy families. Their parents, like mine, all worked really hard to send them to Tara.

They were all very much "good girls." They were respectful to their parents. They weren't bitchy or catty. They weren't mean. While other girls were trying out the thrill of shoplifting or taking a sip of alcohol, these girls were into movies, TV shows, singing a cappella and being a bit different. They weren't like the gossip girls who had to be wearing cool brands like Sportsgirl or Esprit. These girls didn't care about looking pretty or falling for peer pressure. They were about peer support. They were just uniquely and unapologetically themselves . . . and as I got to know them better over the coming months, I got to love them. Finally, I'd found my clique.

I tell my mum that I've made some friends. She gets excited—like *The Price Is Right* excited! "Who are they?" Mum asks, and I describe them. "Oh," Mum says, slightly let down. "What about Lucinda?"

"Lucinda? No, Mum, I told you, she's in another group."

"Why can't you be in her group? You two are doubles partners."

"Yes . . . but that's very different. I'm not pretty and popular enough to be in her actual group."

"Oh," says Mum. What can she say? My eyebrows are growing back real spiky and I have a chain attached to the roof of my mouth!

I have a vivid dream that Whoopi Goldberg (you know, the legendary star of *Sister Act*) pulls up in a limo outside our bush house. She asks me to get inside, she's going to take me to Hollywood. The dream is so, so real, I wake up thinking it must've happened. But how did Whoopi Goldberg know my address? Why would she choose me? I try to forget it . . . for now.

Mum goes to parent-teacher night, looking for intel as to why I might not be popular, and a teacher tells her that I'm still very timid in classes. "Why are you so shy at school?" she asks when she gets home. "The teacher says you go red in the face when you have to answer a question." She says this like it's a really bad thing. She wants me to be "more outgoing." I tell her that at least I'm doing very well with my grades, getting straight A's, but it appears that's not good enough for her. I have to be popular as well.

One day after school she picks me up from the bus stop and says she has a "special treat" for me.

"What is it?" I say, thinking it's a donut.

"You'll see," Mum says.

I start to get nervous; Mum's acting weird. "Mum! Where are we going?"

"You'll see," she says.

We pull up outside the community center. "Okay, you're going in," Mum says.

"What?" I say. "Why??"

"I've signed you up for drama classes," she says.

"What! No! No way!" Drama classes are for boisterous outgoing kids! The "look at moi, look at moi" kids. There's no way I'm going inside. But Mum has a mission—and that is to drop me off at these classes. She gets out of the car, comes around to where I am sitting in the passenger seat and physically drags me out of the car.

"I'm not going in there!" I cry as I latch on to the car door. Mum pulls me. I hold on to the car door like my life depends on it.

"You're going in there," she says. "I've already paid for the term."

She peels off my fingers and literally forces me to the door of the building—like she's a big snowplow moving me forward. I'm crying hysterically by this point. I don't know these kids—this is going to be a complete disaster! Why is my mum doing this to me? I fucking hate her. I hate her so much right now. She pushes me inside the door and a group of gangly teens stop their circular drama game of "zip, zap, zop" and stare at me. I look like I've fallen off a cliff and am crying from the pain of breaking both legs.

"Bye, I'll pick you up later," Mum says innocently as she quickly exits and drives off (probably to get herself a donut from Donut King whilst she waits). I stare at the teenagers. The drama teacher comes over. "Hello, what's your name?"

"Um . . . Melanie. My name's Melanie," I say, instantly adopting an American accent, my now go-to move in situations of extreme social anxiety.

"Welcome then . . . okay, now everybody's going to walk around the space in a character type that I yell out . . . old lady! Go! Freeze. Unfreeze. Drug dealer!"

After the lesson the drama teacher asks, "Where in the States are you from?" It's only at this point I realize that I have been, out of trauma, putting on an American accent. I was just trying to make it through the class. Sure, I like watching Whoopi's movie *Sister Act* and probably sang the songs around our house when nobody was watching—but that was me in PRIVATE. Sure, I entered the talent contest during the school holidays and was writing to record labels—but that was a competition. Now my annoying mother was putting me in a local drama class where I would have to express myself every single week! For no prize. Why was she torturing me like this? (It was like the time during school holidays where she made me take a modeling course at the department store, Grace Bros., and at the end of the week we had to strut down a catwalk in the middle of the store. I only did it because the Bells said they would do it too. For a not-cute kid, it was kind of embarrassing. Slim Liberty seemed to love it and danced her way down the catwalk wearing a fun hat and short shorts like she was young Kylie Minogue! Stocky me chose to model denim overalls—not exactly a crowd-pleasing look!)

Anyway, turns out after a few of these drama classes, I actually quite enjoyed it. I liked that there were a few boys in the class. I wrote in my diary that acting was "kinda cool." And if my anxiety had been at one hundred for that first lesson, that number decreased by like two points every week I returned. The more I pushed myself, the more I used my voice, the slightly easier it got. The drama teacher was nice and encouraging and the other kids were friendly. Maybe we were all dealing with teen anxieties. Theirs might not have been extreme shyness, but I'm sure they all had their issues.

At Tara, Zahra and I were selected for Tournament of Minds—a creative team competition that required both quick intellect and creativity. I wrote our performance piece for the group, and we made it all the way to the state finals. As much as I hated to admit it at the time, and as much as I wished that my mother had more gently nudged me into drama classes, I'm very glad that she did.

That one weekly drama class gave me an outlet to express myself by pretending to be other people. I could hide behind the characters I was playing and act more confident. And slowly, I became more confident myself. Meanwhile other girls my age were starting their rebellious stage, making terrible teen mistakes like crashing Daddy's car or fighting someone with their shoe at a disco . . . but I didn't go through that stage. Now I was onstage—albeit a small one.

While the snakes were shedding their skin on our back porch nightly, I was becoming more comfortable in my own skin.

EIGHT

42nd Street

I hear Mum on the phone. She's talking to our dogs' agent, who I imagine is sitting at a desk with a ciggie hanging out one side of her mouth. "Sue, yep, we've got a callback audition for Sassy, two p.m. tomorrow." "Yes . . . yes . . . okay, we'll be there," says Mum excitedly. One of our beagles, Champion Bayhound So Sassy, a.k.a. Sassy, has a callback for the Sydney production of the musical *42nd Street*. I am thirteen years old and have never seen a musical. I've seen movie musicals like *Grease* and *Annie*, which I thought were amazing, but never a live one.

Mum takes Sassy to the callbacks. There are various pooches vying for the coveted role of . . . um, I guess "dog." The lead actress calls the dog from offstage, and the dog has to run to her. Mum waits stage-side for her turn, patting Sassy and giving her pieces of Schmackos dog treats. I hate the smell of Schmackos on my hand, but I would use this trick too when I was a junior handler. It's our turn to go. Whilst the other little dogs followed their cue, Sassy kind of meanders onto the stage, stops well before the actress and poops. We don't get the job.

Mum is like, "I wanna see which bitch got it," so she buys us all tickets to see the production. Our grandma Gar comes with us too. The whole mission is really to sit in the audience and see whatever dog was cast and know in our hearts that our dog would've been much better.

We arrive at the gorgeous Her Majesty's Theatre in the city. I've brushed my hair for the occasion, wear my best tennis polo shirt and sling a little purse on a chain over my shoulder . . . because let's not be too feral. This is a fancy place. There are large posters and lights out front. The crowd enters before the start time and takes their seats inside the plush theater. They have a candy bar that sells lollies and drinks at really expensive prices (I know how much lollies really cost, remember?). Mum buys the program and quickly scans for the photo of the dog.

Then the real magic happens. The lights go down and the overture begins. Drumroll. Horns. Strings. I can make out the tune to "We're in the Money!" and then the colorful cast of performers sing and dance their hearts out for the next three hours. Who are these talented fast-footed people? Where did they come from? Oh my God, like WOW. Yesterday my mood could best have been described as "a bit goth"; now I'm so happy I'm crying. It's like the music lifts me out of my seat and my soul is flying around the theater. For the entire show I forget about all my teenage problems. The dark cloud around me dissipates and sunshine shimmers through. All I see is sparkle. I want to get up there and sing and dance too. Like someone breaks their ankle and they need a girl—it's an emergency—and so I just run up there and join in the pure joy. I then remember I've had no dance or singing training and couldn't possibly do what these people do—but I just want to be a part of this absolutely amazing spectacle.

"Did you know they do this eight times a week?" my grandma Gar says. She radiates kindness from her light eyes.

"They do that whole thing eight times a week?" I say.

"Yes."

Whoa. How could they create this magic every single day, sometimes twice a day? I'm in awe. I needed this two-act wave of happiness and I have our family's dogs to thank for the opportunity. It's also the start of a new gorgeous matriarchal tradition in my family of going to see musicals—my grandma Gar, my mother, Liberty and me. Over the next few years, we see many shows in Sydney, such as *A Chorus Line*, *Beauty and the Beast* (with Hugh Jackman), *The Phantom of the*

Opera and *Miss Saigon* (where Liberty sleeps right through a massive helicopter landing onstage and I of course make fun of her afterward). In every show I'm transported and transfixed.

I buy every Andrew Lloyd Webber cassette and any other musical theater tapes I can find at Castle Towers and listen incessantly to all the songs. When I have rough days at school, rough days at home, rough days inside my mind . . . I now listen to musicals.

Flash forward to 2003. I am twenty-three and lucky enough to win the Nicole Kidman Lendlease scholarship through the Australian Theatre for Young People (ATYP—the acting school I went to after high school down at the wharf in Sydney). I'm awarded $12,000 to go anywhere in the world to pursue my acting career. "New York," I say to the audition panel. "I want to go to New York." I want to go to New York to see live theater on Broadway, to actually walk down Forty-Second Street and hum that theme song to myself. Also, the Second City, a famous comedy school whose alumni include Mike Myers, John Candy and Eugene Levy, has a branch in New York, so I enroll in their classes for specialized comedy training. We don't have any comedy schools in Australia, so this seems like a smart way to spend Nic's money. I love how I just casually call her "Nic," as if I know her at the time. I don't—I once saw her having dinner with Russell Crowe at Sydney Theatre Company and was walking over to say hello to her and drop off a program for our play, but before I could even get one word out, Russell turned sharply to me and said, "Fuck off!" (BTW, love Russell, he's a classic, such a brilliant actor.)

I'm the last of the sixteen winners of Nic's scholarship and I'm pumped to win, to fly to New York for the very first time.

The classic yellow taxicab drops me off outside my address—Forty-Sixth Street between Ninth and Tenth Avenues. This is Hell's Kitchen. I hoist my extraordinarily heavy suitcase up four flights of stairs to get to the apartment. I'm subleasing for a few months from a New Yorker whom I don't know but who seems like they're not a psycho from our email exchanges . . . and they've promised me that they have hundreds of TV channels. I'm sold.

It's January—so it's brutally cold. I'm from Sydney, where it rarely drops below 47 degrees Fahrenheit (8 degrees Celsius), so I don't know that you need a warm winter coat like a North Face or a Canada Goose. I have one letterman jacket given to me by the Australian Theatre for Young People, but that's it. I'm really not prepared for a bitter New York winter.

I need to get outside, though. I need to see Times Square, to see Broadway, to see Forty-Second Street—the HOME of musicals. I put on four layers of clothing topped with my letterman jacket. Because I'm over 220 pounds (100 kilos) at this point, all the layers make me sweat between my upper thighs as I walk. It's absolutely freezing but I'm loving every second. I round the corner into Times Square and there it is: Broadway. All the lights, all the excitement. It's like Her Majesty's Theatre in Sydney but on steroids.

I stand in the TKTS line, where you can get discounted tickets to Broadway shows. I buy tickets to one called *Urinetown*, a satirical comedy musical. If I walk quickly, I can make the start time. I sit almost at the back of the theater, eating a new sweet I've discovered called Milk Duds. The lights dim. The orchestra starts playing. Yep, it's still there, that incredible feeling where I'm so happy I could cry. I fucking love musicals.

A few weeks later my awesome friend Snickers (whom we'll get to) comes to visit from Australia. We see that Whoopi Goldberg is starring in *Ma Rainey's Black Bottom*, and we buy tickets to see her play a blues singer. I'm in awe that I'm so close to one of my idols. After the show, Snickers and I wait at the stage door with the rest of the crowd. Most of them get too cold after ten minutes and leave. But I'm determined to meet Whoopi. We wait close to ninety minutes. I am so cold that my bogan fringe is sticking straight up in the air, totally frozen.

Finally, the heavy stage door opens and out comes THE Whoopi Goldberg. There she is! My big bust hangs over the silver metal barricade that gives Whoopi a bit of protection from the crowd and a corridor to walk to her waiting town car.

"Whoopi! Whoopi!" I scream the second she walks out the door. I'd kill for an autograph or a picture. "Whoopi, I'm an actress from Australia!" I point to my Australian Theatre for Young People jacket—not that she knows what the hell that is. "Can I get a photo please?" I ask. "Sure," Whoopi says. Then, according to Snickers, I get so god-damn excited that I push over the barricade to get closer to Whoopi, to which Snickers quips, "Rebel!! Don't kill Whoopi!"

Whoopi must have seen this supreme level of excitement before. She must sense that I'm a superfan and graciously takes the photo with me. "Oh my God, we just met Whoopi Goldberg!" "Yes, we did!" says Snickers. We order Mexican food to the apartment to celebrate and somehow, when I bite into a corn chip, one of my incisor teeth breaks in half. It's the snaggletooth that I had a dentist fix with composite to make it look more like a normal tooth. And now the fang is revealed once again.

Snickers is videotaping the whole thing like we're characters in *Rent*. (We watch it years later and laugh about how feral we were.) I look particularly bad in my early twenties—with huge dark circles underneath my eyes—probably because I'm working so hard to become a success and my diet could best be described as CARBS ONLY. I'm freaked out by the tooth chunk falling off, but I'm on such a high from meeting Whoopi, such a high from walking down Forty-Second Street every day, that I don't even care.

Years later, I did meet Whoopi properly when I was a guest on *The View* in my thirties. I told her this story and showed her the photo of me with the frozen fringe. Of course, she wouldn't have remembered the exact encounter but got a kick out of the photo. Love you, Whoopi!

In 2001, when Her Majesty's Theatre sadly closed for good, I bought the original *42nd Street* marquee poster at their closing auction to keep as a memory. Okay, now enough of my dorky musical theater side, reader, let me tell you the story of how I—the mathlete who solved advanced math problems for fun, the girl whose beauty routine only involved a leg razor, the girl who used to eat her lunch in the library every single day in solitude—actually became, to quote *Wicked*, "popular."

NINE

Popular

I'm sitting at the bus stop one afternoon after school in my Tara uniform. Waiting.

I'm fourteen, about to turn fifteen. I look like a woman. My tennis skirt is the largest size they sell at the school uniform shop—the skirts don't get any bigger, so I hope I won't get any bigger either. Not that I'm fat, I'm just athletic. I'm now fully adult sized, but mentally I'm still very innocent. Mum is strict about not letting us watch anything adult on TV, and going to an all-girls Christian high school means that I'm quite protected. I'm not at all like my cousin who at sixteen was already pregnant. That is, as my dad always reminds me, because I'm lucky enough to be getting a world-class education at a private school.

Dad wants me to be the best. He rewards me with a small amount of money if I come first in my grade in a subject. He even offers to buy me my own television if I score five goals in one hockey game. Fuck, I try so hard to score those goals. I literally bash the shins of girls from opposing schools with my hockey stick as I barrel toward the goal with force, playing center forward, bright orange mouth guard in place. I get close but I never score five goals in a single game. (Professional teams on average score three goals per game, so that would've been quite an achievement.) I try, though. I want that TV so bad.

I also go to the Osco warehouse to work for Dad on weekends

and school holidays. I staple packages of birdseed bells together and make $5 for a box of five hundred. Dad normally employs adult people with Down syndrome to do this job (through a positive program that creates access to employment) but allows me to do it too if I want the money. Of course I want the money, so I say yes. Sometimes I rope in some of the Bell girls to join me and we listen to the Hot 40 hits on the radio whilst we do the repetitive manual work. It's hard to use the heavy stapler repeatedly. My hands and wrists ache after a few boxes.

Today is just a regular after-school afternoon, though. I sit on the concrete that was warmed all afternoon by the sun, trying not to tear my blue stockings. If the tear is too big, too noticeable, I'll have to throw them out, and I don't have that many pairs. I have to ration them.

Math homework out. I look at my watch. Where is Mum? She knows what time the bus drops me off and she's not here. Why isn't she here? She's often late. Which I absolutely hate. You only need to look at the definite watch tan I have on my wrist to know that I AL-WAYS wear a watch and am on time for everything. I finish a section of the math textbook. It's starting to get dark. I don't have a cell phone at this point. The biggest tech item I own is my calculator. I could start walking toward our house, but with my heavy bag of books, that could take hours. "Where is Mum?!?" I think/yell in my mind.

I spend hours waiting, until finally Dad pulls up. "What happened to Mum?" I say as I throw my bag in the car. Dad doesn't answer. I'm grumpy as hell as I slide into the front passenger seat. "What happened to Mum?" I ask again.

"Your mother doesn't love you," Dad says, "she only loves the dogs."

My mum loves the dogs more than she loves me? It can't be true, but when your father is saying it . . . you tend to believe it. If only momentarily. Dad then spends the rest of the car ride telling me how well he thinks I'm doing in school and how much he loves me.

He soon buys me a gym membership and we start going together at night to a big newly built gym in Castle Hill. Dad is being . . .

ummm . . . different. I don't remember him whacking me since I became a teenager—maybe because I'm too big now?

Going to the gym was our special daddy-daughter time—lifting weights, doing circuit training and cardio machines. I liked working out. I wanted to be good at sports, and at Tara I played a lot of them—mainly tennis but also basketball, hockey and cricket. And Dad seemed to be in a much better mood when we went to the gym. He seemed to be favoring me. He also used the time to talk shit about my mother. He'd say she was a bad mother, that she'd groom the dogs more than she ever did my hair. He'd remind me how she was always late. "No one else would ever put up with her!" Dad said whilst we changed spots on the weight bench.

My parents were fighting all the time. Mum was slowly trying to return to work as a teacher so she could have some of her own income (my father controlled all the finances), but my father was adamant that she stay at home.

"Oh, and your mother is terrible in social situations, it's so embarrassing," he'd say as we were in the gym sauna at the end of the workout. "Yeah," I'd say agreeably. What else was I supposed to say? I needed him to drive me home.

I knew a lot of what he was saying wasn't true, but I wasn't going to argue with him. I'd seen his temper too many times and thought, "Hmmmm, better not." And this nicer, more improved Dad was better than that exploding red balloon. Now it felt like he was enlisting me to join his side of the battle—the battle between my parents, of course. He wanted to win my vote, and so I was getting free car rides, compliments and now a gym membership.

Weeks later I open the trunk of Dad's car and there is a sports bag that I've never seen before. Did Dad get a new gym bag? I open the bag and it's filled to the brim with . . . cassette tapes. So many cassette tapes. "What the hell?" I don't ask anyone, I just take the bag up to my bedroom. I start playing one titled *How to Win Friends and Influence People*. Hmmmmm, this is very interesting. Why does Dad have this stuff in his car? He's started to take some business courses at a local technical community college and probably borrowed the tapes. They have all sorts of advice—like how to be popular, how to be a great salesperson; they're essentially motivational tapes.

I guess at that time, in the area where I'm from, no one was doing therapy. That was something weird you'd only see mentioned on American movies and TV shows. Clearly my parents' marriage was more than doomed, clearly my father had some kind of mental health issue, and so maybe this was his way of bettering himself? He did want to be better, didn't he? I listened to the tapes religiously over the next week or two. I'd put on my headphones and listen to my Walkman. It drowned out Mum and Dad fighting downstairs.

Then in the school library I read an article that says your personality at fifteen years old will be your personality for LIFE. For example, if you're extremely shy at fifteen, chances are you're never really going to overcome this as an adult. Basically, the message was that when you're young, you're still malleable. You have some hope for change. But does that mean that when you're in your early forties like my dad, you've missed your window? Maybe he's too late? "Hang on, I'm almost fifteen," I think, "so maybe I could change my personality and better my life?" Now I'm getting MOTIVATED!

What did I want in life? Even though I had a group of friends and wasn't a total pleb at school, no one really knew me. I wanted to become popular. Mum would like that. That would make her happy, and she seemed pretty depressed lately. She wanted me to lose a few kilos too. She'd told me that as she herself tucked into a piece of Viennetta ice cream cake. "You'd just look prettier if you lost two kilos," Mum said. At around two hundred pounds, she was overweight and wasn't happy about it. I think she'd been to WeightWatchers or Jenny Craig or maybe both, and I'd gone with her once to some sort of group meeting where the women lined up and were weighed in like they were cattle at an auction as a skinny lady up front recorded the weights and made comments on each one. "Good job, Courtney, that's one kilo down. Someone's been monitoring their points!" Cheers for Courtney. Courtney has a smile on her face like she's single-handedly ended the Cold War.

Mum was trying to help me—she didn't want me to have to stand in the weekly weigh-in line and be guilted to "always take the stairs!" I was still young enough to change! At 147 pounds (67 kilos), I wasn't "fat"— I was stocky because of all the sports I played. I had athletic shoulders. I had muscles from the gym. But I could limit the sweets and junk food I was eating. I could do that, couldn't I? Mum couldn't right now, she was going through a lot, but I could. Other girls in my grade were starting to do it. I'd noticed they were being conscious of the calories they were eating and restricting themselves from certain foods. "I'm giving up chocolate for lent," Haps said. And she did. She was very disciplined. And it didn't even have anything to do with boys! We just somehow had all been sent the memo from I don't know who, Patriarchy Anonymous, instructing us to behave like "women" now that we had adult-size bodies. There were now invisible sticky notes on our fridges, in our lunch boxes, on restaurant menus, saying things like "Little pickers wear big knickers" or "A moment of joy on the lips equals a lifetime of hell on the hips." I thought of that pink hippo toy with the measuring tape around its waist. It wasn't a blue hippo measuring itself, was it? Nope. It was a pink female one. Adult women measured themselves. We didn't want to be big.

However, my number one goal wasn't about losing weight—my priority was definitely to become popular at school. I mean, what teenager doesn't want to be popular? No one wants to feel lonely and be a no-friends Nigel. Earlier in high school I had been desperate for other girls to approach me and invite me into their group . . . but I'd never considered: What if I took active steps to get more friends? What if I took my popularity destiny into my own hands? And now, thanks to these motivational cassette tapes, I was starting to think differently.

With my new bit of confidence from the weekly drama classes, I immediately forced myself to do things that I'd heard on the tapes would help me become popular, like talk to five new people every day. I had to ask them their name and some questions. The first few weeks were painful. I'm sure some girls thought, "Why is this random talking to me?" But then there were plenty of other girls who also felt lonely or ostracized and were grateful to have a chat with someone new. There were foreign students at Tara from Singapore and Korea who normally never spoke to Aussie girls. There were dorks who played in the handbells ensemble who didn't speak to anyone outside their group. I was going to become a connector. I was going to become friends with everyone. The bus was actually a perfect place to strike up a chat. And pretty soon I became the queen of the commute—talking to all girls regardless of what grade they were in, what race they were, whether they were cool or not. I organized Tazos challenges—a game we'd play using tokens from chip packets (and yeah, I ate a lot of chips, so I had a lot of these)—on the bus, which became quite popular. It was silly, but it was a way of connecting with other girls.

I joined more clubs at school. The more you're part of groups, the more you have a sense of belonging. It's also a really easy way to make new friends, because you're forced to interact and work together. I signed up for almost every single activity that Tara offered. To become more confident speaking in public, I started entering the public speaking competitions and joined the debate team. Would my face still go red when I had to speak in front of an audience? Yep, pretty much every time I'd have red blotches on my face or chest or both. The fear and the nerves were intense. But then after a few months I'd win the public speaking competition or high-level debates against other schools—and that feeling was awesome. It took a year but I rose up the ranks to become third speaker on the Firsts' Debate Team (also called the "rebuttal speaker," this was a highly coveted position). I'd get up there with my palm cards and bring it home for my team like I was a quarterback needing to score right before the buzzer—the pressure normally falls on the third speaker and you are the hero if you win . . . and remember, I really, really liked winning, even if it meant passionately arguing the most ridiculous things. "Good afternoon, adjudicator, ladies and gentlemen—quintessentially the fall of Nazi Germany did NOT greatly affect the populism of democracy."

(I always used the word "quintessentially" in debates and essays, even when it was incorrect, because I thought it made me sound super smart.)

I remember a tip on one of my dad's cassette tapes: "Sometimes at first, you must get people's attention. Only once you've got their attention can you then turn it into something positive." It's kind of like the psychology underlining the success of the rapper Eminem. In order to get famous, he did and said outrageous things. Once he got the attention, he then followed it up with hit songs. But without the notoriety first, his songs might never have been hits.

"Hmmmmm," I thought. I'd spent all this time—my whole life really— being a "good girl." Being quiet, polite, respectful . . . all those "good girl" traits. But look where that had gotten me. That hadn't made me popular. I had to turn a bit bad, a bit outrageous. I had to get attention and then use that momentum to get success.

So, I plotted, like I was Macaulay Culkin in *Home Alone*, to get attention. Every girl in Tara would know the name Melanie Bownds.

Now, reader, it's not like I was going to do something super bad like burn down the school whilst laughing maniacally . . . I still was a sheltered student at an all-girls Christian school . . . so here's what I did:

On a field trip for the academically gifted girls to Canberra, the Australian capital, I schemed for me and my friends to smoke fake cigarettes in the parking lot. Smoking was the number one vice banned at Tara. I knew that when the teachers saw their smartest students standing in school uniform, smoking, they'd fly off their rockers. And they did. Our science teacher storms up to us, rips the cigarettes out of our hands and stomps them with her shoes. "Get on the bus!" she says furiously. "I can't believe you girls would do this! This is a disgrace!" Everyone watches as the teachers debate our punishment. They're fuming. Usually, a Tara girl caught smoking in uniform would be expelled immediately—but are the teachers really going to expel the top five academic students in the grade? I think not. We can see the dilemma on their faces. I start laughing.

"What's so funny, Melanie? You're about to get expelled. What are your parents going to say to that?"

I smile. "But we weren't smoking, miss."

"Yes, you were! We saw you! We saw you smoking those filthy things!"

"But, miss, they're not real." The teacher is perplexed. I walk down the aisle of the bus like I'm walking down the catwalk during Paris Fashion Week, holding the crumpled counterfeits. "They're not real, miss. They're fake cigarettes, see?" I hold one out to her. I show her the fake packet. "You can't get expelled for smoking FAKE cigarettes."

I had a point. And the teachers knew it. They hated how I outsmarted them. But they couldn't punish us because we hadn't done anything wrong . . . technically. I'd organized a classic antiauthoritarian stunt and it was funny. The other kids shared the story and word of my prank went viral—this was pre–social media, so it went viral like a mono outbreak. I got my first little taste of attention. And it was almost as good as sugar. So, I plotted some more.

I pushed the mean English teacher into a cupboard, locked her inside and left her there for hours. No one ratted me out either. Our whole class took the detention for it. I also masterminded breaking into the school canteen on several occasions and shared the cookies and chocolate cake with my friends. I snuck into the staff room and stole their biscuits. I would stage various "silent protests" in classrooms and refuse to sit down. Just generally being a smart-ass. I'd play jokes on teachers too. Zahra had an electronic watch that could change the channel on the TV and turn it on and off, and we'd drive the teacher mad with it as she tried to play an educational video. "Hang on, it was working a minute ago!" the teacher would say, confused. We'd all laugh behind her back.

I was becoming a real rebel, like my original name. Now I'd strut down that Tara quadrangle with swagger. All the girls would know me. "Hi, Mel!" I'd high-five them . . . if I felt like it. Those damn cassette tapes had worked. I was now fifteen and I'd actually transformed my life, right before the cutoff date. I was legitimately popular—not with the teachers, of course, I'm sure some of them hated me because of my antics, but with my peers.

I auditioned for the school musical, *Grease*, which the Tara girls were about to perform with the boys' school next door. The King's School is, I think, the oldest and one of the most prestigious boys' schools in Australia—kind of like Eton in the UK. The boys wear military-inspired uniforms. They have shooting ranges and a massive number of football fields and cricket ovals. King's was right next to Tara, but the boys were much fancier than we were. They had more facilities. They had a multimillion-dollar theater to put on stage productions, with a revolving stage and everything, and so they would invite some lucky girls to be part of each production under the tutelage of their legendary Zimbabwean theater director, Mr. Haigh.

Many boys would imitate Mr. Haigh's Rhodesian accent, pretending to be him while yelling incessantly. He was a demanding teacher who put on semiprofessional productions of plays and musicals using only students. He had escaped Zimbabwe during the civil unrest, and I think several of his family members died during the conflicts. He had been a professional theater director back home but now he was an English teacher at King's and doubled as the theater director. He was like a character out of *The Power of One*—a hardened, tall man with moppy brown hair and more lines on his face than were in a play's script. He really cared about us but at the same time was very hard on us. And seeing as I was very hard on myself—with my own loud internal critical voice—it made sense that I idolized Mr. Haigh. I thought he was a genius. He was. I loved watching musicals and now, if I was one of the lucky girls chosen to be in his production, he was going to teach me how to create that magical spectacle onstage.

I wasn't allowed to audition for a main role in *Grease*, because normally those were reserved for the older girls in the eleventh grade (and I was only in the tenth grade), but luckily, I was allowed to be in the chorus. It was exciting for us to be around all these King's boys after being surrounded by hundreds of girls every day.

The boys were so different—smelly and loud and rambunctious. It was like a whole other world just a few paddocks away filled with manly men and boys who wanted to be manly men. Surprisingly it was seen as very manly and cool to be in the plays and musicals at King's—I think because the productions were just so damn good! If you were the lead, you were extremely popular. It was as good as being the captain of the Firsts' rugby team. There was never any teasing, like "You must be gay if you're in the musicals," because the musicals were where boys would meet girls. So, despite some toxic masculinity traits I saw being promoted at King's, at least the boys were encouraged in the creative arts.

My friend Bayella and I were at the back of the theater in the lighting rig watching the principal characters rehearse. We wished that we were the leads. I had wanted to play Jan or Marty. Bayella and I joked that maybe something would happen to one of the lead girls and they would need one of us to fill in. Our fifteen-year-old faces gleamed with joy over that fortuitous hypothetical. How cool would that be? We'd get plucked out of the chorus and into a lead role.

Theater is a cruel mistress, though. Later that afternoon, Bayella and I were standing at the side of the stage in the wings of the theater, waiting to rehearse "We Go Together," when the bulky side-stage television monitor suddenly fell off its shelf and straight onto us. Bayella sadly took the brunt of the weight of the falling TV and really injured her shoulder. I looked at her. "We should never talk ill of other performers again," I thought. "We'll stay in the chorus and give it our all and maybe next year, when we're older, we'll get lead roles." At least we were part of the production. And of course, that meant we got invited to all the cool parties!

Whilst I wanted to do the musical purely to shine onstage, purely to be a part of something awesome, I couldn't help but see that a lot of the girls were doing this to get the boys' attention. They'd twirl their ponytails and giggle when the boys were around. Some would sit on boys' laps during breaks in rehearsals. Some would kiss them. It's like at Tara we were go-getters about to change the world, pouring things into beakers whilst speaking intelligently—but over at King's it was more about which girl was the cutest AND could do the splits!

Mr. Haigh would notice relationships forming and at the end of every production he'd gather everyone onto the stage and hand roses to the boys he suspected were in relationships. Then the boy, in front of the whole cast and crew, would have to hand the rose to his "sweetheart." It was *The Bachelor* before *The Bachelor* even existed. It became particularly interesting when one boy might've dated two girls throughout the run of the show and then it was controversial as to which girl he would choose to get the rose. "Ooooh, is it going to be Erina or Nicki?" Suffice it to say, I didn't get a rose during *Grease*, but I did get one in a play later that year where I was cast in an actual role. It was a Yorkshire farce called *When We Are Married*. Mr. Haigh obviously noticed my star quality and expressive face as I overperformed in chorus numbers like "Born to Hand Jive." Even though I was usually in the back and off to the side, I gave that stage everything I had. And he took notice. And then one of the King's boys noticed me too.

Justin was the stage manager for the shows, and he seemed to like me. He looked like a younger, cuter version of my father. A bit stocky, he was great at rugby and cricket. Plus, Justin obviously loved theater and spent all his spare time there. So I liked him too. He invited me on a date to the movies. Mum drove me, very impressed with this "normal" positive development in my social life. She couldn't stop smiling! Her daughter now had a King's boyfriend. She seemed to forget the awful troubles she was having with my father, an ex-King's boy. She was excited that the shy little girl who always hid behind her skirt was now becoming the popular daughter she wanted (minus the dog-showing thing . . . it was still a travesty that I wasn't winning Best in Show).

While we sat in the back row of the movie theater, Justin touched my inner thigh. I felt titillating feelings I'd never felt before. That was about as racy as it got, I'm afraid to say. I didn't really know what sex was and I wasn't sure what to do on a date with a guy. Bat my long eyelashes? Talk about cricket?

When We Are Married, my first proper play, was a mixed experience. Mr. Haigh almost fired me before we opened for not perfecting the Yorkshire accent. Mum had to call up Mrs. Marshall, the producer of the show. "Please, don't fire her, it'll destroy her," Mum pleaded passionately. "She'll get the accent! I'll make sure she gets it!" Mum was a rock star that day. She stood up for me like nobody ever had before. I do think she saved me—and I'm not sure I would've become an actress if that hadn't happened.

I worked hard on the accent with a teacher from England who would record it onto a cassette tape, and I'd repeat each line incessantly. I still remember my first line of the play because I had to repeat it so many times: "Oh 'ere you are, you gassing in 'ere like you own the place instead of getting on with yer work. She's rung for yer twice and I've just taken in another lot of 'ot water!" Mr. Haigh would sit scowling at me every time I opened my mouth. I'd only really done American accents at the drama classes, never a Yorkshire one, and it was HARD. But I tried.

Justin handed me his rose at the end of the production—that meant we were official. Life was amazing. I was popular. And now I only had about four and a half pounds (two kilos) to lose!

Dad never mentioned anything about the sports bag with the cassettes. He must have noticed that it went missing for several weeks. But maybe he didn't? Maybe he was too angry at his inability to improve his own life. I had improved my life, but at the same time his was going downhill fast. Nanny's dementia was getting worse. One day I found her on my school bus, and she didn't know where she was. It was so scary, I didn't know what to do. Liberty also found her one day walking around the shopping mall lost and confused. Osco Pet Products had a break-in. And with two daughters now at Tara, money was again really tight for my family. Mum was so busy looking after us four kids, she'd often be up 'til three a.m. just doing things. For us.

My father would come home from the warehouse and say to Mum, "And what have you done today, you fat, lazy cow!" Then he'd walk into the living room and say to me, as if he were a completely different person, "Hi, darling, do you want to go to the gym?"

TEN

New Year's Resolutions

Diary Entry: January 1, 1996

(Yes, this is the start of my actual diary in 1996)

<u>Weight</u>: 150 pounds [68 kilos]

<u>Relationship Status</u>: Justin is my boyfriend. We went to the formal together and everything . . . although I haven't really heard from him since we went on school holidays?

<u>Mental Attitude</u>: I can make my own destiny. I am so focused. I'm basically a new person now after coming out of my shell and showing people my personality.

GOALS
New Year's Resolutions

1. To lose weight and become fitter < 67 kg [147 pounds]
2. To be a nicer person
3. To improve my communication skills
4. To organize myself for more study and work more
5. To compete in many areas of sport well

6. Find a way of making money easily
7. Become more independent
8. To network
9. To make myself more recognized
10. To get an opportunity to show my acting skills thoroughly

January 1st, 1996

I'm planning on sticking to my New Year's Resolutions. In my horoscope for today it said that there are good stars for my dreams to come true, but I haven't seen or heard anything happen. I have to stop reading those things but I really hope today's horoscope was right. I've been a good girl. I went for a jog, drank glasses of water, did my schoolwork and tonight we went to Greater Union at Castle Towers, and saw the new James Bond movie *GoldenEye*. It was alright.

January 2nd, 1996

Oh, if only I was a rich woman, but I know money is not the only thing in life. I really do have a strong passion for acting. Well, my diet and exercise is going great. Mum said that she can already see an improvement. WOW!

January 3rd, 1996

Howdy, you know I'm really unsure with what I'm going to do with the rest of my life. It really gives me something to think about. I want a job with good cash, but I want to do something worthwhile, using my intellect and other skills.

January 4th, 1996

Hi, we got some bathroom scales today, is my hard work really all worth it? The answer is of course: Yes! I love the way exercise makes me feel after I've pushed myself and achieved my goal. I'm healthy, well getting there. Haven't heard from Justin? I think we're just friends. USA soon!

BYE, CHOW, CHOW 4 NOW*

My diary is filled with contradictions. Sometimes I'm really confident—winning debates and speaking at assembly, performing at the King's Theatre. Other times, I'm still painfully shy. Some days I'm wildly happy and others I'm depressed and contemplating life. What is my future?

The Justin comment is interesting. I found out a few weeks later that whilst my family was on holiday at Disneyland, Justin kissed my friend Orla at a party. Orla was highly apologetic and told me as soon as I returned to school. I weirdly never had an issue with her over it, I guess because she immediately fessed up. And she was a good girl. She would've never tried to hurt me. I thought Justin was an asshole, though, and so I . . . gave him the silent treatment. He'd rue the day

---

* I was shocked to read this stuff in 2023 when I pulled out this diary that I used every single day in 1996. Firstly, what kind of normal teenager has these goals? "To network." OMG, I'm such a geek!! I can't believe I wrote that. The motivational tapes had clearly kicked in by this point. I was also saddened to see that first on the list, my top priority as I was about to turn sixteen was to lose weight. I was a very healthy, athletic teen girl who played sports several times a week. I didn't realize I'd had these thoughts so early on in my life about trying to lose weight. But this diary is littered with comments such as "I was good with my eating today" and, after eating pizza, "It was nice, not for my size, though."

he "cheated" on me. How dare he kiss one of my friends whilst I was riding Splash Mountain! Fuck that guy. I'm pretty sure I told people I'd broken up with him. That was clearly to save face, because my diary reveals that he called me on the landline to say that he "just wanted to be friends." And then I just agreed.

I sometimes wondered what my life might've been like if our relationship had become more serious. My sister Liberty ended up marrying a King's boy—the first boy she'd ever dated, when she was fifteen. He did lighting at the King's Theatre. That could've been me. In Liberty's case, her young love led to marriage. In my opinion, akin to my mother's story, it was an emotionally and financially abusive relationship.

Both women eventually bravely left these men and showed how strong they were. Both were left with practically nothing and had to rebuild from scratch. Both are incredible, smart women. But how could the same negative things happen to both? They both married a king but never thought of themselves as a queen. Both were treated so badly by men. My life wasn't meant to go down that path. I would refuse to let it.

Justin's cheating, even though it was quite minor, very early on solidified my lack of trust in men. So, whilst my sister latched on to the first boy she dated, I did the complete opposite. I didn't want anything to do with boys after that. I never dated anybody else throughout high school or the whole of my twenties.

I decided I should just focus on myself. I decided to work hard to be excellent and build up my résumé. I decided to make sure that I got into the best college. Boys were a smelly distraction. Girl power.

ELEVEN

Sweet Sixteen

March 1996. I slide into my knitted USA crop top and fasten the buttons on a fresh pair of white jeans. My skin is tanned from all the tennis and basketball I've been playing outside lately. I borrow some of Mum's mascara and blush and just have a stab at using it. This is it. This is my Sweet Sixteen birthday party. I feel fantastic. You know when you look in the mirror and you're like: Dammnnn! I smize and purse my full lips, and dammnnn. Now that my braces are off, I'm hot to trot.

And why wouldn't I be loving myself sick right now?! I'm about to have the hottest sixteenth-birthday party of the year at our new house. Our family moved back to civilization . . . well, back to Castle Hill, to a pretty respectable two-story brick house on a street called Galahad Crescent. It has a pool in the backyard with a waterfall that flows into the pool from a big rock above it (when it's working). It feels like a fresh start, like the fresh start my parents were trying to make with our recent family holiday to Disneyland.

Okay, so back to my sick party. "Oh my God, you would not believe how cool it's going to be"—me to everyone. Basically, every girl from my grade is coming (about a hundred) and basically every boy from King's I know from the theater shows is coming (about another hundred) . . . including the entire cast of our latest production: *Fiddler on the Roof*. I was cast as the ghost, Fruma-Sarah, with one splashy scene where I descend from the roof in a coffin screaming/singing to the character of Tevye, played by a boy named Tim. I have a secret crush on Tim, but I will never mention this to him. "Remember, Rebel, boys suck, and although most other girls are trying to get their attention, you are not" . . . I mean, I guess I am trying to get their attention tonight by wearing this crop top and mascara, but tonight is different, because it's my birthday and I want attention. A little kiss on the dance floor would be great!

We rent a jukebox to play music in our backyard. Dad chose the shittiest music, though, like some band from the seventies called Chicago, so we have to go back and swap it for one that plays cool modern songs like Coolio's "Gangsta's Paradise" (still my favorite karaoke song to date). Thanks for almost giving me a heart attack, Dad!

Mum ships all the dogs to another home for the night so they'll be safe. The paved dog runs become extra dance floor. We want to present an image of a successful family who lives in a nice house. Not an image of "dog people" who make money selling pet products—now available at Franklins discount supermarket. Just an image of prosperity. Like everything is fine with us. My parents are fine. My siblings are fine. And here we all are, putting on this really fun party. Mum gets how important this is to me, for my popularity, and she's worked tirelessly to make the backyard look great. There is not a dog poop within sight or smell.

Even Justin is coming to the party. I still have feelings for him, although I'm not going to embarrass myself and say anything. Now five of my girlfriends like him. Ugh. I have to forget about him. There are like ten of the top King's boy hotties coming to the party anyway. All with abs from rugby or rowing and full heads of hair. The sun is setting, and my life is about to officially be awesome.

Haps, Ann and Zahra come early to be with me before all the other kids arrive. We take a photo out on my deck with a Kodak camera. I love these girls. But this party thing is not really us. Sure, I'm popular now. But as a group we aren't "party girls." None of us ever drink alcohol. For the others it's because of religious reasons, but for me it was seeing Nanny's decay brought on by alcohol. I don't want to lose my mind and start having conversations with a magpie that lives by the toilet. Despite thinking I look hot right now, I always know that being smart is my best asset. I have to protect my brain.

Haps and Ann don't want to mingle with any of these King's boys. They're from a strict Coptic Orthodox community, so if they were going to "get with anyone," that would mean only a guy from their small community after church. They'd have to get married before doing anything physical. Haps and Ann just accept that this is how their love life is going to go (and it will—Haps will get married right after high school to an amazing guy from their community).

Zahra is more like me in that she isn't too fussed with boys because she wants to be a success. We both want to live and work in America one day. We spend our money at a store called Successories, which sells things like motivational calendars and posters of majestic mountains with sayings like "Keep Climbing." It's hard for Zahra to be at Tara because she has a double whammy—she's Indian and Muslim. Like in most places, there's a lot of racism in Australia, and Zahra has experienced it badly. Imagine going through the hardships of being a teenager in high school while being bullied because of your race and religion. Some of the teachers pick on you, even the headmistress picks on you. Zahra couldn't wait to finish high school and get as far away as possible from "this hellhole." (The "it does get better" update: she's now crushing it as a powerful attorney in Manhattan with three beautiful and smart children.)

So, I'm representing the USA with my crop top choice. I think America is the best place on the entire planet after our family trip— pancake stacks everywhere served by people who look like Roseanne. We went to Disneyland—it was my parents' last-ditch attempt to see whether their relationship could work. I was like, "Why are they giving it so many chances?" It's clear . . . it's not going to work.

I'd been given a video camera for Christmas and recorded most of our holiday. Look out, Steven Spielberg, 'cause here's Mel Bownds getting exclusive footage of us walking through Las Vegas hotel lobbies and going, "Ahhhhhhhhh. That's massive." At one point at Universal Studios, I gave Mum the camera to take a shot of me. She was being annoying and not doing what I directed: "Mum, pan from the Mel's Diner sign onto me and then when I start talking, YOU walk backward." She was fucking it up. She wasn't getting it. I got so, so angry that I punched her in the upper arm. Like I completely snapped. Over something so stupid. I instantly felt regret and shame. I didn't want to be like my dad and shake with rage and abuse my mother. I didn't want to be like that at all. I was now totally on her side despite my father's attempts to win me over. I wanted him gone—kicked out. I know Mum did too. I'd heard her crying about it.

That's why I didn't understand why Mum kept "trying" with him. Was it for us kids? So we could stay in our new house? "Make sure you film some of your father," she'd say as I held up the video camera. "Why??" I'd say petulantly. So that we could pretend like we were some happy family? We weren't a happy family. No one was saying "I love you" around here.

Why pretend?

I think I was so angry at Mum on that USA trip for trying to act like everything was fine. Everything clearly wasn't fine. It was so frustrating. Her inability to capture the shot I wanted on the video cam was just the trigger for all my pent-up anger. It wasn't really about the video. Why hadn't she left our father yet? Did she think Tinker Bell at Disneyland was going to sprinkle fairy dust on her head and make everything better?

"Someone's here!" Mum says. Her hands are raw from all the hours she spent prepping the backyard and garden for the party. I look out the window. Oh geez, I better take out the cheese plate and Jatz crackers and make sure the jukebox is programmed to play all the hottest hits first. It's only seven p.m. and the party doesn't start 'til seven thirty.

"That's weird," I think. Hang on, it's a bus pulling up outside my house. I watch as various teenagers get off, but I don't recognize any of them. "Mum, these aren't kids from Tara or King's." Somehow a whole bus-load of gate-crashers from another school has arrived and the party hasn't even started. "Warwick, you go out there!" Mum sends Dad to shoo them away. He gets rid of the strange kids . . . for now.

This is the start of things to come. Apparently, news about my "cool party" spread to kids from other high schools. Mum says it will be fine because she's commandeered some of her dog-showing friends to man our side gate and only allow the invited kids to enter. I'm not sure I'd put too much faith in a five-foot-three, slender, ginger-haired man who shows beagles to act as security—I would've preferred like a crew of big Samoans—but that's all we have. I try to get all the adults to leave when the party starts, because I certainly am not going to kiss any boys in front of my parents, but after that initial busload of crash-ers, Mum says they have to stay. That's actually the right decision!

The night turns into a complete disaster. So many gate-crashers. Our backyard is overrun with hundreds of teenagers who somehow each brought their own body weight in vodka. All the girls from my grade who live on campus (a.k.a. the boarders) have permission to sleep at my house overnight. Toting Sportsgirl bags that clink loudly, they sneak the alcohol into the house, then later bottle by bottle they bring it down to the party, under the ruse of "We're just going to the toilet, Mrs. Bownds."

I dance with some of the boys, trying to have a good time, but I just can't chill out. This is all getting to be way too much.

Then *bang*—from behind me, someone is punched and falls into the pool. A fight breaks out between some of the King's boys and new intruders from another school. Things are getting out of control. My parents call the cops—between them and their friends there are only four adults present—and now there are hundreds of drunk teens in the backyard going wild. Some kids are robbed, some are groped.

The police are called not once, not twice, but three times. We're lucky the teen ragers don't get into our house. I can't even imagine what would happen. Eventually, at midnight, I've had enough and go to bed . . . crying. It was MY party—but I felt a responsibility as the host for all the bad shit that happened and so I didn't have fun at all. Is being popular worth it? Because this is A LOT.

I wake up the next morning, look out the back window and just see empty alcohol bottles littering the whole backyard. There's my lovely mum, braless in her new Disneyland nightie, lugging a large garbage bag, slowly picking them up.

On Monday I return to school and my party is all anybody can talk about. It's legendary—one of those high school parties that people talk about for ages. Everyone seems to have had an incredible time, despite all the drama. I think because most people got fucked up, they don't remember some of the bad shit that happened. But I was stone-cold sober and remember everything. It was scary seeing my peers out-of-control drunk. I feel lucky that at least my sober besties Haps, Ann and Zahra had my back.

I go to our dress rehearsal for *Fiddler on the Roof*. The King's Theatre is now my happy place. I'm hanging precariously high up in the theater rafters in this closed, blacked-out coffin. During my big scene, the coffin is lowered by pimply year-nine boys pulling on a rope system. Then on my exact cue, timed to the music, I BUST out of the upright coffin dressed as an old ghost and start singing, then I run high-energy around the stage for the rest of the song. I go full out ALWAYS. I want to impress Mr. Haigh with my charisma and so I BRING IT!

I did it successfully a few times in rehearsal but now, for our dress, we have an audience. Something must've happened technically, because as the coffin lowers a little bit, I bust out like I'm supposed to on my cue—not knowing that I'm still almost ten feet (three meters) up in the air. OH shiiiiiiiiiit!

I'm falling. I realize the bloody coffin is nowhere near the stage floor. Once during rehearsals, it was like two inches off the ground, so when I popped out, I just took a slight step and was fine. But this time, with all the smoke and lighting effects for the dream sequence, I bust out of the darkness and then free-fall toward the stage. I reach back toward the coffin with my left hand to try to stop my fall but that only serves to scrape my skin all down my wrist. There is nothing to hold on to. I fall. SPLAT. I hit Teyve's bed frame and then I tumble onto the revolving stage. The crowd gasps. The orchestra stops. People think I'm dead. This is *Fiddler on the Roof* and I just fell from the ROOF!! I feel immediate pain in my ribs and my wrists. Mr. Haigh yells for everyone to stop and rushes onstage to help me. He also yells at the pimply stage crew boys for fucking up. "What the bloody hell are you doing!"

I start to move so that people don't think I'm actually dead, although I'm sure that rumor has started. Mrs. Marshall takes me to the medical center with another mother, and miraculously no bones are broken. I get away with just bruised ribs, a sprained left wrist and some scratches.

The next night, I'm back at the King's Theatre, singing "Tradition" with my bandaged arm up in the air. Despite the injury, I wasn't going to miss opening night. I'd have to be dead to not perform my role in our high school musical.

Everyone thought I was a legend for surviving the fall and still showing up to perform. In one year, I had gone from one of the most unpopular girls at Tara to one of the most popular. I had done this. And I didn't even have to drink or smoke or do drugs to be cool! (Sure, I might've locked a teacher in a cupboard, almost destroyed my family's new home with my party and then almost killed myself in a musical number, buuuuut I was there, crushing it!) This was my first sweet taste of fame.

TWELVE

Head Girl

You know how you have that kid that you're always compared with when you're younger? To me, that was Lucinda. (Recap: I knew Lucinda from Castle Hill Primary School because our family had sold her family a beagle, and I liked her because she had the world's neatest handwriting and, like me, played tennis.) She was blond, pretty, tan—good at sports AND smart. My mum wanted me to be her, I'm sure. She would make comments every now and then like "Why can't you be more like Lucinda?" or "Lucinda's got a boyfriend, so how come you don't have one?" It was like Lucinda was the measuring stick of how well I was doing in my life. An all-rounder, very good at pretty much everything and very sociable.

What mother didn't want her daughter to be like that?

Even when I was socially ostracized at Tara, Lucinda would extend an olive branch every now and again. We were tennis doubles partners for years. She'd invite me to her birthday parties. One year her birthday was a talent show and you can bet that I performed a rap medley wearing a baseball cap backward.

Back in our first year of high school, a history teacher explained that our senior year at Tara would coincide with the school's centenary, which made us a special graduation class. Therefore, whoever was elected head girl for the class of 1997, well, that was going to be truly special. Being voted head girl was like being voted most popular and class president all at once by your peers. As head girl you get to lead the school assemblies, you coordinate the formal (prom) and other events—you are essentially the student body leader. You have power, you have prestige, AND you get to wear a special badge. It was clear that Lucinda was being groomed to be our head girl. She was the obvious choice. She was classic. I was unconventional. She didn't get into trouble with the teachers. I challenged them. But I had to take a run at head girl. I had to throw my brimmed school hat into the ring. Sure, I wasn't everyone's cup of tea, but I was now really well-liked. And so here we were, Lucinda and I, former doubles partners, now neck and neck in the race for head girl. The vote would take place at the end of year eleven, but which one of us would win? I had to. I had to prove to my own mother that I was better than Lucinda.

I decided that I wanted to leave home and actually live on campus. Tara had just expanded their boardinghouse and the senior girls all had their own brand-new bedrooms. Haps started boarding first. I saw how much she loved it and so I begged my parents to send me.

Becoming a boarder was like having a slumber party every night with twenty of your friends. Dinner was in the dining hall promptly at five thirty p.m. every night. I loved that. Structure. Routine. Sometimes at home we wouldn't eat 'til nine p.m. because poor Mum would be too overloaded. At boarding school, I had a schedule; I could study more, do more. It was awesome.

When I got word that there was a place for me in the Tara boardinghouse, I said yes without hesitation. I felt guilty leaving my three younger siblings behind. There was a lot of fighting going on. But I knew I had to help myself if I was going to do well in my final exams. I wanted to make something of my life, and the family drama was going to suck me into the same depressed hole that now engulfed my mother. I thought, "It'll be okay, because when I'm rich, I can help them all." I knew I was being mega selfish but it would help everyone in the end.

There were weird boardinghouse rules to get used to—you weren't allowed to leave food on your plate in the dining hall unless the most senior girl at your table gave you permission. If she said you had to eat it, then you did. Every dessert, no matter what type it was, had to be eaten with a fork and a spoon. When a more senior girl was walking toward the boardinghouse entrance, the junior girl had to hold the door open and was only allowed to enter if the senior girl said, "Go through." Lucky for me, I only boarded when I was more senior, so most of these rules bent in my favor.

We were only allowed to watch thirty minutes of television each night in the common room—which was probably good for me as I was a bit of a TV addict. We would normally watch *Heartbreak High*, a local drama about kids in high school. Zahra and I had done work as extras on the show and sometimes we were clearly in the back of shots, which made us look super cool. We'd made about $100 a day and gotten to ditch school, so we really enjoyed it.

Mr. Haigh, now my mentor, said I was the gutsiest actor he'd ever worked with and decided to add a special production of the Jean-Paul Sartre play *No Exit* into the King's School theater season. It's essentially a three-person, very complex play that we were to perform in the round. This would make it more intimate.

My character in *No Exit*, Inez, was a lesbian. "Huh?" I thought. First, how were our very conservative Christian schools putting on a production where one character is clearly gay?! It goes to show you the power Mr. Haigh had as a respected director. Second, wait a second, why did Mr. Haigh cast me as the gay character? Did he see something in me that . . . was a bit gay? Tara Anglican School for Girls had zero out lesbians at this time. Of course, there must have been lezzies there. My money, for a start, was on the short-haired PE coach ironically named Miss Dykstra. The tennis coach who loved to pat us on the butt was also suspect. But no one was OUT. No one even talked about being gay. But here I was, at sixteen, given this incredible responsibility to play a lesbian character in an exceedingly difficult and complex play.

I sat in my new boardinghouse bedroom—which consisted of a single bed, one built-in desk with shelves, a desk chair, one computer and one cupboard that held my school uniforms and a few other sets of casual clothes. There was a window with bars on it . . . I guess so that we couldn't escape at night to see the King's boys? As I was learning my lines for *No Exit*, I couldn't help but think, "Is there something lesbian about me?" Rumor had it that one of my good friends had left the school because another girl had said that she had a crush on her. She literally changed schools to avoid a potential lesbian encounter. Then another girl was clearly going through some things and had shaved her head Britney Spears style. She was then forced to wear a beanie every day at school until her hair grew out. Because short hair was seen as "unladylike."

Our headmistress, Dr. Shatford (who, FYI, had a very short haircut herself and was unmarried), was horrified when she came to see *No Exit*. I loved that Mr. Haigh pushed boundaries in this way. It was certainly not appropriate for us to be doing this material, but we did it anyway. And we did it to such a high standard that we were asked to put the play on professionally in the city, which we couldn't do because we were all students and had exams, but it was cool to be asked.

The night Dr. Shatford came, I made sure to be especially lesbian—when I had to stare into my co-star Eliza's eyes, I lingered for a long time. I really made it seem like I was going to kiss her. We were directed NOT to kiss. My lips just had to get really close to Eliza's and they did. Plus, I added swear words into the heated scenes just for extra dramatic effect. But what could the headmistress do? I could get away with it because I was onstage. I was playing a character. It wasn't really me. But the act of doing all this, in this ultraconservative environment, was so gutsy.

One day during lunch, Eliza yelled out across the quad, "Mel's a lesbian." I'm not sure why she did this. Why was she hanging over the balcony yelling this out at me as I was walking below? I was momentarily stunned. For any other girl, being labeled a lesbian would have been social suicide. I mean, it was considered a sin; that's what was preached. That is why, even though I suspect at minimum 10 percent of my classmates were gay, no one ever came out. No one dared. But somehow I was popular enough that I could just make a quick-witted joke back up to Eliza. "You wish!" I said. I laughed it off. But later that night in the privacy of my dorm room I pondered what she'd said—was she targeting me? I didn't get it. Luckily some other boardinghouse drama unfolded—like how the year twelves were going to haze us one night soon and we all needed to sleep together in the common room for protection—and no one remembered Eliza's comments. (They did haze us—tied us all up with rope and paraded us around the school in the early hours of the morning, hosed us and threw flour and birdseed on us. Eliza got the most.)

Then suddenly, it was the end of year eleven, time to vote for head girl. I had campaigned over several months, taking part in lots of school spirit activities and talking to as many girls as I could. See, in Australia, you can't appear too full of yourself, but my résumé was looking good—I was the school basketball captain, I was on the state-finalist Mock Trial team, I was in the Firsts for debating (meaning the school's top team), I'd won public speaking competitions, I was the lead in the school play, I did handbells and choir, I played multiple sports and I was one of the top girls academically. Sure, I'd been a bit of a menace to some teachers and had shocked everyone by playing a lesbian—but that's just a bit of fun, isn't it?

Everyone knew it was essentially a two-horse race. Me vs. Lucinda.

Zahra thought I could win. "I think you're going to get head girl, Mel, you deserve it," she said supportively, "but the teachers could rig it and give it to Lucinda." I'd done all I could. At Tara, every achievement was rewarded with a "pocket"—embroidery commemorating your accomplishment that was added to the pocket of your school blazer. My blazer read like an essay. I was decorated. I definitely had a shot.

Girls cast anonymous votes in boxes. The teachers made sure to emphasize how important this vote was because it was the school's centenary. Each student had one vote, but the teachers' votes counted as two.

The whole school was seated in assembly as the results were read by Dr. Shatford. "Our centenary head girl will be . . ."

"Please let it be me, please let it me," I thought.

"Lucinda Marblethorpe," said Shatford as she shat on my dreams.

All the girls politely clapped as Lucinda's cute, pretty friends all screamed and hugged her.

"Ughhhhhh," I thought. Was I an idiot for thinking I could get it? Was it just always going to be Lucinda? Because girls like Lucinda just seemed to get everything. Then later that day, it was announced that I had been voted deputy head girl. I wasn't top dog, but out of all the eligible girls, I was the second-most popular student in the whole school. And I still got a badge to wear on my collar. On the front cover of the book about the school's history, published that centenary year, I am pictured standing outside the gates of Tara with Lucinda and some of the other junior girls. There we are with regal looks on our faces. Privileged white private-school girls.

Later that night, when I was finally alone in my dorm room, I cried. My mum had called—I now had a cell phone that I'd wear on a belt on weekends. She was proud of me, but she also begged me to return home. She "needed me." I knew what she meant. She needed my support whilst she was dealing with my father's outbursts, but I just couldn't. I couldn't be there for her—not this coming year. I had all my senior exams to crush over the next twelve months and I needed an outstanding mark on my final exams to get into an excellent college. To do that, I was going to have to say goodbye to the King's Theatre productions for good now—even though the ABC (the excellent government-funded TV channel) was going to make a television documentary about the next one, the musical *The Mikado*. I was going to have to let down Mr. Haigh because I had to sit in that boardinghouse room and study my ass off. Now was the time to prove that my parents' investment in me would pay off. Acting was a waste of time. Acting wasn't going to be a career. I had to get 100 percent on all my exams. I had to be perfect.

Getting a medical or law degree was my ticket to success. I was sure I didn't want to become a doctor, though, because I couldn't bring myself to dissect anything in science class; it was just too gross. Law school became my goal. I put "99/100" on a Post-it note in my dorm room above my chunky computer. It was the mark I needed to get accepted into the top law school. If I did that, then I could get a job at a top law firm and make my family proud. Then maybe my life would be exactly like an *Ally McBeal* episode. Hopefully, I could win cases by day and sing at the piano bar at night.

I studied so hard that year that my eyesight deteriorated, and I needed glasses. I memorized hundreds of pages of material per subject whilst eating Tim Tams. I wrote countless essays. Even though math came quite easy, I still did as many practice exams as I could find. I was supremely focused. Nothing was going to stop me from reaching my goal. Not even what was going on at home. 99/100.

Mum finally kicked Dad out of the house on Valentine's Day 1997. She'd finally mustered the courage after all those awful years and wised up to the fact that she deserved more. I was so proud of her. It must've been extremely difficult. Ironically, that day—before knowing their marriage was about to end—Dad had sent her flowers. He'd never done anything romantic for my mother in the twenty years they had been married.

I did score in the top 1 percent of all students with my final Higher School Certificate results, with a 98.9 Tertiary Entrance Rank (the equivalent of a Universities Admission Index of 99.3, which is pretty much akin to the current system). With that mark I could get into any law school I chose. There wasn't a huge celebration when I got my excellent final marks. It was expected. My family had sacrificed so that I could have an education. Now I had it. I didn't leave the boardinghouse until a week after my last exam. Most girls are out of there immediately, running out like animals escaping a bush fire. They race home. I took my time. I walked out the sandstone Tara gates and it was anticlimactic. High school was over, but now what the hell was I going to do?

I chose the University of New South Wales and an arts/law double degree. I had several scholarship offers—one was from the Australian Army for their Intelligence Corps—but I turned them all down. Because despite getting into the course I wanted, despite doing so well on my exams that I was now on the traditional track to legal greatness, I wanted to do something crazy. Now—and I don't think anyone could've predicted this—I was going to leave everything and everyone I'd ever known behind and go to Africa . . . by myself.

THIRTEEN

South Africa

Africa! Plot twist, I know! How did that happen? Well, long story short: In my final year of high school, I was a witness in a major crime squad investigation. I seemed pretty badass having police pick me up from school several times in their squad car and drive me down to the court- house to testify. I've never told anybody any details about the case and never will. But I did provide evidence as I felt it was the right thing to do, even though it was hard being a minor and testifying as an adult, in person, in the same room as the accused. A man connected to the case was very impressed with how I handled myself and recommended that I apply for the Rotary Youth Ambassador program. I hadn't heard of it before but learned that it was a year-long program for outstanding high school graduates, essentially a "gap year" before starting university. If you were selected, you were sent to a foreign country to "spread inter- national goodwill," which basically meant giving speeches, doing a few charitable things and also experiencing the host country and having a cultural exchange.

Most of my classmates were going straight to law school—literally like 90 percent of the girls from my year went to different law schools after graduation—but I did like to be different. In the first sentence of my final high school report card Dr. Shatford wrote: "Melanie is a non-conformist." (Which I think wasn't supposed to be a compliment at the time, but I took it as one.) I wasn't going to be like other girls. So, I decided to apply to become a youth ambassador.

Now that I was going out into the real world, who was I? The fact is, I didn't know. I didn't have a clue. I watched so much *Oprah* that I wanted to have a "purpose." I wanted my life to mean something, but I didn't know what that was. At least if I took a gap year I would have a little bit of time to figure things out.

When I got to know more, the Rotary Youth Ambassador program sounded amazing. They selected the best and brightest from our area of Western Sydney to go off to different countries. I was like the lead character in *The Book of Mormon*, hoping for Orlando, USA! Or somewhere cool like that. The selection process was very intense. I had to prove that I was a good public speaker and that I would represent Australia well, in that I had good values and morals.

They had lots of rules, but the biggest was called the four D's: no drinking, no driving, no dating and no drugs. Lucky for me, none of that was going to be a problem. I was a perfect candidate for the program. I was selected, but my first country offer—and you only really got one offer in this extremely competitive program—was to go to South Korea. Not exactly Orlando! They were going to put me in an intensive language-learning school for a month before sending me to live in South Korea for the rest of the year. However, languages don't come easily to me—so purely because I feared a massive language barrier, I rejected their offer. They were shocked. I thought I'd never hear from them again.

But then the Rotarians came back and asked, "What about South Africa? Would you go there?" They wanted to give me a challenging country, not an "easy one like America or Canada."

Mr. Haigh had shared crazy stories about Africa—some positive, some negative. He drove a little Jeep painted like a zebra around King's. From a distance, looking through my boardinghouse window, it looked like a zebra running through the grass fields. So even though Africa seemed like a crazy idea, because of my connection to Mr. Haigh, because I looked up to him so much, I thought, "Yeah, okay, why not give Africa a go?" It would be an adventure. It would be like *The Lion King*. I love that movie.

Turns out it was NOTHING like *The Lion King*.

South Africa was only a few years post-apartheid, and Johannesburg, where I was heading, had the highest rape and murder rate in the world. But oh no, here's me thinking I'm going to be singing in the bush with Pumbaa.

I was given a new blazer to wear—my official youth ambassador blazer, green with a yellow Australia-shaped name tag pin above the pocket. The Rotarians came to the airport on January 1, 1998, to help send me off, along with my family.

I looked over at Mum. She was crying her eyes out. I didn't quite understand why and thought she was overreacting. "I'm going to be fine," I assured her. She cried like she'd never see me again. But to her credit, she let me go. She allowed me to travel halfway around the world to a country where I literally didn't know a soul and would have to live with strangers.

My father wasn't there. We weren't talking now. It was clear to him I had chosen my mother's side, despite his efforts to brainwash me, and so now he was trying to punish all of us. He would do random things—you never knew what day he was going to show up. One time we were having a garage sale to make money (because Mum was now raising four kids on only one public school teacher's wage; Dad had set up the family business so that Mum had no access to the money). We were selling things like the old hammers we used to use to set up Petcetera Etc. "Two dollars each!" Dad came over, became livid that we were selling something that was apparently "his" and walked inside, grabbed the first thing he could find—a pen—and gouged Mum's favorite wooden coffee table in the living room. Gouged it right down the middle in a fit of anger.

Another time, he walked into our house whilst we were having dinner, grabbed two newly born beagle puppies from the litter box by the scruff of their necks and swung them around, threatening to take them. We kids cried and screamed. "Dad! Don't!" we pleaded. We feared he'd kill them in front of us. They were so tiny. They were also worth about $750 each and Mum was selling them. Dad knew this. Eventually he put them down and instead took a framed picture off the wall, which he said was valuable. (It wasn't!) Nothing we owned was really valuable except for the house itself, but it was some small win for him apparently. Piece by piece he would try to make Mum rue the day she'd left him. But his actions only turned us kids against him and left him with nothing.

Dad got his brother to call up Mum's new job, teaching at Parramatta West Public School, and say all sorts of disgusting things about her, trying to get her fired. Who would do that? I found out later that Dad's verbal campaign against me was to tell my younger brother and sister continuously that I was selfish and didn't love them. Just like how he'd told me that Mum didn't love me, only the dogs. Despite all the crazy shit that was going on, Mum still made my younger siblings Anna and Ryan stay with him on weekends. I could never understand why. He was clearly unstable and now he was living with his demented mother, which couldn't have helped. Mum would never badmouth our dad. She thought it was the "right thing to do" to allow him to see the younger kids. But Libby and I had definitely cut him off. We weren't going anywhere near him.

My father did agree to keep paying for private school fees (although smart Liberty applied for and won a 50 percent scholarship at Tara, which helped) and had promised my younger siblings that they would get the same schooling I did. On this point he never faltered. Yet part of his plan to hurt my mother was to ruin Osco Pet Products, a business that had been thriving, that should've been worth seven figures. My mother was technically the director of Osco, so he was determined to run that into the ground. He bought himself a BMW and started gambling again . . . all whilst we were selling our personal items on the front lawn for $2 each. Mum wanted us to stay in the nice house for as long as possible, but we all knew eventually Dad would take it away.

So here I am—walking through security at Sydney's international airport. You know, just popping off to Africa amid the family chaos! I board the Qantas plane. Rotary provides a small monthly stipend for being part of the program, but my grandparents Gar and Poppy paid for my economy plane seat. I have one suitcase and a carry-on. My district sent one boy and one girl—yes, it's all very *Hunger Games*—and so on the plane I meet my male compatriot: Nicholas, a.k.a. Snickers, a boy with spiky hair from Western Sydney full of cheeky jokes and love for Belinda Carlisle and Bette Midler.

Snickers and I sit together on the plane, wearing the same green blazers, both our faces freckled from the Australian sun. We want to make a difference in the world, we want to have fun, we want to find ourselves on this adventure.

"Hey, I'm Nick," says Snickers as we shake hands like professional youth ambassadors do. We talk about where we went to school, and I tell him I attended Tara. "So, you're a massive bitch then!" he says, only half-joking. I ask him why he thinks that, and he tells me about a debating competition where he went against a team from Tara and was convinced they cheated. Snickers went to a very rough public school and has a real fly in his face about people who attended private schools. He thinks Tara girls are all stuck-up, privileged bitches. I want to tell him that my upbringing really wasn't posh, but he isn't buying it. During the flight we bond over a packet of Burger Rings (burger-flavored chips). We're more similar than we both know. This is the start of a lifelong friendship.

When we arrive in Joburg, I quickly say goodbye to Snickers as he's staying about ninety minutes away with his host family. I'm actually stationed in the far east in Vanderbijlpark, an industrial city in the Vaal Triangle, the territory where a lot of the Boer Wars were fought. Nick got a more upscale central suburb, I got Vanderbijlpark . . . which . . . umm . . . has a steel factory.

My host family, the Du Rands, pick me up at the airport. They are speaking English, but I can't understand anything they are saying because of their thick Afrikaans accents. I just smile, and as soon as I get into their car to drive to my new home, I almost instantly revert back to my shy self. I'm in another country with another culture. I've never seen a real gun before and now there are multiple guns between the front seats. It's more than overwhelming.

I lay in bed that first night after the Du Rands offered me pizza topped with banana for dinner, and I was thinking, "Why do they put bananas on pizza?" (I'm a pineapple-on-pizza girl myself.) More important, I was thinking: "Why on earth did I do this? This is absolutely mental." It's not like I could call anyone and say, "Hey! Sorry! I've changed my mind!" I didn't have a cell phone. I didn't know where I was. It's not like I could Google anything as I didn't even have access to the internet. I couldn't buy a plane ticket home. I didn't have any money. I just lay there . . . thinking I'd made the biggest mistake of my life.

Guns really were everywhere. There was barbed wire on the top of house fences. There were vicious-looking guard dogs trained to only attack Black people. This place was full-on, and I'd only been here half a day. I was told that if I was walking by myself, I had to carry a weapon that was basically a wooden baton. I guess I was supposed to hit someone over the head with it if they tried to attack me. Break their skull? When I was in the Du Rands' house by myself, I had to wear a panic alarm necklace to press in case of an intruder. Luckily, I never had to use either.

The Du Rands had two teenage daughters, Marion and Stephanie, who were nothing but kind and welcoming. I was just this random Australian girl who had been sent to live with them and I don't think this family had really wanted to have an exchange student of sorts living with them. They were somehow, last-minute, just lumped with me via the Rotary Club. Mrs. Du Rand, in a very nice way, had told me that there'd been some mix-up, but they'd agreed to host me.

"Oh great," I thought. "They didn't even want me." And now here

I was, and I was nothing special. It's not like I'd smuggled a cute koala in my suitcase I could show off at parties. I was just . . . me. Melanie Bownds. Average height, average build, average looks . . . smart, but you couldn't tell that by looking at me. I wasn't particularly fun or funny.

Snickers was living it up with a family that really wanted him—they wanted a boy from Australia! He was cracking jokes and making friends left, right and center—I was sure of it. I didn't have Snickers's natural charisma. What on earth was I going to do? The only way to get out of the program was to be sent home in disgrace. For a girl that meant either breaking one of the four-D rules or getting pregnant. I wasn't exactly going to do that. Two of my teenage cousins now had babies and their lives didn't seem great.

As part of the cultural experience, I got sent to the local high school, Transvalia, and to my delight found another boy there from the Rotary program—he was Australian too and his name was also Nick, so let's just call him Hot Nick from Tasmania. Because let me tell you, Hot Nick was handsome, and he had one of those deep, rugged Aussie voices that seems to tenderly caress your ears! Plus, he was a brilliant student and, no surprise, also going to law school after this year in Africa.

I kind of instantly became obsessed with Hot Nick and was so thrilled to have another Australian at the same school as me. He was genuinely lovely and so intelligent. We played chess and chatted away in the school library. It was a little weird being placed in a high school when we'd both already graduated. We didn't have any real schoolwork to do, so we just bided our time until we could go on the big trips with the other youth ambassadors and experience more of South Africa. I discovered the library's collection of videos and watched everything by their most famous comic, Leon Schuster. This guy is a comedy genius—and was doing movies like Johnny Knoxville's *Bad Grandpa* and comedy character work like Sacha Baron Cohen way before they were doing it.

I found laughter. I needed it—which I think is why I was drawn to watching Leon Schuster. My father had been a huge fan of British comedies, but I never wanted to watch them with him. He'd watch *Only Fools and Horses* or *Fawlty Towers* and liked Monty Python. I was more taken by the Nickelodeon channel. But now, sitting in the library all day, half a world away from my family and friends, I turned to comedy. I'd watch those Leon Schuster videos in the school library and just laugh so hard. I also learned a lot about racial tensions in South Africa from his work. I then watched every single Jackie Chan VHS I could find, because I became obsessed with him when the Du Rand daughters invited me to join their karate class. (Yes, this is how I first learned nunchakus.)

I would spend the rest of my days writing people back in Australia long, somewhat sad handwritten letters. Girls from Tara, my family, the Bells, Mr. Haigh. Being so far away gave me new perspectives. I missed my friends. Friends are important. I loved my family so much. I was so grateful for everything my mother had done for me. She loved me so much that she allowed me to go on this crazy adventure because it was something I wanted to do. And the questions I'd keep contemplating in my head were "What am I going to do with my life?" and "What is my purpose?"

On my eighteenth birthday, I received a package from Mum with a silver Tiffany necklace inside. She must've spent all her savings on that—or got a credit card to afford it—and boy, did I treasure it. It was my first real piece of jewelry. But apart from that, I spent my birthday alone in the middle of South Africa, waiting for Oprah to come on the television and inspire me.

Two months passed and it was time for our "tour" around South Africa with the other youth ambassadors. This was where we'd all pile into a bus and sightsee together—visiting touristy places like Robben Island, the prison where Nelson Mandela was held; Table Mountain; game parks; and Kimberley's Big Hole. Yes, there is an underground mine and open pit called Kimberley's Big Hole, and it made us laugh every time someone said it. Most of the youth ambassadors were incredibly loud and confident. At Tara, when we had to change clothes, we used our school dress like a tent canopy. No one ever saw our naked bits. But these Brazilians and Europeans seemed so free with their bodies. Not self-conscious at all. They told me they'd go naked in saunas!

I was most impressed with the female Canadian ambassador, Lorelei, though. If I wished at school I was more like Lucinda, I wished during exchange I was more like Lorelei. She was just so confident. She could walk up to any stranger and start a conversation—a meaningful one. Lorelei was into Snickers, but Snickers was into Jarle from Norway. It was a bit of a love triangle, and I was just the fourth wheel. If we had been in a massage train, I'd have been the one on the end giving and not receiving a massage from anyone. But boy did we have fun—going to an ostrich farm, going to a winery in Cape Town, going to Planet Hollywood in Cape Town (which was bombed the very week after we were there, and several people died . . . did I mention this place was dangerous AF!).

Whilst we were all on the bus together traveling from place to place, Snickers and I would share headphones as we listened to our cassettes filled with pop songs. We also had songs passed down over the years from former youth ambassadors, which we'd belt on the bus. "Exchanges, exchanges, a long way from home, we're highly obnoxious so leave us alone. We drink when we're thirsty, we drink when we're dry, we drink 'til we're bottomless and then we get hi-hi-hi. We are exchanges, exchanges, we live it up, we screw it up, we fuck it up we do, so pass another [beer brand] or two, or three or four or a couple more." I'd sing along heartily like everyone else even though I'd never had more than a sip of alcohol in my life.

As we drove to KwaZulu-Natal, a coastal South African province known for its beaches, mountains and savannah, I was sitting with Snickers and Lorelei in the backseat of the bus. Everyone had partied a little too much the night before (somehow the "no drinking" rule seemed to be overlooked), but I was the only sober square who had gone to bed early and seemed to be awake.

We were stopped at an intersection when suddenly, I saw a mob running toward the bus carrying large sticks. "Oh no! They've got sticks." Then I saw another pack of people chasing the first group—but this second mob had guns and started shooting. They were shooting in our direction. It was like everything was taking place in slow motion. "Oh no! They've got guns!" Then, "Everybody down!" I yelled with clear intention. Everyone got down on the floor and the bus driver sped through the red traffic light. Shit like that happened in South Africa A LOT. But I was glad I saw it coming and warned the bus driver. None of us were harmed but I'm sure people back at that intersection didn't fare as well.

Later that day, we swam with wild dolphins off the coast of KwaZulu-Natal. It was majestic. I'd experienced two extremes of South Africa in one day—the wild rugged beauty and the wild violence. This country had both. Light and dark. Like what I had. I felt like I had so much light from my mother, from gorgeous Gar and her side of the family, and so much dark from my father and his side of the family. I was a combination. I was a contradiction. I could be so shy at times and then at other times strangely brave and give a speech in front of a thousand people. I could be so smart at times and at others very naïve. And the two sides battled inside me over which one would emerge. Witnessing violent situations in South Africa did put into perspective all the incidents with my father back in Australia—it might've been awful, but at least no one was getting killed. Australia seemed like the safest sanctuary on earth. No wonder it's nicknamed "the Lucky Country." I now felt really lucky to have grown up in a country where education was free, health care was free, where there was true law and order.

I remember Mrs. Du Rand, my host mother, telling me, "Still waters run deep," which is how she described my personality. I had a lot going on inside. But outside, people couldn't really tell what I was thinking or feeling because I'd internalize everything. On the outside, even in a traumatic situation like the bus incident, I just seemed still. I wanted to share more with people I met, but I couldn't. I came from a family that didn't speak about emotions and personal things, so I couldn't express things like they could.

My first game park experience was with my host family. Mr. Du Rand had organized for me to shoot a warthog with a high-tech bow and arrow (because I had softly expressed that I was kinda against and scared of guns). So, as my initiation into the "real" South Africa, I was tasked with shooting a warthog and then watching it be skinned for food. Instead of singing with Pumbaa, I was now crouching behind a bush, waiting to kill him.

I was instructed on how to hunt properly, how to shoot to kill. After what seemed like hours, I shot a warthog dead with one shot. They said I needed to smear some of the blood on my face as it was my first kill, and this was apparently important. I did. It really wasn't my thing to kill an animal (take me back to the dog shows!), but I was experiencing their culture. Apparently, the fee for the hunt went toward the preservation of the game park, to protect more-sacred animals—so at the time it wasn't seen as a bad thing. The warthog was later roasted.

"Don't you want to try some of the warthog?"

"Um . . . no thanks . . . I'm vegetarian."

On the subsequent "Northern Tour" with my fellow youth ambassadors, we visited Kruger National Park and went for a walk with a lion and an elephant. I was like, "Is this dangerous? You know, just walking with a lion and an elephant?" There were no leashes, no guns here. What if these animals went rogue? Hakuna matata? The South African guides were like, "Ach, no, it's fine. Just don't run away from the animal because then they will think you're prey. Then you'll be dead."

So, a bunch of us were just walking around a game park with a lion and an elephant. No biggie. Except it was a massive biggie. It might've been the most magical experience of my life. A semi-wild lion and elephant roaming around the game park with a bunch of international kids as the sun set. Wow. We also saw hippos and rhinos. It was insane.

At one point the guides told me to touch this big electric fence, which was meant to keep rhinos out of our camp. I touched it and it felt like every bone in my body was breaking. And then they all laughed, and I was like: "Geeeeeeeeez." (South Africans do have quite a dark sense of humor.) That part wasn't so magical. Neither was the fact that when we got back to camp, monkeys were rifling through our luggage . . . apparently looking for food or prescription drugs. We shooed them out.

The tours were so much fun that sometimes we'd fully forget about the dangerous stuff happening around us. Stuff that if my mother had known about, she would've called for my return immediately. In post-apartheid South Africa there was violence like taxi wars, where different local tribes were fighting over the transport routes. From their bakkies or minivans, they would just shoot each other over disputes. I saw many dead bodies on the sides of roads, many images that I've had to subsequently block out of my mind because they're just too disturbing. I'd never seen a dead body until I went to South Africa, and the image was awful. People at this time were getting carjacked or killed on the street just for their watch or a piece of jewelry (I very rarely wore my Tiffany necklace). Three times during that year I was caught in crossfire—luckily, I never got shot myself.

Working with the Rotary Club that was sponsoring me, I helped rebuild a rape crisis center. Rotarians are so amazing in their ability to give back to their communities, and this was one of the club's projects. Sadly, soon after we finished, it was bombed because some of the men in that township didn't think rape was a crime. Then we had to rebuild it again. "Ach, this country is so different to Australia," I said in the slightly South African twang that I'd now adopted. From speaking basic Afrikaans daily and even some Zulu, my accent changed a bit.

While most days were either boring or dramatically violent, there were of course so many amazing experiences. Like the time on the Northern Tour when I got up super early and climbed one of the Drakensberg mountains, and when we got to the top—right at sunrise—we saw wild baboons. Majestic. These were adventures I could never have experienced if I'd just gone straight to law school.

One time I was dared to go into a cage with a leopard. Why? I don't know, South Africans had a pretty dark sense of humor, as I've said, but I did it. It was quite a large cage, more like a grassy enclosure, with one adult leopard inside. The leopard seemed to be asleep on a small tree. But at the game parks I hadn't seen a leopard, because they're rare and hard to spot. When would I get this opportunity again? I stepped into the cage. It was crazy. Again, if my mum had known I was doing this, she would've died. I could've died. But the guides had said that as long as I didn't run away, if I wasn't frightened, then the animal wouldn't think I was prey. So I breathed from my gut, like I'd do when I was nervous before hitting the stage at the King's Theatre, and I moved slowly inside. Let's be honest, I only took one or maybe two steps into the cage and I stood there for maybe a minute in silence. But I did it. I faced this leopard. It looked at me with its gorgeous light eyes. I stared back. So strong, so beautiful. I looked at its coat. It was light AND dark. It was a beautiful mixture of both.

FOURTEEN

Malaria

Apart from the youth ambassador tours that were organized by Rotary, I was also invited on a three-week excursion with about sixteen students from Transvalia High School, traveling north from South Africa through Zimbabwe, Mozambique and Malawi, all the way up to Cape Maclear, Lake Malawi. This was going to be a very rugged trip, unlike the youth ambassador tours. We traveled in the back of what looked like a converted cattle truck. And we slept on the ground in tents. This wasn't about visiting touristy spots—this was a real African bush adventure. I was excited and bought tan corduroy shorts and a bush hat for the occasion (did I mention I had zero fashion sense?). For the most part, there were no showers, no toilets, no luxuries. We brought all the food we needed in the bottom of the truck, a few clothes and our tents. And we were off. My host sister Stephanie came on the trip, and so did Hot Nick, but the rest were mainly girls from year eleven whom I didn't yet know.

We bounced around as the cattle truck puttered through the thick African bush. On the first night, when I was lying on the ground in my sleeping bag, I heard the laughter of hyenas. It was so creepy—were they going to come and eat us in our sleep? "Ach, no," our South African driver said. "If you're close to the campfire, the animals won't come and eat you. They're scared of the fire." I nudged closer to the campfire. "Hmmm, okay." I really needed to go to the toilet right before I fell asleep, but I was terrified to move away from the fire. I somehow held it all night.

There was a lot of time spent driving and I struck up conversations with the girls. Whilst they mainly spoke Afrikaans, they all studied English at school and were intrigued about my life in Australia. One girl, Lilliene, was super friendly and so cool. Like a lot of Afrikaner girls in that area, she was a bit of what I called a "glamazon." A lot of the Afrikaner girls really did have the body type of Charlize Theron, tall and athletic. (Lilliene was smart too, and if my memory serves me right, I think she became head girl/school captain the following year.) I felt like I had found a group with these girls, and it felt awesome—I became the funny Australian exchange student among the Afrikaner glamazons (I guess those Leon Schuster videos had rubbed off a bit and I was exercising my comedic muscles for the first time—mainly by telling half-exaggerated stories about koalas and kangaroos).

At one point, we're driving on a bumpy dirt track, and we hit a branch with a wasp nest, and it falls into our moving truck. Although there's a roof on the truck, the sides are all open. The giant nest falls right next to my legs and the angry wasps start swarming out.

The wasps—lots of wasps—fly up my baggy corduroy shorts, and I freak out.

"Ahhhhh!" I scream, and in a panic, I jump off the moving truck with wasps crawling up my shorts. Some of them sting me in the commotion. I take off my shorts in front of everybody, including Hot Nick. If it weren't so painful it would be a hilarious comedy scene.

"Ahhhhhhh!!" The stings really hurt. These African bush wasp fuckers are really hard-core. The bites on my legs start turning into welts. We're in the middle of nowhere, in the veldt. Our guides give me some kind of super-strong antihistamine in case I'm allergic to wasp stings. I pass out from the strong drugs.

I only remember waking up in the tent the next day. But I don't know how I got there. At least the stinging welts had gone down. I remember soothing myself with a Coca-Cola and what we call in Australia hot chips (thicker French fries). Even if you were in the middle of nowhere in Africa, somehow you could always find someone selling Coca-Cola and hot chips.

After so much travel and gossiping, we got to our destination, the stunning Lake Malawi. Wow. "Why aren't there any adults around?" I asked. There were only kids in this village, no local adults anywhere. Our South African driver said, "Well, they've all died of AIDS."

The children carved pieces of wood and soapstone to sell to earn money. I loved their initiative. I of course bought as many as I could humanly carry. I told myself, though, that when I was successful, I would give back to the poorest of the poor, to kids like this. (And that's why I've since donated a lot of money to the School of St. Jude in Tanzania, which provides poor local kids a bright future through education. It's an amazing school, GOOGLE IT!)

We kept all our food underneath the cattle truck. We'd cook in large cauldrons and just eat and drink very simply. It was mainly stews or sometimes a cornmeal porridge called mieliepap. One of the girls had a hidden stash of chocolates and she became queen bee because of this. I literally would've done anything for chocolate on most of those days. I would've picked sand out of her toenails for hours. Luckily, because she thought I was cool and funny, she'd share with me. We swam in Lake Malawi, which was just gorgeous.

One night as we were driving back through rural Mozambique, it was getting dark quickly. We didn't make it to the campsite where we were supposed to stay for the night. Our drivers, who I believe were ex–South African military guys, were like, "Okay, well, we're just going to have to make camp here by the side of the road, hey? Do NOT go more than a few feet from the road." "Why?" I asked. "Land mines," they said. "So, if I have to go to the toilet?" "Do it right here unless you want your leg blown off." This was the third week of our trip—we were filthy from all the adventuring. We didn't really have the energy to properly set up our tents, which had mosquito protection. That night,

I just slept underneath the truck. I woke up the next morning and one side of my face was in the dirt; the other side, the one that was exposed to the air, had about fifty mosquito bites.

During my year in South Africa, I knew that malaria was an issue—I knew that I was going in and out of malaria zones all the time with the constant traveling. I decided not to take the antimalarial tablets. They made me nauseous, so I just decided to take the risk. And now I'd been bitten dozens of times on my face. I thought to myself, "Geez, there's probably a high chance that I could get malaria from this." But malaria can take about two weeks to develop in your system, so I felt fine for now. I just hoped that the bites would go down quickly.

As we bumped around in the back of the truck, I clutched a set of soapstone rhino bookends wrapped in a sweater. I didn't want them to get scratched because they were a present for my grandmother Gar, a treasure from one of the deepest parts of Africa. Being out in nature, away from any supermarkets, meant I couldn't buy blocks of chocolate or processed junk food. Apart from the rare Coca-Cola, I was mainly eating unprocessed whole foods. I wasn't wearing any makeup, I was naturally contoured with dirt from all the not-showering, and my jaw looked snatched. My curly hair was blowing free in the wind as the truck moved. My face and arms were sun-kissed from being outdoors. Lilliene looked at me, smiling, and said, "You look more and more pretty every single day, Mel." In the depths of the African bush, without any modern comforts, I was happy. South Africa had been hard, but this trip was joyous. I knew that some of my hardships in Australia really weren't that bad in comparison—not compared to AIDS devastating communities, not compared to African poverty, not compared to the violence that was happening on this continent. I'd always had a place to live, I'd had food, I'd had electricity and running water and toilets. I'd had a world-class education. Sometimes you need to take a huge step away from your situation to see it clearly. You can't see the whole chessboard if you're stuck looking closely at one piece. I felt like I could view my life now with the clarity of the water in Lake Malawi. The adventure to Cape Maclear had made me feel "clear."

Later, at sunset, when we stopped on a deserted Mozambique beach to camp, I walked away from the group to write in my diary and to reflect. "What am I going to do with my life?" I looked out as the waves crashed. As the sun set, the water got darker. I wanted to do so much, but what did I actually want to do and how do I do it? Life could go in a million different tangents from here. It got too dark, and I went back to the group.

The next morning, we head toward the South African border. As we're driving in the afternoon these African guys come along next to us on their moving truck, yelling, trying to get our attention. I notice that these guys have big guns. They yell out, "Eh! Your truck is broken! You have to get off the truck." And I'm thinking, "Hang on. This is weird. Our truck is moving—it's clearly NOT broken."

"STOP! Get off your truck! Your truck is broken." They're demanding now.

And then our drivers stop. (We only have two male Afrikaner drivers/chaperones with us.) Why the hell are they stopping!? Who are these guys?

We get ushered onto their truck and taken somewhere, which I can only really describe as an outdoor bar-type place in a small village in rural Mozambique. The men with guns act casual, like nothing is really happening. Like we're not being kidnapped right now. But I kind of feel like we're being kidnapped right now. What is happening?

Our two drivers are trying to keep us calm. "Look, it'll be fine. Don't worry about it." But now I'm getting suspicious, especially when they start plying the glamazons with alcohol. Most of these girls are only sixteen years old.

I'm starting to get very agitated. A lot of the kids accept the alcohol. A lot of them are thinking this is just some unexpected delay, and so why not have a cheeky drink? I'm the only sober person. Am I the only person who thinks this isn't right? We should be almost home by now. People were expecting us to be back tomorrow at the drop-off spot inside South Africa.

"Why have they taken our truck?" I try to stop everyone from drinking the free liquor, but that's like trying to stop me from eating chocolate.

It's now getting dark and the men move us to a shell of a house. It only has concrete floors, a few concrete support beams and a roof. There are no walls, windows or doors. No furnishings, apart from an old chair or two. There's a black cauldron heated by a fire underneath, where these men who reek of BO are cooking something weird. We are now in some creepy abandoned house and these men with guns have our passports. Our drivers collected them earlier in the trip "for safekeeping." Holy fuck, I'm in the middle of fucking nowhere and I think I've been kidnapped! I'm without my passport and I definitely think I'm the only sober one here!

My heart is racing. Is there going to be violence, or, even worse, sexual violence? I'm really not sure. I'm guessing these guys are locals from Mozambique, but I don't know. They're toting AK-47s. We don't have any weapons or any form of communication. And my few months of karate training really aren't going to help us right now. We all sit together on the cold concrete. I have the idea of linking arms because it's getting late at this point and some of the girls are sobering up and starting to view the situation the same way I do. I'm afraid one of the men will separate one of the girls from the group. Only bad things could happen then. I saw the *Oprah* episode—"never get taken to a second location." We are now at the second location!

I tell the other girls how scared I am and how dangerous this situation could be. I don't know where our drivers have gone. We take turns sleeping whilst others stay awake watching—watching these smelly men with their strange cauldron. They offer us food, but I don't really want to take any. What if it's poisoned? What if there are drugs in it?

Rebel's parents' engagement photo, 1975. Warwick and Sue.

Baby Rebel, born at 14 Montague Street, Balmain, Sydney.

Young Rebel in the garden, Sydney.

Rebel's preschool photo
with younger sister Liberty,
Castle Hill, Sydney, 1984.

Castle Hill Primary
School, first-grade
school photo.

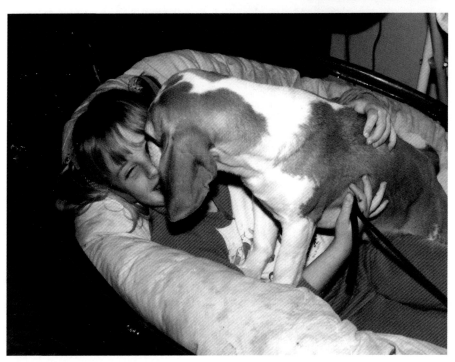

Rebel with champion Nangunyah Casablanca, a.k.a. "Cassie."

Young Rebel with her toy collection. Cabbage Patch toys called Rupert and Nathan, kookaburra hand puppet and Pound Puppy. Castle Hill, Sydney, 1986.

Rebel's first visit to Disneyland, age eleven (with bum bag).

Rebel and family boarding *Fairstar*, "the Funship."

Standing outside Nanny's house at Blue Bay, drinking Slurpees.

Rebel surfing, 1993.

Rebel's second visit to Disneyland with family, 1996. Back to front: father Warwick, mother Sue, Rebel, Ryan, Liberty and Anna riding Splash Mountain. (And yes, we coordinated to go different angles to get the photo right!)

Rebel with Tara friends
Haps, Ann and Zahra,
tenth grade, 1995.

Rebel's Sweet Sixteen
with Tara friends Ann
and Zahra, March 1996.

Rebel performing the character Inez in the Jean-Paul Sartre play *No Exit*, the King's
School theater, 1996. *Photograph from Tara Archive Collection*

Christmas morning,
Castle Hill, 1996. Rebel,
Liberty, Ryan and Anna.

Rebel's twelfth-grade
school photo, just
prior to graduation,
Tara Anglican School
for Girls, 1997.

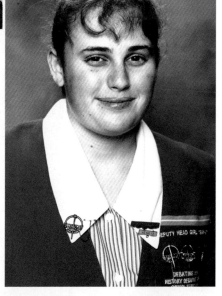

Walking with an elephant in the
game park, South Africa, 1998.

Rebel with rhinos, South Africa, 1998.

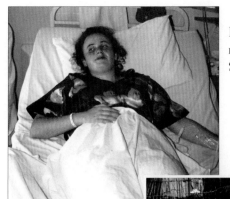

In the hospital with malaria, Vereeniging, South Africa, 1998.

Rebel patting a lion in a game reserve, 1998.

Ostrich farm, South Africa, 1998.

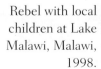

Rebel with local children at Lake Malawi, Malawi, 1998.

Rebel preparing to shoot a warthog in a private game reserve, South Africa, 1998.

Rebel with mother, Sue, at Sydney airport after returning from her year away in South Africa, 1998.

Rotary district meeting address after returning from South Africa, 1998.

Main publicity image used for Rebel's first play, which she wrote, produced and co-starred in, called *The Westie Monologues*.

So, I act like the team leader and tell people not to eat anything. The group listens. I'm good in a crisis. Still.

The next day, most of the African men return, along with our drivers. "Your truck is fixed now," their leader says. "You can get back on your truck." So, without questioning anything, we all just gratefully board our truck and our guides drive off. By my estimate, it has been almost twenty-four hours—almost a day since we were low-key kidnapped.

I didn't want to question anything too much or too loudly. But something weird had clearly taken place. I kept my mouth shut because we were not physically harmed. It was always a bit of a mystery as to what had happened. We arrived in South Africa a full day later than planned, but somehow once we crossed the South African boarder word had reached our parents and host families that we'd be late, and it didn't seem like that big of a deal.

Years later, I randomly watched a documentary about how illegal things were smuggled into South Africa by the Afrikaner Resistance Movement—known as AWB—using cattle trucks like the one we traveled on as students. During those years, the Afrikaner nationalist group was secretly planning to overthrow the new African government. Was this what had happened? Were we used as glamazon mules to smuggle things into South Africa?

By the end of our trip, the bottom of the cattle truck, which had been full of all our food, was really a huge cavity. After I saw this documentary, I pieced together what I think happened. The group of African men took the truck away from us, and while we waited, they filled the empty space with something illegal, like guns or black-market diamonds, or who knows? Things that weren't supposed to be smuggled back into South Africa. And that's why we weren't harmed. They used us. We didn't look suspicious. We were just a bunch of white kids on a school trip who, unbeknownst to us, had been turned into mules. Our drivers did have a slightly dodgy vibe—they were jacked like military men usually are and not very talkative. Why did they not freak out when our truck was pulled over by strange men with guns? Perhaps the incident wasn't sinister—wasn't connected to the AWB or anything like that. It could've simply been a way for our drivers to make some extra cash by transporting goods. I'm really not sure. I was just super grateful that no one was harmed. (I will never again give my passport to ANYONE for "safekeeping," though.)

I got back from that trip and I was so dirty, so filthy, that I had a bath and the water turned black. Black bathwater. There was just dirt in every crevice of my body from spending over three weeks in the African bush.

Once I cleaned up, I tried to get back to my normal routine in Vanderbijlpark, and then I was in an aerobics class, literally doing the grapevine, when I realized, "Oh, crap. I don't feel too good." With the whole kidnapping thing I had forgotten about the fifty mosquito bites, but my body hadn't. I started to feel really, really sick, like pains all over my body and a fever. I was just out of it. I moaned all night as I tried to sleep. I was clearly very ill but couldn't get out of bed to fetch anyone. Mrs. Du Rand took me to the local hospital early the next day, and it turned out, yes, I did have a very, very nasty strain of malaria, and so did Dolinda, another girl who had also been on the trip. Dolinda had taken the antimalarial tablets, but this strain was resistant to those tablets. So even if I had taken them, there's probably a good chance that I would have gotten sick anyway.

In the hospital, I was in so much pain that they gave me some kind of morphine-type drug immediately—it was like a river of relaxation flooded into my body. Now I was really out of it. I was floating.

Dolinda and I were both hospitalized and ended up recovering in the same hospital room. Malaria is not like a cold or flu. It is a life-threatening disease caused by a Plasmodium parasite, transmitted by the bite of the infected mosquito. To me, it's a bit of a "voodoo disease" in that you kind of feel like you're out of your body. It's like your body is over there, but you are a meter away, sweating and some-times shaking. It is like no other sickness that I've ever experienced.

I think I scared my mum half to death, because after I had spent a few days in the hospital, she apparently called and I made no sense whatsoever. I don't have memories of those calls, but many years later, she told me this was one of the most difficult times in her life. Her oldest daughter was in a life-threatening situation, I needed her, and she didn't have the money to fly over to see me. She also had my younger siblings to look after. Mum says it was terrifying to be so far away without the ability to do anything. At least I had travel insurance as part of the Rotary program and was in a great hospital. But the reality is, I could've died. To kill the parasites now multiplying in my blood, I had to take these awful quinine pills every two hours, and they would make me gag. Still, to this day, I have trouble swallowing pills.

I'm not sure whether it was the medications or the malaria, but I lost my hearing for the two weeks that I was in the hospital. And whilst I was lying there in terrible pain, lying on that hospital bed in my silk Mickey Mouse pajamas, not being able to hear anything . . . I had the hallucination that was to change my life. I dreamed that I was an actress. And I was so good that I was at the Oscars, and I actually won an Academy Award!! My name got called and I walked down the aisle in front of everyone. I went up onto the stage, and instead of giving an acceptance speech, I did an acceptance RAP, which went something like:

"Listen up, y'all, I've got something to say, it's about this award that I won today. I want to say a few words of thank-yous and of gratitudes—"

. . . and then I can't quite remember any more than that. But I recall it all so vividly. I had never been to the Oscars, obviously, though I'd probably seen bits of it on TV. And now I had this full-on, full-blown hallucination that I was an incredible Oscar-winning actress. It was so, so real; it truly was like I was there.

When I had been on that deserted beach in Mozambique asking the universe about my life . . . was this hallucination the answer?

When I got out of the hospital I started saying, "Guys, I think I have to become an actress now." And everyone's like, "Ach, no. The malaria has affected your brain. You're not an actress." Nobody thought I could be an actress. (Except for Snickers, who for my twenty-first birthday amazingly made me my own gold star with my name engraved on it, so that one day I could put it on my dressing room door. He gave it to me as we had a quiet birthday celebration, just us two, by the Parramatta River in a bush cave. Snickers believed I could do it. But literally nobody else did. Not even my own family.)

But I'd had the vision. I said, "I have to go back to Australia, and I have to become an actress. Now!" And they literally looked at me like I was insane. I wasn't crazy. I'd watched a lot of *Oprah*—that was the one thing that got me through a lot of very lonely days in South Africa. *Oprah* would come on about three p.m. and I always made sure to rush back from school or whatever I was doing to watch her. And Oprah would say that sometimes the universe gives you small whispers and then the whispers grow, louder and louder, until it's like a load of bricks being dumped on you with the message. Oprah would say, "You've got to listen to the universe." Whether this hallucination was like a divine message from above or whether it was my subconscious pushing past my fear and surfacing my real passion for acting, I can't really say. I just knew I had to follow this dream.

However, I never thought a girl like me could have a professional career in the entertainment industry. I had been accepted into the best law school in Sydney. I was going to become a lawyer, surely. That was the safe bet. But now I knew there was this other tangent: acting. In horse-betting terms, I was going to put money "each way," on law school and on acting, just to make sure I had more chances of winning. I would still go to law school and play that good-girl game, just in case the acting didn't work out. But I was going to try acting. I was going to ditch the name Melanie for good. Melanie died in that Vereeniging hospital along with the malaria. I was done for good with boring, shy, nobody Melanie. I never wanted her to resurface again. I was going to make that vision come true. I was going to officially go by Rebel now—the name my mother gave me at birth. (I didn't change my name legally until a few years later because it was a bit of a hassle to change all my documents.)

I left South Africa a month early so that I could audition for Australia's big drama school NIDA—the National Institute of Dramatic Art—where famous actors like Cate Blanchett and Mel Gibson had attended.

I was the skinniest I've ever been when I returned—and people were like, "Oh my God. You look fantastic!" and I was like, "Yeah, thanks. I almost died." Malaria was the best bloody diet. But you know, not advisable. Trust me.

At the NIDA audition, there seemed to be about a hundred people that morning who were gathered in the main foyer and then split into groups. Then, after some waiting around, inside a bare acting studio I performed two monologues in front of an audition panel whilst the other hopefuls in my group watched from the side, waiting for their turn. I didn't even make it past the first round. A lackey holding a clipboard addressed the auditionees, who sharply turned and stopped their conversations about "headshots" as soon as the lackey entered. "It's a NO to these people, thank you so much for your time."

Everyone on the NO list gathered their things and left slowly whilst the other lucky ones who were successful and on to the afternoon session stayed firmly seated, as if it were a game of musical chairs and there was no way in hell they'd give up their precious spot. Thousands auditioned; only about twenty-five per year were eventually chosen after multiple rounds.

I walked to the bus stop trying not to cry. Even though the rejection stung worse than a hundred wasps. There's something very humiliating about being asked to leave a foyer because you're clearly just "not good enough." You hope maybe the lackey has made a mistake and accidentally read your name out on the NO list when you should've been a YES. So if you walk away slowly enough, maybe they'll realize the mistake. I looked back several times at the lackey whilst I was leaving, but they didn't give a shit. I was rejected. I was not good enough.

It wasn't nuts to follow this vision, right?

Later that month, the Rotary Club who had sponsored me asked me to give a speech about my experiences at their dinner. It was my last obligation as part of the program. I didn't hold back and talked about every harrowing African moment. It was a dramatic monologue worthy of a callback, but there was no audition panel now. It was a bunch of older white businessmen enjoying their steaks and dinner rolls. After my speech, someone took notice, though. The Rotary district decided to no longer send girls to that part of Africa. I'm not sure if that decision has ever been overturned.

My green youth ambassador blazer was covered with pins and patches from people I'd met and places I'd been. But the biggest thing I took home with me, apart from over one hundred pounds (almost fifty kilos) of soapstone and wooden gifts for my family, was a near-death experience that would incredibly change the course of my entire life.*

---

* Side note: I do want to thank all the amazing people who helped me in South Africa, especially the Du Rand family, who showed me so much kindness. To everyone at Transvalia and my fellow exchangees and the Rotarians—I owe you so much for this life-changing experience. Even small interactions and small acts of kindness meant a great deal to me.

FIFTEEN

Becoming a Fighter

Okay, so this South African story needs its own special chapter. While I was living in South Africa when I was eighteen, I trained at the local Japan Karate Association Shotokan karate center in Vanderbijlpark under Sensei Mike Dukas. And I was really enjoying it. I had graduated from white belt to yellow belt and my sensei told me that there was a novice all-style martial arts championship coming up in a few months. Would I like to represent the dojo? Little did he know that I loved all things ninja growing up, like *Teenage Mutant Ninja Turtles* and the Japanese television series *Monkey Magic*. Who didn't?

So, yeah, when invited to represent my dojo in Johannesburg in the novice competition, I said, "Yes, Sensei." This was before the malaria hallucination, so I thought, "Maybe this is my destiny . . . to become a champion fighter." Maybe this was my secret calling? Being a female Aussie ninja! Or perhaps this was the same misguided calculation that inspired me to start the gangsta rap group with my sister Liberty.

Okay, so I digress—where was I? Oh yes, me being a ninja.

I would train quite hard for months, the *Karate Kid* theme song and Spice Girls' album playing on cassette on my Walkman. Since I didn't have actual schoolwork to do at Transvalia, I had a lot of free time to train and became pretty ripped. I had quite big shoulders from tennis and now my legs were getting strong from doing drills like duck walks and lunges across the mat. My stomach was flat and toned. Karate training was great—I was really in peak physical shape, with great muscle tone.

In the tournament, there were two categories. The first, called kata, is where you perform a series of set solo moves for the judges. The second, called kumite, is where you fight against an opponent.

On the day of the tournament we piled onto a bus, the whole team from our little karate school, and headed west to Johannesburg. I was looking every bit the suburban ninja in my gi, my light brown hair slicked back with cheap hair spray into a serious low ponytail. (I only really had two hairstyles: high ponytails for parties, low ponytails for entering high-stakes novice martial arts championships.)

The tournament was held, I guess, in like a local high school gym. I felt like I entered in slo-mo. "That's right, motherfuckers, I'm here to take you all down," I thought. "I am the baddest bitch in here. Yeah-yeah!" You know that feeling you have like you've walked out of a spy movie and slip on your sunglasses and walk to your car like you're being followed by operatives but at any time you are ready to attack with your high-level skills? It was like that feeling—I was now a full ninja. I was ready to destroy.

We were in this high school gym and first up was the kata section. I did a series of moves, like I was shadow fighting, by myself, ending my little routine with a guttural "KIAH!" I projected right to the back of the auditorium, like Mr. Haigh had taught me. I loved kata. To me, it was like putting on a show, and I knew how to do that. I knew how to pretend to be tough. Swift arm movements: check. Great footwork and knee bends: check. Fierce facials that would've won a cheerleading competition: check.

I won the gold medal, beating out twenty other girls in my category. I'm sure all those bitches were looking at me thinking, "Ach, nee, where did this girl come from?" Here I was. The surprise ninja packet from Australia.

Then, in the afternoon, it was the kumite, the fighting section. If there had been commentators, they'd have been like, "And now, taking the floor, fresh off her gold-medal domination of the kata, weighing in at just under sixty kilos, deadly, like an Australian spider, it's Melanie Bownds!"

But of course, this was a very low-rent event, so there were NO commentators. Probably one hundred to two hundred spectators, though. In my mind, I was in the final scene of *The Karate Kid*, but in reality, there were fewer people and no movie magic.

I was probably tapped to win after my fierce performance in the kata. But what my competitors didn't know was that I'd never been in a competitive fight before. We'd done some sparring training, but guys and girls never hit you with full force in class and definitely never hit you in the face. I'd received a few bruises from training, but nothing really that bad. Training buddies would "tap" you rather than really punch or kick you.

I'd never been in a fight in real life either—nope, fights had completely escaped me. Then here I was, about to compete in the kumite section of the novice championships.

My opponent in the first fighting round was a girl from Soweto who, and this is no exaggeration, was built like a tank. Now, I'm not sure if you know much about Soweto, but it's probably the most notorious township in Johannesburg. It was a "hardened environment," to say the least, a slum designated for Black people when the whites were running South Africa. The place of the Soweto uprising where schoolchildren protested the Afrikaners' laws.

Now here was this Black girl, for whom maybe fighting was her ticket to a better life. And here I was, a private-girls'-school-turned-exchange student from Australia who thought it would just be fun to pretend to be a ninja. I sized up my opponent. "Yep, she's still a tank." She glared at me fiercely.

I tried to be tough. Like in the leopard cage: "Do not show fear." I did want to win. I'm a competitive person, remember (just ask anybody who has ever played Monopoly against me), and I had trained really hard for this. So even though I was up against this heavier, muscular girl, I was like, "Well, maybe I can take her?"

The referee blows his whistle and we move toward each other and start the first round. At this point we're more dancing around the fighting square. I'm heavily left-handed, so I fight southpaw. We're both throwing a few punches and front kicks—just feeling each other out really. About a minute passes and the referee blows a whistle to end the first round. Neither of us landed a decent blow.

I turn to head back to my corner of the fighting square. And right as I turn my face, when my opponent has left my peripheral vision: BANG! I feel this giant force hit my nose. The Soweto girl sucker punched me when I wasn't looking. How did the referee not see this? It was so dirty. She whacked me right on my nose with a massive punch, made worse by the fact that I didn't see it coming. The pain is instant. It stings so badly. I know people will read this and think, "Well, what did you think was going to happen in a fighting tournament? You're going to get punched in the face!" But the unfairness of it, that she hit me whilst I was not looking, makes the sting extra painful.

I start crying. Sobbing, really. It's embarrassing. My sensei is in my corner—he's a black belt and looks like a South African, slightly hotter, slightly younger Mr. Miyagi. He looks like he's been in many fights. If shit went down, you know he could handle himself in two crafty moves and a strategic leg swipe. But here I am, really not representing.

The tank girl smiles at me from her corner as she wipes some sweat off her forehead. I really want to quit. That's it—my ninja days are over. I'm not joining the TMNT. My sensei tells me I can't quit because it would "bring shame on the dojo." I really don't think I can go on, but he says, "Well, if you really want to get out of the fight, the quickest way possible is to just lose three rounds."

After almost six months of training, I get back in the ring, still crying, and I let this Soweto girl land three clean hits on me—trying to protect my face from her tree-trunk arms, but letting her hit my body so that she'll win three clear points and therefore win the fight. Then I cry for three hours straight. I cry all the tears that I probably should've shed in my childhood but have instead internalized. Tears about my father's treatment of my family. Tears about Nanny being destroyed by alcoholic dementia. Tears about being alone, afraid. It all just comes out. I don't think I've ever cried publicly before . . . except for when Mum was pushing me through the doors of that first drama class.

Luckily my nose was not broken. And even though I love karate, I love the discipline, I love that self-defense can give you self-confidence unlike anything else, I hated being punched in the face. And I vowed never to go into a fighting tournament again. Would I do a kung fu action movie now? Hells yeah. In movies when you do stunts, you're usually not even making any contact whatsoever. So that would be really fun (although on the last night of filming an action film last year I was accidentally whacked in the face by a stuntie holding a fake gun and needed three stitches in my nose). But if you've ever wondered why I have random nunchaku skills, well, it's because of those months of karate class in South Africa. I tried being a ninja, but that life was not for me.

When I think back on this story, I feel like it was a bit of a metaphor for a lot of my life. There were many times when I was metaphorically punched unfairly in the face. And in most of these situations, I would just cry and not fight back. And then came 2015. I was riding high, starring in the number one movie worldwide: *Pitch Perfect 2*. I could not have been hotter by Hollywood standards. I was getting offers for every big comedy film. Then, on the very weekend the movie was released, dominating the box office with a $70 million take in the US alone, Australian tabloids owned by Bauer Media launched a series of negative articles depicting me as a serial liar. I guess they couldn't really invent bad things like a DUI arrest, mental breakdown, drug habit or secret baby, because the truth was, apart from my cheeky antics at high school and the occasional cheeky joke, I was squeaky clean. All I did—all day, every day—was work hard on my career and try and build a better life for myself. But because I was the most popular Australian that week and because of God knows what toxic jealousy that seems to drench women's magazines like it's a leaking free perfume sample, they attacked my credibility. They attacked my authenticity, which is something I hold very dear. They claimed my life wasn't really my life.

I remember sitting in a New York hotel room, crying in the corner after reading the articles. I received dozens of messages about them just from family and friends who had my cell number—so I imagined these stories had a far wider reach. I tried to avoid looking at my devices, but the next workday, it was on American radio as I was being driven to work. The kind driver heard the negative discussion about me and quickly turned it off. I was absolutely devastated by these nasty articles. Were they just waiting in their troll-holes until I was starring in a number one movie?? And then BANG! They were going to pull the "let's bring her down now" trigger and release this nonsense. In Australia we have something called "Tall Poppy Syndrome," which is where people get attacked because of their achievements and/or success. It's as if the "poppy"—in this case, me—dared to grow taller than the other poppies in the field, and so thereby, following some weird toxic egalitarianism logic, certain people took it upon themselves to "cut me down." In their eyes, they think: "How dare she be successful? And as a woman, how dare she be proud of her success?" Tall Poppy Syndrome was particularly vicious in Australia toward women, fueled by these gossipy tabloids that were running rampant with untrue stories. A girl that was working for a different Australian media company had confessed to me a year later that the week prior to these articles, her team, knowing *Pitch Perfect 2* was going to be massive, had had a meeting led by their female boss in which the topic of conversation was "How can we bring Rebel Wilson down?" It's awful to hear something like that—that groups of people I've never met (apparently this group was mainly composed of women) were plotting to destroy my reputation. Meanwhile here's me, getting up at five a.m. every morning, working hard and just basically trying to make people laugh.

One source in the first Bauer Media article was a former classmate at Tara, the same person who bullied my friend Zahra for being Indian and Muslim. I had only one class with this girl, Jerry-Jane, throughout the whole of high school—so she was never a close friend of mine. I believe she had given completely false quotes to the magazine and supplied them with some pictures of me at school.

The resulting articles claimed things like my name wasn't my name and that I had lied about my age, my family and background. Bauer, the publisher, clearly refused to let the facts get in the way of a "good story." One of the follow-up articles, written by Australian "journalist" Caroline Overington, even implied I could be lying about my own father dying. It was disgusting. It conveyed that nothing I say about myself can be taken to be true unless it had been independently corroborated. (PS: Why on earth would I make up that my own father had died?? A simple Google search that would've taken thirty seconds could find his funeral service program online!)

This whole thing stung way worse than that massive sucker punch to the nose in Johannesburg.

Jerry-Jane was paid for her "story." Her information was false—either made up or misremembered. Friends from Tara had warned me about her, saying she had developed a weird jealousy, comparing her life to mine after seeing me on billboards and on television. "Why's she famous? There's nothing special about her!" Jerry-Jane had said to other Tara classmates. She'd sit at home and see me crushing it, first in Australia, then overseas, and she was envious. She would post about me on weird internet message boards. She was not the only one—there was also a time when my crazy uncle Robert was also posting vile things about me online on forums such as Facebook. They couldn't handle the fact that I had come from a very similar background, yet here I was, confident and successful out in the world.

The magazine had advance legal warning about the original story supplied by Jerry-Jane, yet they still published it. I guess negative stories sell more copies of magazines? That was clearly their business model—negative stories, particularly those targeting female celebrities, sold more copies . . . so that's why they'd write them. In my case, there was a complete disregard for journalistic ethics and the facts.

However, this time, I wasn't going to back down from an unfair punch. I wasn't going to sob in the corner inconsolably. Nope. Now I was thirty-five, twice the age I had been in South Africa (and almost twice the weight), and I was ready to fight back. Like a legally trained ninja in the shadows, I waited to see if there was financial and reputational damage from the articles. I was hoping there wouldn't be, that people wouldn't believe these published lies, but the stories had been picked up widely overseas and I lost millions of dollars in deals. It's difficult to prove who didn't offer you a job because of these articles and the associated negative press, but suddenly all the big movie offers dried up. It wasn't a coincidence. The tide had changed on my reputation, and my career was being sucked out to sea. And so, I sued Bauer Media.

Suing a billion-dollar media corporation is not for the faint of heart. Rarely had anybody successfully challenged them. They were bullies. They were ruthless. Even Gina Rinehart, the richest woman in Australia at the time, had not won her case against the Australian press. But I was determined to stand up for myself and restore my reputation. I hadn't worked so damn hard to be a professional actress every single day since I returned from South Africa just to let some toxic magazine try to bring me down, all so they could make money. Bauer Media should've settled out of court—the court accepted it was a very clear-cut malicious defamation case—but what followed was a month-long high-profile court case that was on the Australian news every night!

I personally was on the witness stand for seven days proving my life story. I was and am incredibly proud of my life story, proud of my authenticity. To be called a liar, to be cast as untrustworthy, was something I couldn't stomach. I was at the top of my game when *Pitch Perfect 2* came out. (That movie remains to this day the most successful "musical comedy" film of all time. Note: this is a separate category from "musical" films because it's comedies that contain musical performances.) It was the pinnacle of my career. I should've been feeling on top of the world. Instead, people turned against me, people thought less of me, and the professional and personal repercussions were awful. I am not perfect. But I clearly wasn't some serial liar.

I took to the witness stand to prove them wrong. Day after day answering a constant barrage of questions. When I arrived in Hollywood, I was mysterious about my age. That wasn't a lie, that was a good business strategy. The older a woman is, the less chance she has of breaking through. Everyone knows that. Hollywood is obsessed with youth. So, no actress is rocking up to Hollywood proudly displaying her use-by date on her chest like a piece of meat in the grocery store. The name on my original birth certificate was Melanie Elizabeth Bownds but I officially changed it to Rebel Melanie Elizabeth Wilson before I became a professional actress. So, throughout my professional career my name was always legally Rebel Wilson. And of course, my father did die, and I did get malaria, and grow up bogan, etc. While all these things could be easily proved by hundreds of witnesses, Bauer Media was going to make me sit on the stand and endure the ordeal of talking about everything. Everything personal. Everything about my business. Everything about my family. Proving EVERYTHING. The one thing that could not be proven 100 percent one way or another was whether or not I am a distant relative of Walt Disney.

As I mentioned earlier, when I was about six years old, my grandma Nanny told me that my great-aunt Lillian Bounds was married to Walt Disney. At one point she even had a family tree drawn up to prove it. This was well before the internet, so I have no idea how she knew—but at one point in my childhood she was trying to figure out whether our family was entitled to any of the Disney fortune. Apparently, because we were related to Walt via marriage, we were not entitled to any Disney money. I just thought it was awesome to think that we were related to Walt in some small way, and this is what spurred our family's huge love for Disney. I still don't know as a certainty whether Lillian Bounds is a great-auntie of mine—I guess only a DNA test would prove that—but I know a man named James Bounds appears on both of our family trees (the spelling of my family's last name changes from Bounds to Bownds over the decades).

Regardless, what was true is that I believed Nanny's story. I even had a poster of Sebastian the crab from *The Little Mermaid* on my boarding-house dorm room wall and would drive other boarders crazy with my constant singing of Disney songs. I had no reason to doubt my grandmother as a child. (PS: I am very willing to do a DNA test to determine this once and for all, and I will always absolutely adore all things Disney.)

During the trial, Bauer Media tried to further smear my name—and, in my opinion, they tried to intimidate me at every turn, even resorting to dirty tricks. My legal team was informed about a dinner party right before the trial that members of the Bauer legal team attended and at which confidential figures about what I earned per movie were discussed. Bauer didn't want me to stand up for myself, because that could inspire other people to do the same. If the grubs that worked there couldn't write filth about people, then, well . . . they were out of business. So, they fought hard, even though they were clearly on the wrong side of the case. I know lawyers must fight for their clients, but it appeared to me that their legal strategy was oddly mean. I felt that it was as vicious as the defamatory articles themselves. I'm on the stand, tearfully talking about how my father died of a heart attack, how painful it was to read these awful articles inferring that I made up his death, and one of the Bauer team closest to me is sniggering. They are laughing six feet away from me as I'm describing one of the worst days of my life.

Bauer subjected me to repetitive question after question, dragging out the proceedings, trying to sling mud at me when it was clear they were going to lose. At one point I said in open court something like "I know you're getting paid by the day, but I've already answered these questions and you keep asking them." They were trying to wear me down like I was a pair of jeans and maybe at some point a hole might form in the crotch. But there were no holes. And I have stamina. I answered every single question. The billion-dollar company with a super expensive legal team and huge international resources could not fault me.

To make matters worse, though, a stalker showed up in the middle of the trial. Dressed in a suit, he was somehow allowed access to the courtroom with flowers and a note for me. He hugged me and kissed me on the cheek. I opened the note in my holding room during one of the breaks. He wrote that he was going to kidnap me, take me to his farm and chain me up in a bedroom. Eventually I was going to "learn to love" him. The police detained him when he showed up the next day, but it was so frightening that this man had gotten close enough to kiss me on the cheek.

Whereas I had family, friends and colleagues to testify for me, Bauer had basically no witnesses for their side. Jerry-Jane obviously wasn't fronting up to defend a story she made up. The "journalist" Caroline Overington took to the stand and never apologized or retracted any statement that she had made despite the mountain of evidence against her (the judge took a particularly harsh view on this in his judgment). Another "journalist" who had written one of the articles appeared and started crying only when she spoke about having had people write negative comments about HER—the irony being of course that she had written negative things about me. I was thinking, "So how do you not understand the hurt and distress you caused me? You think just because I'm a celebrity that I'm not human, that I don't feel things . . . and that somehow gives you the right to make up crap about me?"

The few Bauer witnesses made me want to vomit a bit in my mouth, having to sit there and listen to them. Although I did have to laugh when, in the eleventh hour of the trial, they called some random person to the stand who had nothing to say. It felt like their last-ditch attempt to try and slam me, and like all their other attempts, it failed.

After the month-long trial, Bauer Media lost. The full jury in the Victorian Supreme Court found that the articles had defamed me. Furthermore, it was defamation which was motivated by malice, which is an extreme form of defamation. The Honorable Justice John Dixon of the Supreme Court of Victoria wrote in his judgment that publicly branding me a serial liar "was an extremely serious thing to put against the plaintiff not just without a legitimate basis, as the jury verdict made clear, but with malice."

Justice Dixon awarded me nearly $5 million in damages, an

extremely fair and accurate amount. You could tell I'd lost that amount of money (probably more) from the negative press because when my reputation was restored immediately after the verdict, my earnings instantly improved. I went back to earning millions of dollars.

This was a massive damages award for Australia—something like four times higher than the previous Australian record for damages—and so my team and I knew that (even though we believed this amount was fair) it was likely the amount would be reduced upon appeal. In the end, Bauer still had to pay me $600,000, which all went to charity (mainly the not-for-profit Australian Theatre for Young People and the School of St. Jude in Tanzania), plus they had to pay millions of dollars for their own legal bills and about 80 percent of my legal bills.

For me, this defamation suit was never about the money, it was about finally standing up for myself. One day mid-trial, a woman and her two tween daughters were watching me give evidence and approached me at the end of the day. The mother said that they were waiting to give their evidence in their domestic violence case in the neighboring court and that the tween girls gained confidence from seeing me on the stand, answering questions from the lawyers. It was these small interactions that made it seem worth it. I stood up for myself and beat a bully.

My dear Australian agent Jacinta Waters said that I walked a little taller after that court case. Like physically, I held myself up more after that experience. I was so grateful to my legal team—who I think are the smartest and just all-around great people. They were by my side every step of the way. As a result of my case, ethics in tabloid journalism in Australia was given a wake-up call. In my opinion, because of their huge financial losses from my case, Bauer Media had to shut down many of their gossipy publications Down Under. So I may have lost that one fight in Johannesburg, but this fight in Australia, where my whole career and reputation were on the line—this fight where it really mattered—I won.

Don't be afraid to fight back. Block. Kick. Punch.

SIXTEEN

Rejection

Diary entry: November 23, 2001

<u>Weight</u>: 165 pounds [75 kilos]

<u>Relationship status</u>: Single and not even a mingle. I'm too focused on "making it."

<u>Mental attitude</u>: Total and utter rejection after just being rejected from the National Institute of Dramatic Art (NIDA) for the fourth year in a row. They only hold auditions once a year. Being rejected for a fourth time means I am never, ever going to get into this school.

Today I got rejected from NIDA for the fourth time. I am so upset. I am searching for answers and am in a haze of confusion—what should I do with my life? Why is this happening? Why, when I've put so much work and energy into being a fantastic performer, do I fail to get into drama school? Why don't they like me? Am I really all that fantastic, or do people lie to me? Do they pretend that I'm good? Do I just think that they're telling me that I am good, when I'm really not??

I don't know what to do? Why do I focus my energies on something that isn't going as planned. Why do I have these tears?

Why don't they love me. Why don't I have somebody to love? What's wrong with me? Why won't God give me a break? Why won't God give me a sign. Should I know when to give up? Should I give up now? What should I do? What is my future, and what path should I take. I can't understand this life.

I'm broke, fat, ugly and have no one showing me the light. I can't see the light. I'm sure as hell not in the light.

I've wanted so bad to go to NIDA and become a "proper" actress. I wanted to write to Lorelei or Lilliene or someone like that and tell them that my dream has come true, that I got accepted into the best acting school in the country. I want people to be proud of me.

Why am I so pathetic right now? What is in store for me now? Why is this the way that things have to be? Why am I so scared—why do I hate myself and yet love myself? Why do I have so many gifts and yet at this time they seem not enough? Why am I chasing my dreams that may never come true? Why do I brag and boast? What can I show the world? What is the world to me? What am I supposed to do? What are my options? Tell Me. Anyone. Please. Please. Please. I beg you. What should I do?

I write this, crying, as I'm sitting at the Pizza Hut all-you-can-eat buffet on George Street in Sydney. Out of the thousands of people who auditioned for NIDA this year, I made it through to the callbacks but then got cut. I told everybody I was going to be a professional actress and the only clear path I knew was to get accepted into this prestigious drama school. Then I could graduate, get an agent and start working. I spend all my money on acting classes and audition prep. I have several casual jobs—one at a sunglasses kiosk in the middle of Castle Towers, one at a video store and yet a third at a cinema. I am on government assistance too because I'm also a law student and have such a low income. I work 'til midnight almost every single day. I have no social life. I just work on "making it," on getting accepted to this one drama school, only to be told, "You don't have the voice for Shakespeare," or "You're not what we're looking for."

It's embarrassing getting rejected for the fourth year in a row. Everybody knows how much I want to get into this school. I was performing with the Australian Theatre for Young People—I performed at the Opera House in a play called *Birds* and in a Nick Enright play called *Spurboard* at the Sydney Theatre Company, which also toured regionally. Yet this prestigious school does not want to admit me, and my only response is . . . to eat pizza. To eat a ton of pizza. This is now my ritual after each rejection from NIDA. To take the bus into the city and eat pizza until I can't feel the pain of rejection anymore. Then, when I can barely move, I'll take two more buses to get home to the hills. I can't understand why I was given the Oscar vision when nothing seems to fit with that storyline. Nothing seems to be going right.

In early 2002, out of desperation really, I put on my own play, the first that I had ever written, called *The Westie Monologues*. I wrote it in two nights whilst I was also working a reception job at the Australian Theatre for Young People (because in exchange they gave me a small salary and free acting classes). The play has five girls playing thirteen different characters that are all based on either my life or that of people I knew growing up in the western suburbs of Sydney. It's a series of monologues and funny little songs that weave together at the end. Since the prestigious drama school didn't accept me, I'm basically forced to create an outlet to show people what I can do as a performer. I had one meeting with an agent who told me, "No. Sorry. We can't see you being on *Home and Away*." (This is the big soap opera where stars like Melissa George, Isla Fisher and Chris Hemsworth had their start. The women were basically hanging out on the beach in bikinis, which clearly wasn't me. I wasn't going to ever be cast in that show.) Rejected!

I use $2,000 I have saved to produce *The Westie Monologues* with two friends and cast myself in one of the roles. It becomes the most noticed show of the Sydney Fringe Festival and goes on to play at the Belvoir St. Theatre, and then executives at the television station Channel 7 give me $90,000 to put it on professionally at Parramatta's Riverside Theatres (just down the road from Tara). A TV writer/director/actor named Paul Fenech comes to see me in that show and offers me a role in his new feature film . . . aaaaaand, no joke, that film is called *Fat Pizza*. (Oh, the irony!)

Then it's once again time to audition for drama school: November. What do I do? I've technically worked professionally as an actress, and due to the success of my first play, I did get an agent. Do I try one last time?

I can't let go of my dream of becoming the next Dame Judi Dench. I want to be a serious actress. I want to be taken seriously. My hair is now dyed black with supermarket hair color . . . because I am so fucking serious.

I audition at NIDA for the fifth time. It's now been five whole years since I returned from South Africa. Five years since I had the vision to become a professional actress. I was once a private school girl but now I'm sleeping on a thin mattress on the floor of my sister Anna's tiny room in our shit house. (Mum eventually lost our nice house in the property settlement with my father, and since I'm the oldest and, according to Mum, "should've left home by now," I don't get a bedroom.) There aren't enough rooms, so I share with Anna and my brother lives downstairs in a windowless corridor we call "the dungeon." I spend all my money on law books, acting classes and starting my own theater production company. I can't afford to move out; it's too expensive to rent in the city. Some semesters I don't have enough money for my law books, so I read the library's copy and photocopy chunks to read when I'm working late at the cinemas. My grandparents lent me money to buy a used car but there are days when I have to choose between petrol and food. I'm on the struggle bus constantly. I'm investing all my money into my university degree and my acting skills . . . but nothing seems to be paying off. I have a credit card debt of $10,000 and am unable to make the monthly payments. Mum can't help me. Our electricity is being cut off . . . again. She's worried about that.

That year at the NIDA auditions, I make it through the rounds to the final fifty. The NOs walk past me at each cut and I hold on to my seat. I know they choose around twenty-five students, and some are kept as reserves in case someone rejects their offer. I know that now you find out whether you've been ultimately accepted by a letter in the mail. The audition couldn't have gone better. I couldn't have shown more enthusiasm or skill. I wait. I don't receive an offer.

I am rejected. Again.

I, of course, find my way to a Pizza Hut.

Many years later a man on the NIDA audition panel told a friend of mine that I was "too good" and I "didn't NEED to go to NIDA." That's why they didn't accept me that final year. I call bullshit on this. For whatever reason, I just didn't fit their mold of what an actress should be. Well, now I was ready to break molds.

For our five-year high school reunion, Lucinda organized a dinner in Darling Harbour, but I literally didn't have the $55 to attend. It was so embarrassing. The deputy head girl didn't have $55 to her name. I felt like the biggest failure. But I wanted to keep up appearances, and I wanted to see all my old friends from Tara, so I gate-crashed.

At about ten p.m. I rock up coolly, going, "Hey, Luce, what's up?" I drift around the tables because I don't have a seat. I smile as I hear about everyone's jobs at mid-level law firms. I hear about their partners, who they all think are awesome, even though those dudes would probably much prefer to watch a game of cricket than do anything nice or helpful for them. I get the feeling that these girls are getting the raw end of the deal, but they are all doing what is "normal," what is expected of them. Soon there will be marriage and kids. The horses are off to the races and here I am, five years after leaving school, not having left the stalls.

"How's the acting going, Rebel?" Mousy says to me.

"Great! Heaps good. I'm basically starring in a movie that's about to come out called *Fat Pizza*. Soooo, yeah, things are going really well." (PS: I have like two lines in that movie.)

I dip out and sit by myself out near the water. Feet dangling over the sandstone edge. When I look straight down at the dark water below it is like I am looking into a black mirror. What on earth am I doing with my life? Ugh.

SEVENTEEN

Getting Fat

Something is wrong with me. I'm looking at my forearms and the dark hair sprouting all over them. And I've got these dark . . . I guess you would call them sideburns . . . on both sides of my cheeks. I'm much heavier now. I've put on about sixty-six pounds (thirty kilos) in the last year. I'm like legit fat now. And I have pains in my stomach. Something is definitely wrong with me.

As a kid, I knew my auntie was what you'd call fat. And I knew it was seen as a bad thing. She was laughed at as she waddled down the street in Rooty Hill, Sydney. I saw it, I heard it. And yes, "waddled" is the best way to describe how she walked. I'm not trying to be mean. I loved Auntie Sandra. She was sweet, had a great sense of humor and worked looking after kids with Down syndrome during the day. Auntie Sandra used to make these huge multilayered trifle desserts when we'd visit her house—a layer of custard, a layer of cream, a layer of cake. She'd go to the local donut store in her muumuu (plus-size fashion really was limited back then) and buy a garbage-bag-size sack of donut offcuts for $2 and an industrial-size tub of Betty Crocker icing and eat it while sitting in front of the television. Like me, she had an unlimited ability to eat sweets. Auntie Sandra, with her sweet jolly face, was on the extreme end. She probably weighed about 440 pounds (200 kilos).

When I started rapidly gaining weight, when the scales tipped over

220 pounds (100 kilos), I started to worry. What was I going to do? Was I going to retreat to a small country town, like Auntie Sandra, so that I wouldn't be mocked? So that no one could ever really see me?

Mum was sick of my bad eating habits and she constantly let me know about it. One time I came home from a night shift at Greater Union cinemas with a fresh pint of Baskin-Robbins ice cream, my reward for working so hard. I'd been at law school all day and worked at the cinema all night. My plan, obviously, was to sit in front of the TV for the next hour to mindlessly eat the whole pint and then fall asleep on the mattress on the floor in Anna's room and wake up and do it all over again.

Mum spots me as I walk up the stairs carrying the ice cream. Some sort of cookie-dough flavor—my favorite. It was like I was carrying gold—this ice cream was super important to me.

"What have you got there?" Mum says.

"Nothing," I say as I go to the kitchen to grab a spoon.

"What is that!?"

"What!? Nothing."

Mum sees that it's a pint of Baskin. "You don't NEED that!"

She swats it out of my hand like an NBA player making a steal, grabs it and throws it in the grotty trash bin.

"Hey!! What did you do that for!" I'm now about as angry as I get. This ice cream was my lifeline. It's sweetness that saves me at the end of a long day. My feet are sore from standing for hours as an usher at the cinema, my brain is sore from studying at law school and now my mother is depriving me of the one pleasurable thing in my life.

The ice cream is unopened, so I try to rescue it from the garbage.

"No!" Mum yells. "You're not having it!"

"I bought it, it cost me like ten dollars!"

"You're not having it. You don't NEED it!" She keeps saying this. That I don't NEED it. She's also very fat now. What the hell does she know?! I do NEED it. With all the constant rejection trying to be an actress and the constant stress of trying to earn money and keep up with law school, this ice cream is the only thing that's keeping me going.

I try to grab it from the bin but Mum jumps in, blocking me like she's on defense in the paint.

"Mum!" I yell. "I want it. It's MY ice cream!"

But she physically blocks me. It's like right now she's got extreme physical power. The only other time she exhibited this superpower was when two beagles were fighting at my grandma's house and were somehow attached by a metal chain. It looked like one of the dogs was going to kill the other one, which couldn't escape because of the chain. So, Mum raced over and, in this emergency, somehow had the brute force, with her bare hands, to break the chain and save the dogs.

I try to get past Mum, but she is not letting up. She's angry. I'm even more angry. Mum's a far cry from her ballerina body. She hates the fact that she's fat. But she seems to hate it even more that I'm fat. "You're young," she says. "You can do something about it!"

"Why don't YOU do something about it!" I scream in her face, and walk off to Anna's bedroom. I slam the door.

I don't get my comfort that night. "Fuck you," I think. Next time, I'll just eat the ice cream before coming home.

When I was performing in *The Westie Monologues*, I'd cast a girl named Lucy, who at the time of the first production weighed far more than me. Lucy was hilarious, a fantastic and endearing actress, and in the show, she would get a ton of laughs. More laughs than me. Sometimes I'd watch her and think, "Why is she getting more laughs?" I'd written the roles fairly equally in terms of jokes and comedic moments. She was brilliant, but I realized it also had something to do with her size. Then I took a course at university called Comedy and Power and it became clear to me that the psychology of comedy is that people like to laugh at people that they DON'T want to sleep with. They are more likely to laugh at someone who has some kind of physical irregularity—being fat, being super tall, having a big nose. Stuff like that. As I rapidly started gaining weight in 2002, I was like, "Well, fuck you. Fuck you to all those diet-obsessed people, fuck you to people who think women must be skinny . . . I'm just going to be fat. Because guess what? It's going to be awesome for my career. I can lean more into comedy and be the funny fat girl. Fuck you, fuck all of you. Fuck that agent who said I could never be cast in a bikini in *Home and Away*. I don't want to be on that dumb show anyway. Fuck those wanker drama schools who don't see me fitting their mold! I'm allergic to mold! I'm going to be a comedian and I'll show everyone just how fat and funny I can fucking be."

Then . . . I feel them again. These stabbing pains. I think maybe I have something stuck in my stomach. What is it? This time it lasts for days. I decide to go for an ultrasound at the local hospital. I'm just in too much pain.

Turns out the pain is coming from my ovaries because I have a cyst or had one that burst or something. "You have something called polycystic ovarian syndrome—PCOS," the doctor says. Basically, she tells me, "Just take this pill for the rest of your life. And that should stop the symptoms that you've been experiencing." The dark hair on my arms and on my cheeks, the weight gain—they're all classic symptoms of PCOS. I get my prescription for Marvelon 28, a birth control pill, and I start taking that daily. I tell Mum and she tells me to be more disciplined with my eating. "Why don't YOU be more disciplined with your eating and set a good example," I think. "You're the mother!" We're all on the struggle bus right now since my dad left our family with nothing. It's crowded and the windows are busted. Meanwhile Dad's driving a BMW.

Later that year I am cast in what I call "my big break!" It's a series of commercials for Australia's biggest telecom brand, Telstra, that are commercial tie-ins with *Australian Idol* (that show has become a huge hit!). I play Rachel, a teenage girl obsessed with *Australian Idol* who creates little skits in the basement with her cute friend Jen to promote

Telstra. It was a bit *Wayne's World*. But somehow with this job, I hit the jackpot. I'm paid about $90,000 for a few days' work.

I walk into the bank to pay off my $10,000 credit card debt. The bank lady looks at me and says, "What, you want to pay it off in full? Like . . . all of it? Did you win the lottery or something?"

"Yes!" I say.

I finally move out of my mum's house and rent my first-ever apartment, in Newtown, Sydney. I spend $10,000 filling it with new but cheap furniture. I buy my first bed, my first couch, my first little square dining table with two chairs. My first washing machine. Wow, my first apartment. Tensions with Mum peaked right before I moved out. Apart from weight, we'd also fight about my need for quiet so I could write. I am a very slow reader because I have something called subvocalization, and I also can't read or write if there's any noise or distractions around me. As a family we only had my one computer from high school, which lived in the kitchen. Often if I wanted to concentrate, if I wanted to write a new play or work on comedy material, I'd have to get up in the middle of the night, like at three a.m., when everyone was asleep. Often, though, Mum was still on the couch or pottering around tackling an endless list of tasks for the dogs or for us kids. I'd selfishly yell at her to let me work in quiet. You'd think I was writing the Constitution with how militant I was about having that quiet space to write. I was so focused on making it, and so frustrated with how long the process was taking, that I would get angry at her very easily. I guess I was frustrated with my life, and she was frustrated with hers. We butted heads. Not only do we look alike, but we have some very similar traits, which caused us to clash. Moving out was the best thing for both of us. I was twenty-three and it was definitely time.

I go on my first solo grocery-shopping trip. I'm cashed up and I can buy whatever I want. Not the cheap mince that Mum would buy—I can buy the four-star or five-star ground beef. I can buy as many tubs of ice cream and packets of Tim Tams as I want and now nobody can stop me. This is the start of my professional acting career (although just in case it doesn't work out, I still take a few courses each semester at law school). I have my own apartment in the city and can finally quit all those side jobs that are sucking my energy. I did love working at the cinemas, though—and was still working there when *Fat Pizza* was released in April 2003. People would come out at the end of the movie, and I'd be there holding out a big black garbage bag to collect their rubbish, and they'd be like, "Weren't you just in that movie?" and I'd be like, "Yeah."

But now I have money and, amazingly, no debt. I decide that with a big chunk of the money—like $35,000—I'm going to treat my whole family to a big international trip. I know that I probably haven't been the easiest person to be around the last few years, I know that Mum can't afford to take my young siblings anywhere, so I spring for an epic trip—New York for Christmas, then to Washington, DC, to see the White House; to Disney World in Orlando (I knew I'd get to Orlando at some point!); and then to Thailand for a relaxing beach holiday. I pay for everything. Flights and hotels and transfers. New York hotels are really expensive, so we "do a dodgy" and enter the lobby in groups of only two or three at any one time so the hotel doesn't tweak that there are five people in one room. But we all love seeing Broadway shows! In Washington, DC, we walk to the White House, stand outside and say, "Yep, there's the White House," and then it's too freezing so we immediately walk back to our hotel.

At Disney World we alternate turns riding the motorized scooter (a.k.a. the "fat cart") to take a break from all the walking. When I'm having my go in the "fat cart," people look at me. "What's wrong with her?" I'm sure they're wondering. What's wrong with me? I am legit fat, spurred on by PCOS. But who cares, because I'm a professional actress now. I'm also what you might call a comedian. I'm literally laughing all the way to the bank.

When I get back from the family trip, I sit alone in that Newtown apartment pretty damn proud of myself. I pat myself on the back fat.

Go, you good thing!

EIGHTEEN

Women Aren't Funny

Turns out my small cameo in the film *Fat Pizza* was so memorable that I was asked to be in the TV show of the same name. I play Toula, the overweight girlfriend of Habib, a drug-dealing pizza delivery guy. I make myself as fat and sloppy as I can. I wear unflattering eye shadow colors and ill-fitting tracksuits. I eat donuts regularly to gain even more weight. We film a scene at a newly opened Krispy Kreme store and in each take I inhale five fresh donuts. Most actors would only take one bite of food per take—even using a spit bucket after the director yells "CUT!"—but here I am, just "going for it."

Mum refuses to allow *Fat Pizza* to play in the house. She doesn't want to see it because I look gross and she disapproves of my swearing in it. (Yes, I swear now, because I also learned at university that certain words are funnier than others—for example, "fuck" has that strong K sound, which just makes it funnier, a clean sound to get a laugh on.) It's my first television show and I'm the first lead female character, but it's banned from Mum's house. I flaunt my fat stomach on national TV and Mum absolutely hates it. I'm deliberately making myself look bad for comic effect—but Mum doesn't understand. She just sees her daughter looking unsightly. I see an opportunity to break out.

I was the first recurring female character on *Fat Pizza* who wasn't a sexy blond bimbo. Toula was a Greek gang girl from Sydney's western suburbs whose catchphrase was "Oh my gawd!!!!" The ongoing gag was that my boyfriend Habib was ashamed of me because I was over-weight, and he'd try to hide the fact that he was dating me. Cue the many, many derogatory jokes about my size and appearance. I knew the jokes weren't directed at me personally—my role was to be the big fat whale that got laughs. And I was willingly playing into that. It's not like I was the only one getting mocked. The little person was hired for their physicality, the Asian guy was hired because he was Asian, the Muslim guy was hired for gags because he looked like a terrorist. This is just how it was. I was determined, though, to give my character some more depth. I also tried to hold my own among the guys, mainly improvising my own lines, hoping to get one joke on camera during a twelve-hour workday—because, trust me, no one's going to just hand you amazing jokes or material. No, no, honey—not if you're a woman in the early 2000s and starting from the bottom in television comedy. You have to push your way through the door and keep the door ajar with your fat foot before they close it on you again.

Fat Pizza was a hugely popular series in Australia, and there were some lovely guys on the show, like Tahir Bilgiç and Rob Shehadie (who played Habib and Rocky). Those guys were always so respectful. But the show was far from sophisticated or glamorous. Toula eventually got her own all-female gang in the show, called the Pussies. We made appearances on the side in nightclubs—and once in a strip club—and were often paid for these gigs in cash stuffed in brown paper bags. We filmed regularly in sex stores—not sure why, just that the boys thought it was funny. One time we filmed at a porn agency in LA, and the boys would get off on asking the porn stars questions about their work and giggle like teenagers at their sexually explicit answers. Pauly asked me to improvise with the owner of the porn agency, telling him that I wanted to join. Of course, I was rejected in the scene because I was too fat. Silly me, to think I was desirable.

I felt like the girl who had gained access to a special men's club and it was all just mucking around with the boys. Just jokes. It was very clear to me what they found funny, and I went with it. There were some amazing TV shows that were female led—like *Absolutely Fabulous* (starring my UK idols Jennifer Saunders and Joanna Lumley), which I found on VHS when I worked at the video shop, and *Kath & Kim* (Gina Riley, Jane Turner and Magda Szubanski—women who literally paved the way for someone like me to even exist in the industry). But I wasn't lucky enough to be in one of their shows. I was in a boys' show, so I had to take their fatphobic jokes right on my double chin.

One time, while filming an episode about a road trip down to Melbourne, we stopped near Canberra in the middle of nowhere. It was just bush. Pauly had seen a dead kangaroo on the side of the road . . . roadkill. He thought it would be funny to shoot a scene where a kangaroo attacks him as he takes a piss on the side of the road. So, he picks up the dead kangaroo and gets a chain saw out of one of the vans (one of the other lead characters, Bobo, was notorious for having a chain saw to deal violently with issues), and then in front of us he saws off the dead kangaroo's arms and legs. He does this so that someone can then hold the arms on either side of the camera and move them like a puppet's arms so that it will look like the kangaroo is boxing and then later kicking him.

I'm horrified and decide to just sit inside the car. Next thing I know, a man in uniform approaches Pauly. "What's going on here?" he says. He's some kind of highway patrolman dressed in a ranger outfit. He says that a passing car called in a disturbing scene taking place on the side of the road. Pauly is often almost arrested whilst shooting the show, but at least this isn't the police. The patrolman sees blood everywhere from the chain sawing and the strewn limbs of the kangaroo. He starts to tear up. "Why would you do this?" he says. Pauly talks his way out of it, and we quickly pack up and burnout out of there.

People would tell my mother about scenes in the show when she was at work, and she'd call me later and say, with that same sound of hurt in her voice: "Why would you do this?"

"Mum! You don't understand! It's FUNNY! It's comedy!"

At least I got to travel to Italy with the show and go to Naples, the birthplace of pizza. "Oh my gawwwd," I said as I chowed down on a heavenly margherita pizza with ricotta cheese in the crust. That week we were being shown around town by a Mafia boss's son (who wanted to get into entertainment), and so we had access to all the best local restaurants. I would only order margherita pizzas, though . . . because literally my diet at this point was carbs and cheese and various combinations of the two. No one ever said to me, "Hey, Rebel, why don't you eat a salad!" All people cared about was that I was fat and funny. And I was doing both of those things very well. Toula was becoming a bit of a sensation! The whale was developing quite a large fan base. I now had actual storylines, like getting married to Habib on the show. I started writing a new one-woman stage show to capitalize on this fame. I was debuting it at the Melbourne International Comedy Festival and tickets were selling out.

Pauly came up to me on set and said, "You try too much."

Why was Pauly now criticizing me? I'd been loyal to him for three seasons, showing up whenever he needed me on set. The reason I was always doing more was because, as a woman, I needed to do more. I needed to come up with ten times more jokes than the boys in the hopes that I'd get some screen time. I needed to try harder just to wedge myself into scenes where I didn't naturally fit because all the boys were taking up the space. Pauly obviously didn't understand that, but I will always be grateful to him for giving me my start in Australian television.

Playing Toula actually helped keep me from getting mugged. I was out with Snickers one night and we were parked at Bondi Pavilion on Sydney's famous Bondi Beach. We'd gotten some dinner (margherita pizza for me, naturally . . . my order was as predictable as my upper-lip sweat) and it was late now, maybe around eleven p.m., and we were walking to the car to head home. Just the two of us chatting about how we wanted to do important things in the world. Snickers had graduated law school and was working as an attorney but also doing pro bono work for Indigenous Australians in his spare time. I was . . . ummm . . . running around in a pink tracksuit saying racially stereotyped jokes. But I wanted to do more. It's just that being part of this boys' club made a career in comedy seem like this massive mountain to climb, and I was just at the gift shop at base camp and already exhausted.

Over the years, Sydney's eastern beaches had had violent clashes between white Australians and gangs of young men who were, at the time, often of Lebanese descent. Even though my character Toula was of Greek descent, I was a white Australian and so was Snickers. As we neared the car a group of about twenty Lebanese guys approached us. Snickers and I both froze. We knew about the tit-for-tat violence that was occurring on the beaches at that time. Were we about to get bashed up? Mugged? These were all big dudes spoiling for a fight. In a split second I adopted Toula's voice and her physicality. "Oh my gawd, you guys, what are youse up to?" I walked toward them, like I'd learned in South Africa's game park. Never turn your back, never show fear. I walked toward the whole pack of them, half lit by the streetlight, half who were hidden in the shadows. "Have you guys had a good night? Oh my gawd, youse are so cute. Can I get your number?" One of the Lebanese guys then recognized me: "Oh my gawd, it's Toula!" "No way, bro!"

"Yeah, oh my gawd, it is me, Toula. How are you guys going?"

One guy grabbed something out of his large fanny pack. I internally freaked for a second, thinking he was going to pull out a weapon, but it was a camera.

"Sick. Can I get a photo?"

"Yeah, oh my gawd of course!"

I took a photo with some of the guys, and then Snickers and I quickly got in the car and drove off.

"We almost got rolled!" Snickers said.

"I know!" But being Toula had saved us.

My next big job was on a weekly television sketch show on Network Ten called *The Wedge*. The producers were looking for comedians who could write and perform their own material, and I'd caught a lot of people's attention with my sold-out one-woman show, *Confessions of an Exchange Student*, at the Melbourne International Comedy Festival.

I was also getting notice as a new stand-up. I didn't really like doing stand-up, though, and I only performed in more "theatrical" venues rather than rougher venues like pubs. Frankly, it was terrifying. Like, you're standing up there with a microphone and there's nowhere to hide. What if someone throws a beer bottle at me? What if they heckle me and I don't have a witty retort in the next 0.6 seconds? So as soon as I booked this next big television gig, I quit stand-up. It just didn't feel as right as acting but I'm glad I gave it a try . . . and I got to do some cool gigs, including big comedy galas and a live-taped television special with comedians from the UK and US like Alan Carr, Russell Howard and Craig Robinson.

When I was cast on *The Wedge*, I was the only lead female writer/performer employed on the show. The rest were guys. We all pitched characters and scripts we wanted to film, and I came up with some good ones, including Lucy Webster, a schoolgirl who gives webcam direct-address monologues about all the teenage dramas in her life.

I also created and performed as Fat Mandi, a British teenager who had been sent away by her parents to fat camp, which she thought was for teens celebrating their girth. So in the sketches, Fat Mandi rebelled against the weight-loss system and encouraged the other fat kids to do the same. And then there were Karla and Kiki Bangs—Karla was a dominating dance mum who ran a dance studio, and her daughter Kiki was the least talented in the class but somehow always ended up front and center in the routines. I played both roles.

The Wedge was filmed in Melbourne, which is more than five hundred miles from Sydney, so most of the first season I flew back and forth to shoot. Eventually I bought my first home in Melbourne and moved there officially. I paid $380,000 for a pretty modest two-bedroom apartment on Brighton Road in Elwood. From my first season on the show, I'd saved enough for a 10 percent deposit but then had to mortgage the rest. I thought I was pretty adult now—I was twenty-six and owned my first property!

I was becoming popular on *The Wedge* and some of the men working on the show didn't exactly like the power I was now wielding. To be honest, I think they were a bit shocked. I had two of the three highest-ranking characters on the show: Lucy and Fat Mandi. I'd hear gossip that some of these men thought I was "getting too big for my boots," and they didn't want this "to go to my head." It seemed clear that their plan was to keep my apparent ego from getting too inflated by diluting my presence on the show. This made absolutely zero sense to me. Did I ask for more money for the second season of the show? Yes. But I felt I was worth it . . . plus I now had a mortgage to pay because the show required me to move to another state. But these guys seemingly HATED having to pay me more and I felt like they were now trying to punish me.

I was well aware that I could be replaced at any moment. Some of them were also very open about the fact that the only way women could be funny was to be in bikinis or skimpy outfits, and so they weren't fans of my funny, brash female characters. There was a running joke between us castmates that a bunch of these men would gather to watch the edits of the sketches we'd shot that week and whenever there was a hot girl in a skimpy outfit, they would say creepily in a very low voice, "Yeah. That's funny." Those sketches started making it on air, and my sketches of characters that had ranked high in the first season were not even shot. It felt to me like my female empowerment and body-positive messages weren't what they were looking for.

I was starting to become known as "ballsy." It felt to me that the male writer/performers were able to speak up, but when I did it, it was seen as disrespectful.

For months, I would just sleep half the day in my designated office in St. Kilda because no one was scheduling my sketches to be shot.

There was nothing for me to do. I'd write scripts and they'd get ignored or rejected.

One day, after a three-hour nap on the floor, I confronted one of my friends in the production team. It just got to a boiling point that day—I'd moved my whole life to Melbourne, I was being paid a great weekly salary and they weren't even using me? Like, what the fuck? I blasted my friend in the office—which wasn't exactly fair, but the men themselves were . . . I don't know, at an expensive boozy boys' lunch at Di Stasio across the street (which is why, I believe, some weeks in season 2 we had no budget for sets or costumes—I wondered whether they were blowing the budget on their boozy lunches and/or on blowing something up their noses?). The one man I'd bonded with from season 1, Australian comedy legend Ian McFadyen, who had been so supportive and helpful with the creative, left after the first season. (I missed him, he was incredibly kind.)

"What the hell's going on?" I yell at my friend in the production office downstairs. "This is ridiculous! Why aren't any of my sketches being scheduled!" I yell as I point to the production board of upcoming shooting days. I'm completely red in the face. I never, ever yell at people (everyone who knows me and has worked with me knows this). But this situation just seems so wrong. To me this is level one hundred. I feel like my dad when he used to snap. This is me snapping. I am furious.

My friend tries to say some bullshit like maybe my scripts weren't "developed" enough. In this moment, I can't believe she's siding with those dickheads. Later I'll come to realize, maybe she has a mortgage as well. But I'm so upset with her response that I'll never really speak to her again. It's too painful. She's a dear friend and she had aligned herself with the other side.

The Wedge was canceled after its second season. We shot fifty-two episodes, which is a lot for an Australian show, but in my view the quality of the show had diminished substantially. One of my very talented male co-stars, Jason Gann, was given his own spin-off show. I left doubting myself, doubting my talents, doubting whether I would ever get a chance at doing my own comedy my way in a world where men called all the shots. To get your own TV comedy show in Australia was a ridiculously hard thing to achieve.

It felt like only two people a year would get that golden opportunity. But at twenty-eight, I finally got mine. I used my brain and ground out six original episodes for a musical comedy show based on parts of my own life called *Bogan Pride* for SBS, working with a great writer/director/producer, Tony Ayres, and his partner Michael McMahon. I loosely based the mother character in the show on Auntie Sandra. I wrote original songs and had a blast making it. Finally, I'd found supportive male producers . . . was this because they were gay? (Hi to all my gay besties out there, whom I adore!)

It was this show that got me to America. I don't know how it started but people in comedy in Hollywood had been handing around the DVD of *Bogan Pride*, and through that I'd been invited to have a representation meeting in America with the William Morris Agency (which later became WME). It wasn't a guaranteed offer of representation, but . . . it was a meeting! It was a chance. In Hollywood! The biggest boys' club there is!

I had to wait until I finished law school to go. Even though I was probably the most recognizable actress in Australian comedy at this point after appearing on thirteen different TV shows, there was still something inside me that said, "Graduate from law school. You never know when you might need that." What was supposed to be a five-year double degree from the University of New South Wales took me ten whole years to complete! It was a marathon effort. At one point when I was living in Melbourne, I would wake up at about four a.m. every Tuesday and drive to the airport, fly to Sydney and take law school classes back-to-back all day, then fly home to Melbourne by about nine p.m. and drive home. It was exhausting. But I didn't want to be like my father and drop out of college. I wanted to complete the degree even though at times it was insanely tough. My mother, siblings and grandparents Gar and Poppy came to my graduation. I'd bought a golden silk blouse with a tie front to wear under my gown because I thought it looked "legal." Mum took photos of me holding my degrees. "No, smile nicely," she'd say. She was very proud of me. I could tell because of how many photos she was taking. She wasn't so much a fan of *Bogan Pride*, where in the very first minute of the show, I paraded around a public swimming pool with fake black pubic hair sticking out of my swimming costume. "That's not funny," she said, staring at the merkin. But she was super happy for me to graduate from law school. That was something I could fall back on if this crazy phase of being a comedic actress dried up.

Why would you want to be a woman who is laughed at?

Why would you want to wear short shorts so that your fat thighs are on display? Why would you want to make yourself look uglier than you actually are? Why would you want to be loud and draw attention to yourself?

Mum didn't get it. Other girls my age were getting serious with their boyfriends. Some were starting to have families of their own by now. But not me. Now, in 2009, after graduating law school, I could finally GO TO HOLLYWOOD! I had one whole meeting waiting for me.

On the eve of my departure, I'm offered a huge three-year contract to join a dramedy show called *Winners and Losers*. It's a solid, well-paying job, but I turn it down. Now, this is a gamble—but, as you've seen, gambling does run in my family.

I sell everything I own in Melbourne, including the apartment (making a nice little profit as I sell it for $520K—go, girl!). I sell my computer and my little Citroën car that I love. I sell my used cheap toaster but autograph it so I get twenty bucks for it. For all her criticisms, Mum comes down from Sydney to help. She's always a champion helping me move. And living separately helped us get close again. Over one weekend we get rid of everything. There is no coming back. I'm going to Hollywood, and I'm going to make it.

"Am I good enough?" I think. When I worked at the cinemas, I watched every comedy movie I could. I actually got busted by my manager one time for watching the films when I should've been cleaning. These Hollywood movies were mainly led by men. But I wanted to do movies—I'd had a little taste of Hollywood being in a movie called *Ghost Rider*. I had a scene with Nicolas Cage and Eva Mendes on a huge set they'd built in Melbourne with a turned-over police car that had smoke coming out of it. It was mega exciting! It was Hollywood. I was instructed not to comment on Nicolas Cage's hair and then, of course, in the first minute of meeting him, meeting an actual Hollywood star, I touch his hair and realize it's a wig. He gives me a strange look. Whoops!

If I could go to Hollywood and get in one movie—only one—then people would respect me. Then maybe Mum would see that this isn't just some silly misguided phase. I would be legit. I'd be next-level.

I'd show all those people back in Australia who doubted me. All those people who didn't cast me, didn't green-light my material, didn't respect me. They just fueled my hate-fire. I'd show them that I shouldn't be kept away in a back office like a comedy-writer-performer version of *Cinderella*. I'd show them that I am a WOMAN and that I am FUNNY.

NINETEEN

Bridesmaids

I know I don't look like your typical immigrant searching for the American dream, but I am. To quote from *Miss Saigon*, "What's that I smell in the air, the American dream!" That's me 100 percent. I'm twenty-nine, soon to be turning thirty. I pack one suitcase, a pillow and a doona, take every cent I've earned in my Australian career to date and move to Los Angeles. LA, baby!

I really didn't know anyone in LA. But there was one girl, a fellow Australian actress called Monique, whom I'd known from past work. She'd moved to LA a few years earlier and said that I could sleep on her fold-out couch in the living room of her shared apartment for $100 a week. Bingo! Thanks, Mon. I'd asked another friend, Josh Lawson, for advice on how to tackle America. He'd been successful in booking acting jobs there. He said, "Sell yourself. If you're not confident in yourself, then how can someone else be?"

My first day in Hollywood is a complete disaster. I get off the plane after fifteen hours or so and I feel gross. Like the contents of a lunch box that's been left in your school bag all day unrefrigerated. I pick up my rental car and then drive, without navigation (car GPS systems are new at this point), to Monique's apartment complex in Los Feliz. I eventually manage to find it, hours later, because yes, this is a foreign country and all I have is one set of printed driving instructions to help me get there. When I finally arrive at the apartment, um, crap—Monique isn't here? I sit on the stoop and just wait. (I don't think my phone was activated yet or something weird.) So, I sit there on the steps, momentarily homeless with my one suitcase, pillow and doona. I sit for so long that I get a parking fine outside because I'm parked where the curb is painted red and apparently that means you're not allowed to park there.

Monique eventually comes and I find my designated couch upstairs. I place my large box of chocolate Caramello Koalas in Monique's fridge. The Caramello Koalas literally took up a quarter of my suitcase. Monique looks at me strangely—I'm bringing a whole box of chocolate when I could only fit such a limited number of things in my suitcase. Never underestimate my love of chocolate, Mon.

I later found out that Monique was in this Overeaters Anonymous group and she wasn't supposed to eat any sugar, as it was triggering. So she really wasn't impressed with me bringing such temptation into the house. She used to be bigger, but I'd noticed she had slimmed down a lot now that she was in America. She was so tiny now and she obviously wanted to stay that way. Was that what Hollywood demanded? She weighed and measured all her "healthy" foods with a small scale—even on the day I took her to Disneyland as a thank-you, she brought her carefully weighed low-glycemic-index food. I, of course, downed several churros, Rice Krispies Treats, soda and ice cream because that's what all normal people do at Disneyland. Isn't it?

Meanwhile I was living my large life, loving being fat. For my whole twenties, I hadn't dated anyone. Did I care? Nope. Okay, I had been incredibly lonely, I had yearned for love from somebody. I am human. But when it came down to it, I didn't want to date anyone because I was so focused on making it as an actress. I didn't wanna waste time saying to someone, "Hey, babe, how's your day going?" I had built up and carefully maintained this barrier around me—this barrier of fat. It said, "Don't you come near me, romantic partners. No, no. This is a closed shop. I can be your fat funny friend, that's a role I'm comfortable with. But I will not have romantic distractions. I do NOT want a part-ner who, like my father and mother's relationship, might come into my life only to destroy me. I'm so fucking lonely, though. Nope—change your mindset, Rebel. I'm not lonely; I'm focused. I have to sacrifice. No social life, no love life, no worries. I'm focused like an Olympic athlete. My mission: to get in one Hollywood film."

I was going to sell myself in Hollywood as Australia's female Jonah Hill. Yep, that was me!! That was my plan. (Note to readers wanting to make it in Hollywood—never try to sell yourself as an actor who can "do everything." That's like being a restaurant that serves everything: burgers, pizzas, steaks, seafood, pancakes etc. . . . those restaurants are never really any good. Better to be specific.)

Monique was a very talented actress, far better than me, actually—she'd graduated from NIDA—but she wasn't making much headway here. Hollywood was a hard town where everyone wanted to make it in the entertainment industry. Even Badrid, the weird creepy old guy who lived in the building, supplied cars for movies and wanted to be in them.

Day one in Hollywood, I'm living right off the famous Hollywood Boulevard—on a couch. Not a glamorous start. But day two is a new day. Day two is different. Day two I get up and spend ninety minutes showering and straightening my hair—it crackles under the intense heat of the GHD flat iron. I get a massive amount of underboob sweat. Damn it! It's because of the heat-styling instruments. So I "whore bath" my boob sweat with a washcloth. No matter what the tempera-ture, I always seem to feel hot at my size. I'm a slut for air-conditioning wherever I go.

I put on my best posh Mickey Mouse T-shirt (posh because it has sequins on it) with jeans, my straightened hair now up in a youthful high pony, and head to the ginormous Hollywood agency now called William Morris Endeavor (WME).

WME is in Beverly Hills, right next to Rodeo Drive, and is arguably the best acting agency in the world. Their office is a bit like a space-ship, with high-tech elevators flowing Beverly Hills–looking people to different floors for their powerful meetings. There are a number of swanky good-looking receptionists at the front desk who are all incredibly busy directing phone calls and validating parking. I walk up to the desk and say, "Hi, I'm Rebel Wilson. I'm here to see Stephanie and Kami." The girl smiles at me, probably thinking, "Who is this random?"

The two agents agreed to meet with me in person, I think so that they could judge me in the flesh and decide whether they actually want to represent me. (I mean, no pressure, Rebel, but you sold everything you owned and moved to the other side of the world hoping that this meeting would go well. Let's bloody hope it does!) This meeting is my big chance. Actually, my only chance . . . as this is the one and only meeting I secured before coming to the US.

I meet the ladies in a fancy spaceship meeting room. Agent Stephanie represents people like Robert Pattinson, who is a big star at this point from his role in *Twilight*. During the meeting, another agent, Tabatha, who represents Jonah Hill, sticks her nose in. Does she smell talent through her black blunt fringe? She'll think about it. (For a year. And then once I'm a breakout star, she'll say she wants to be my point agent.)

I tell agents Stephanie and Kami about how I'm definitely the new female Jonah Hill (selling myself . . . obvi). I see the agents looking at me. I'm experienced with both stage and TV productions, but I'm a big girl and there aren't many of them in Hollywood. Still, I not only act but also write and produce. I can create content, and that's valuable. I see them pondering my potential and future in their minds. Boob sweat starts to drip again and then they say, "Well, we don't really have anyone else like you on our books," and with that, they agree to represent me.

I am unique. And whoa! Being unique has paid off. When I was an actor at the Australian Theatre for Young People, I was labeled as two things: unique and ambitious. Neither was really meant as a compliment at the time. But now both seem to be paying good odds.

I dance all the way back to Los Feliz, sending a kiss to the Hollywood sign through my rental car windshield. "Hollywood, do-do-do-do-do-do-do, Hollywood!" I sing. I lie on the fold-out couch and eat ten Caramello Koalas. This is it. I've made it in Hollywood. I am IN. Everyone knows that to make it in Hollywood you need good agents—this is the only way to get into the rooms to get the good jobs. So strategically, being represented by WME is absolutely amazing.

Monique comes home. "You got signed by WME?" she asks.

"Yeah," I say.

I can see Monique can't make sense of this. She lost weight to make it in Hollywood. She's been here for at least a year and the best she's gotten is some shonky audition that could've been a ruse for porn. How did I just get represented by WME after being in America for less than two days?

My new agents sent me out on what's sometimes known as the Water Bottle Tour of Los Angeles. It's where they send you to all the different networks, movie studios and casting agents to have introductory meetings so you can sell yourself and tell your whole life story. In exchange the other person offers you a bottle of water. I told them stories of growing up in the bush and my adventures in Africa. I had thirty minutes for these folks to "get to know me," and so I was going to be entertaining AF. You never know where a general meeting can lead.

And then once the "Hey, I'm new in town, you should hire me, I'm amazingly talented although no one in America has hired me yet but I will be super famous" tour was done, my agents started putting me up for auditions. Pretty much every day I had an audition. Monique would look at my "sides"—the pieces of paper printed with your audition lines. The fact that things were happening for me seemed to boggle her. It seemed to make her more neurotic with her eating.

I had multiple auditions with director Cameron Crowe for the Matt Damon movie *We Bought a Zoo*. I mean, can you imagine, my first Hollywood movie would be doing scenes with Matt Damon! I tried so hard but the role was then offered to Scarlett Johansson. Ugh.

I tested for a TV pilot with Debra Messing—"testing" is where you're among the few finalists for the network and you sign a big contract right before you enter the room for your final audition so that if you get chosen, you're hired right away. At the time signing a $30,000-a-week contract was pretty fucking exciting. I was testing against Anna Camp (whom I would soon work with on *Pitch Perfect*) and Melissa Rauch (who went on to co-star in *The Big Bang Theory*). Melissa got the role. The pilot, to my knowledge, was never picked up, though. But at the time I was devastated to find out I didn't get the job. I remember crying when my agents told me it hadn't "gone my way." It was huge money. Life-changing. But sometimes when one door closes, another door has a gold star with your name on it.

My thirtieth audition, close to my thirtieth birthday, was for a comedy film called *Bridesmaids*. The script was written by Kristen Wiig and Annie Mumolo, and it was awesome! Full of hilarious FEMALE roles! It was directed by Paul Feig and produced by Judd Apatow, with casting by the genius Allison Jones—who was one of the lovely people I'd met on my Water Bottle Tour. These guys had done a TV show called *Freaks and Geeks*, which had launched the likes of Seth Rogen and James Franco. Jonah Hill had broken out after one scene in Apatow's *40-Year-Old Virgin*.

I knew this audition was my chance. Out of those first thirty projects I auditioned for, this was the best one. I just knew it. Allison had called me in to audition for what was to become Melissa McCarthy's role, the character Megan. Melissa was probably always going to get the role because she was more age-appropriate and was also a close friend of Kristen and Annie and they had wanted to work together. But I guess the studio insisted on seeing some alternative choices because Melissa was not the huge star she is today, and so I was brought in to test.

I head over to Sony Pictures Studios and am led into a room where Kristen Wiig herself is sitting on a stool in front of a camera. Paul, Judd and Allison are on the other side of the camera. They tell me, "You're at a wedding with Kristen, go! Improvise!" And so I did. I improvised my heart out. For ONE HOUR. I don't really remember anything I said exactly—I just remember that at one point Kristen and I were miming snorting cocaine through our belly buttons in a pretend bathroom.

When an audition goes on for a whole hour, you know you've done well. Normally Hollywood auditions last five to fifteen minutes tops. I guess they liked me enough that even though I didn't get the role of Megan, the team decided to add me into the movie as another house-mate for Kristen to play off. They called and said, "We'd like you to play the sister of a British actor, Matt Lucas." "Matt Lucas! Oh my gawd!" Matt was another comedy hero of mine, and weirdly, a few Christmases ago my dad had given me his doll from the *Little Britain* comedy series. I didn't really see my father much except for special occasions like Christmas and birthdays. Over the years my anger to-ward him had turned to pity. He had no one in his life, just Nanny, who didn't even recognize her own family anymore. "Hello, dear," she'd say when you came up to her, smiling. I could tell in her eyes she had no idea who I was. She'd known me as the teenager who'd started at Tara—but now this extremely overweight thirty-year-old blond woman was a stranger to her.

On the rare occasion when I would speak to Dad, he would smile eagerly. Like a keen work-experience kid trying to make a good impression. He asked me about my life, but I only ever gave him the very basics. I was always guarded. The separation battle between my parents had lasted seven years, and the legal fees meant Mum was left with absolutely nothing—so I wasn't about to just freely give him anything . . . even if it was just tidbits about my life. And then, because I'd usually see him on Christmas or a birthday, he'd give me a gift, and that at least filled up five minutes of the awkward time. Recently he'd given me the Matt Lucas doll because he knew I now liked comedy too. (Mum always said my father was a little bit psychic, and this was a very odd coincidence. For a year, I'm looking at this Matt Lucas doll on my shelf, and then I not only get cast to play his sister but actually later live with him. Apparently, Dad would always have vivid dreams and wake up and say something like "So-and-so just died," and then they'd find out the next day that the person had died.)

I'd actually had a dream that we were at Nanny's house, and I confronted him about all the pain he'd caused me and the rest of the family, but he couldn't handle it—he shook with rage. His hand started shaking and he grabbed the first thing he could clutch from the table, a fork, and stabbed me with it. I woke up in an awful sweat. After that I thought, "There's no way I am ever, ever going to confront him." Instead, I'd just try to bear these uncomfortable "special occasion" interactions. Happy Christmas, Dad. Here's your pair of socks that I've put zero thought or effort into. Dad never apologized for anything, and I never told him how I really felt—that's how it was.

Before filming for *Bridesmaids* started, Kristen Wiig took all the girls from the film in a party bus to a strip club called Hollywood Men. It was the craziest fun night—as you could imagine, being in a party bus with Kristen, Melissa McCarthy, Maya Rudolph, Rose Byrne, etc. Strippers gave us lap dances, and there was a lot of drinking and dancing, and Kristen bought me a Hollywood Men souvenir tank top that was way too small for me—but I wore it with pride anyway.

On my first day on set I was called in at four a.m. for my character, Brynn, to get her tattoo. Originally the tattoo was supposed to be "hip-hop Garfield," but apparently the artwork didn't get legal clearance, so they had to change it to a very nondescript ugly "Mexican drinking worm." A fat thing that looked like it had just slithered out of a tequila bottle and was ready to party! All week I couldn't properly shower because they didn't know what scenes I would show the tattoo in, and so each night I had to wrap my torso in cling wrap so the tattoo didn't come off.

Matt Lucas was such a comedy talent, such a gentleman, and it was an honor to film a week of scenes with him and Kristen. Matt and I ate ice cream sundaes every day on set together at lunch like two little giggling schoolkids. We both shared a massive love of sweets. I was the most junior actor on that set—it was full of comedy heavyweights—and yet Matt and Kristen could not have been more welcoming or inclusive. I was allowed to say whatever jokes I wanted—and trust me, that freedom doesn't always happen. By the end of the week of filming, apart from laughing at the wackiest of improvs between us all, Matt also asked me to be his real-life roommate after renovations in his West Hollywood house were completed. I, of course, said yes. I was itching to get out of the apartment complex in Los Feliz where the creepy guy Badrid would always offer to give me back massages . . . One time I was in so much pain when my back went out, I allowed it. He made a few weird sounds as he was massaging my lower back . . . ummmm . . . well, at least it was cheaper than going to a chiropractor? Unlike in Australia, I didn't have any health coverage in this new country.

I got paid $3,500 for *Bridesmaids*, a fee that I then had to pay directly to the Screen Actors Guild (SAG) to join the union. So really, I got paid nothing. That didn't matter to me. The experience was everything! Working with Paul and Judd was incredible. I was on my way to becoming the female Jonah Hill. (PS: Jonah, if you're reading this, I hope I don't look desperately uncool by writing this. I just always thought you were excellent and made great career choices. My new inspo is British actress Olivia Colman, but back in the day it was you, Jonah.)

It took a year after I filmed my scenes in *Bridesmaids* for the film to be released, in April 2011. That was one of the loneliest years of my life. I really didn't know anyone. Monique had returned to Australia, disappointed, and I still couldn't move in with Matt because his renovations were taking forever (don't they always!). I bought a car from another Australian actress for $500. Nicknamed "the Red Rocket," this car was soooo old it literally trembled when you sped up to enter a highway.

Once I'd paid for rent, I only had $60 a week to live on. I'd use that to buy groceries and see one movie at the cinema every week. I didn't go out to cool places like restaurants and nightclubs. I didn't really make any cool Hollywood friends. I was just living by myself, and it was lonely as hell. When I got the lease for my own apartment, I paid $500 for a secondhand bed, a mattress and a chest of drawers from the previous owner. I found a discarded ironing board out back near the trash and brought that upstairs to use as a television stand. I bought my first TV during a Black Friday midnight sale at Best Buy. And for months I only had one camping chair that had a cup holder on the armrest, which I'd bought at Home Depot for $10. I eventually bought furniture, but it took a few months and I had to really budget. Every cent I was spending was my entire life savings. It was like I was a sieve and right now money was just flowing out of me. Ten thousand dollars for a US O-1 work visa. Gone. A five-thousand-dollar deposit to rent an apartment because I didn't yet have a credit rating in the US. Six hundred dollars to get my hair dyed at a salon so it looked good for auditions.

People think it's glamorous moving to Hollywood. I'd thought it would be too. I'd found a decorative plate at Nanny's that had the Hollywood sign painted on it, and when I moved to Melbourne I had it hanging above my bathtub. I'd imagine what it would be like living there—being on studio lots, waving to Tom Cruise whilst being on a call with Steven Spielberg. But the reality was, I was living by myself in a small one-bedroom apartment. There were eleven Armenians crammed into the apartment to my right. In the one to my left lived a lady with so many cats that even with the door closed you could just smell the stench of cat waste. My free escape would be to go on a walk up to Griffith Park and stare at the real Hollywood sign. It wasn't just on a plate anymore. It was right in front of me. And that was beautiful.

One day I eat a whole family-size pizza for lunch and wash it down with a large bottle of Diet Coke. Then, of course, I feel guilty. I feel like a pig eating that much. "I've gotta go walk it off," I say to myself. I put on my leggings and start walking up the hill. Up past the house that was apparently used as the home of Ian Ziering's character's on *Beverly Hills, 90210*. At the top of the hill, forty-five minutes later, I blow a kiss out to the glorious Hollywood sign.

As I'm coming down, my stomach starts to really hurt. I have been diagnosed with irritable bowel syndrome (IBS) and am mildly intolerant to gluten and dairy. Not that it stops me from eating the foods that I want, though! I just eat my way through it, even though it's clearly causing a lot of inflammation in my body (hence the back pain). "I'm not going to be one of those weird people like Monique who goes to a restaurant and says 'I can't have dairy or gluten.' Fuck those annoying people." I'm just going to eat whatever I want and suffer the consequences. It isn't every day that I have an IBS attack. But today, as I'm mid-hike in Griffith Park, is such a day.

I must walk through a few residential streets before I get to my apartment complex. "Holy shit, I'm not going to make it." The pressure inside my bowels is just too much. There's no toilet in sight. There are just houses on either side of the road. Should I knock on one of the doors? Who would let me in? A random Australian girl, sweating, wanting to use their toilet. I think of Melissa McCarthy's scene in *Bridesmaids* where she shits in the sink and says, "It's coming out of me like lava!" That is me right now. I am about to explode. There is no time to think, and I'm still about ten minutes from my house. So I walk behind a small shrub in someone's front yard, pull down my pants and shit right in their front garden. A car drives down the street and stops right in front of the house. They turn off the engine. I am still mid–poop stream. I can't move. I'm frozen squatting there. What if they see me? What if it's Ian Ziering (joking)? What do I say? I think, "I'll just yell out, 'I'm pregnant!'" Maybe that could be a rational excuse for this gross behavior, I don't know. The guy gets out and luckily walks across the road to a different house. Phew. I pull up my pants and walk away from the crime scene. I am disgusted with myself. Disgusted that I ate like that and then behaved like this. This whole thing would've been preventable if I'd just NOT eaten the whole pizza for lunch. But it's like I never learn. A few days later I'll be back eating a similar type of meal and trying to walk it off again.

I was just surviving in America on not much money and it was (pun intended) shitty.

I'd get really pissed off at myself sometimes for buying cheap junk food, and on several occasions, I would throw it all out in the trash bins. I'd put dishwashing soap on it before I discarded it so I couldn't go rescue stuff from the bin later on. But then a few days later it'd be like I didn't remember, and I'd buy more chocolate and ice cream from the store. I was in a vicious cycle where this bad eating was ruling my life. I'd be "good" and exercise during the day, but at night, when it was just me in the small apartment, I'd watch trashy TV while trashing my body with junk food. I'd then call myself terrible names and feel depressed. It was a cycle that repeated day after day. I wasn't socializing, so there was no one to snap me out of it. There was no one to witness my terrible habits, so they just got worse. I'd moved away from everyone because I had this mission to "make it," but it was so brutally hard. Even though I had good representation, even though I'd booked my first movie, none of that really meant shit. I needed that movie to be released, and it was going to have to be a hit for it to even mean anything.

I score a few small TV gigs whilst I'm waiting. A guest-star role in a comedy called *Workaholics* where I meet this dude Adam Devine (my future "work husband"). As he's feeling up my boobs while I'm dressed as a Juggalo, I think, "Wow, this guy's really funny." And then a guest-star role on a CBS sitcom called *Rules of Engagement* where my co–guest star in the episode, the iconic Joan Collins, confuses me for the lunch lady. "What's for lunch?" she says to me as I'm waiting at the catering table. "Oh . . . um . . . I don't know. I'm also an actress in the show." She half-scowls at me and harrumphs off.

I traveled back to Australia several times to tie up some loose ends with the sale of my Melbourne apartment. I also wanted to see my family. I visited Nanny, who was now in a dementia ward because she had deteriorated so much. She had a huge cancerous mole cut out of her nose, which made her look a bit like Voldemort. Now she seemed completely gone. Like there was no life in her eyes and she had barely half a nose.

At the dementia unit, there were strict instructions on the front door not to let any of the patients out. When we entered, I realized why. The patients were like a pack of zombies. It's seared into my memory. I'd never seen anything like it. They were people, but no one was home in their brains. Nanny was in a shared room. Mum and I tried to find her but she wasn't in her room. I saw she had one small cupboard, the size of a high school locker, where two of her outfits were hung up. She had one nightgown. One blanket. That was it. She'd had a house, a beach cottage and a farm with horses. She'd had china tea sets and a collection of long necklaces. Now she had nothing. She didn't even have her own room.

We went looking for her with a nurse from the ward. We found her in a common room, sitting by herself in a chair. Completely out of it. "Hi, Nanny," I said. She didn't really speak now. There were no hilarious stories about someone calling her for a job or about her going overseas. She just looked at me blankly and didn't say a word. Mum said, "You better say goodbye. You probably won't ever see her again."

It was terrible to see my grandmother like this. "Hi, Nanny, it's me, Rebel." I crouched down next to her and held her hand. I didn't even know if she knew I was there. "I love you, Nanny."

I wish the alcohol hadn't taken her. It robbed me of at least sixteen years with her. She never knew that I became a professional actress. I think she would've been delighted with that. I think she would've boasted about it around town. I held her crepe-skinned hand and slowly stroked it. "Goodbye, Nanny, I love you so much." I didn't know what else to say.

When I returned to America Nanny had her ninetieth birthday. Dad and some other family members took her out to a local park. They tried to smile with her for photos around her cake, but she looked like her soul had already left her body. Two weeks later I got the call that she'd passed away. I didn't know what to do. I didn't have the money to return to go to her funeral, so I hiked up to Griffith Park. It was a quiet weekday, and at the top of the loop it felt like no one else was on the hill. I sat down under a tree and said a prayer for Nanny. I thought of the fun times I'd had with her and what a character she was. I thought of how she'd died. Alone. Not knowing where she was. With a demented old man in her room trying to steal her blanket. Oh, Nanny. If you had lived in a different time, maybe you would've been an actress or a comedian. As I was thinking about her, in what felt like total silence, I looked over my right shoulder and I saw a mountain lion. Standing there looking right at me. I kept very still, and I stared back at it. Its eyes reminded me of Nanny, of that cheeky look she used to have as she'd be drinking and placing bets on the horses over the landline. That look she'd have as she was cooking me pancakes.

After about a minute, the mountain lion turned and ran the other way. It disappeared. I couldn't help but think that it was Nanny's spirit sending me the message that she was now free of her awful self-inflicted disease. I walked down the path and blew a kiss to the Hollywood sign before walking home. I love you, Nanny.

The release of *Bridesmaids* was now approaching. I'd waited a whole year for this comedy to get released into the world. I thought: "Is four scenes enough to get noticed?" I was running low on cash. Since I was in the US on a work visa for the arts, I could only earn money as an actress, and I'd only made a few thousand dollars for each of those guest-star roles. Ten percent went to my agents, 10 percent to my manager, and then there were taxes as well (which, once I started earning real money in the US, were close to 50 percent because I am Australian). Even though I was being very budget conscious, I was quickly becoming broke. I'd also given myself a one-year deadline to make it in Hollywood. Otherwise, I was planning to move back to Australia and resurrect my career there. It had been over a year now, but I wanted to see how *Bridesmaids* had come out.

Turns out it's a huge hit, and turns out my four scenes are enough to get me noticed! Better than noticed! I am deemed a "BREAK-THROUGH." Agent Tabatha now deems me worthy to speak to. She says she wants to be my point person. Wow! A breakthrough! The only thing I've ever "broken through" is a glass coffee table in Canberra—I sat on it at Mum's friends' house as a ten-year-old whilst we were there for a dog show and, I think because of my weight, smashed it. But now I've broken through in Hollywood. I attend the premiere and get my photo taken with the whole *Bridesmaids* cast on the red carpet. That weekend, I go to Hollywood ArcLight Cinemas to watch the film with a crowd. I wear a baseball cap and sit in the back incognito to watch people's reactions. People are really laughing, especially at me.

I booked six movies in the two weeks after *Bridesmaids*, purely on the buzz and success of that film, one of which was *Pitch Perfect*. Boy, did that movie pay dividends!

I can't thank Paul, Judd and Allison enough for casting me in the film. They pulled the trigger on me. They gave me that first opportunity in Hollywood that changed the trajectory of my whole career. I think they're all geniuses and I'm eternally grateful to them. And to Kristen Wiig and Matt Lucas, who were so kind and supportive.

After the premiere I return to my one-bedroom apartment in Los Feliz. The Armenians are still up fighting about something. And a guy downstairs is watching porn really loudly. It has been such a big night, but now I'm by myself again. I can't wait to kick off the high heels, because they are literally killing me. I take off my purple dress and shapewear. I remove my makeup and take out the hairpieces. I look at myself in the mirror. "See, women are funny!" I say to myself. Then I head to the freezer, pull out a pint of ice cream and celebrate by eating in front of the TV in an oversize Disneyland nightie until I can't stay awake anymore.

TWENTY

Pitch Perfect

"Du-do-do-dooo, do-du-do-do-do." I'm singing a cappella to Bruno Mars's "Just the Way You Are" in perfect harmony with an unlikely gaggle of girls in the bottom of an abandoned swimming pool in the middle of the night. We're absolutely freezing our tits off. But we're loving it!

Six months earlier, the writer of *Pitch Perfect*, Kay Cannon, had either seen footage of or heard about my improv skills on the *Bridesmaids* set (yes, I always improvise on comedy sets to try to improve my role; even though some may call this "scene stealing," I more like to think of it as "embellishing"), and she'd reached out to me on Facebook. "I've written a character called Fat Amy and I don't want to offend you, but I think you'd be perfect for the role." She was right. I was insanely perfect. And I wasn't offended by the character's name at all (remember Fat Mandi!). When I read Kay's excellent script about the world of collegiate a cappella I thought, "Fat Amy is my favorite character." She wasn't the lead. On paper she was only like the seventh- or eighth-biggest character, but she had spunk! She had potential. And I could embellish that!

I still had to audition, though. I went in to meet with the director, Jason Moore (a big Broadway director), and producer Elizabeth Banks. I always get nervous for auditions. You go into a normally cramped room and act with no props and usually there's just a "reader" sitting to the side of a camera on a tripod filming you. You try to make a lit-tle small talk, like "I was in an a cappella group in high school called Twelve Voice where we wore peasant blouses and long velvet skirts and sang church hymns at funerals. Wasn't exactly a great crowd . . . ha! By the way, I think this script is really great!" I give the casting team the "eyes" that I used to give the dog show judges in Junior Handlers. "Give it to me," I project. Post-*Bridesmaids*, my audition success rate was now 100 percent, so I did feel supremely confident.

I sang the Lady Gaga song "The Edge of Glory" using my own body for percussion whilst singing—I do this cool little "slapping-my-chest clicking-clapping" thing to create a beat. I made them laugh. I could sing. I was fat. I booked the job instantly, and to my knowledge I was the first person cast in *Pitch Perfect*. Fat Amy was born.

I auditioned with an American accent, and it was only later in boot camp that Jason heard me speaking with my real voice and decided that Fat Amy would be much more distinctive if she was Australian. I really wanted to play American. I'd been practicing my accent and had already recorded all my vocals with an American accent. Jason, who is an absolute genius, was right, though, and I'm glad I listened to him. Besides, it is a hell of a lot easier to improvise in your natural accent . . . and I would be doing a lot of that on this set. I also wanted to wear zero makeup as Fat Amy, again, to make myself as unattractive as possible, because that's comedy, right?? But Jason and our gorgeous makeup artist Debbie strongly advised against this. "You need SOME makeup!" they said encouragingly.

We were to film in Baton Rouge, Louisiana. I'd never been to the South but was really excited to go. They were putting up the cast in a place called the Hilton Homewood Suites. It wasn't that fancy but it had a regular bed plus a pull-out bed in the living room, which meant that I could invite my mum and Liberty to visit. This was my first film role where I was "run of picture," which meant that I was in enough scenes that I had to be there through the whole month of rehearsals followed by two months of filming.

Now, a bit of a complication—I had been given a weight-loss deal with Jenny Craig in Australia before booking *Pitch Perfect*, and I had to take it because, well, I needed the money. Weight-loss deals can be lucrative, and second, I was putting my body on the line for comedy— doing things like high-energy comedy dance routines and stunt falls— and that was occasionally causing me pain, especially in my back.

"Maybe I should lose weight?" I thought. And then I looked at all those zeros on the offer amount and thought, "May as well give it a crack!"

I had already lost close to twenty-two pounds (ten kilos) by the time I started *Pitch*, following Jenny Craig. I really liked their plan—it was working for me at the time, and I was feeling better physically. I had to film an initial commercial announcing I was on their program. They made me sit on a couch and eat ice cream from a large bowl. It was the Hollywood version of what I was actually doing every night— but instead of a Disneyland nightie, I wore a cute fluffy robe and had my hair blown out and makeup on. I was directed to "look sad" as I shoveled the ice cream into my mouth. It felt a bit yucky filming this, like my private moments were now being shared with all of Australasia. The behavior I was ashamed about, the behavior I did in secret, was now openly being shown to people. Yuck. But when I looked at my bank balance: yay!

Being a lawyer, I noticed that my *Pitch* contract stated that I wasn't allowed to drastically change my appearance for the entirety of the shoot, including potential reshoots up to a whole year later. It meant my weight couldn't fluctuate more than ten pounds (around five kilos) either way from when I was cast in the movie. "Oh crap! I better start eating donuts!" I thought. I got out of my Jenny Craig contract and forwent most of the money they were going to pay me. I only got paid for the first commercial, which was a small percentage of the total fee.

If the role of Fat Amy had never come along, I would've stuck with the Jenny Craig deal and probably would've successfully lost the sixty-six pounds (thirty kilos) I had promised them. But it was such a conscious effort every day to lose weight; it was really hard and it was much more fun to let loose and go film this incredible movie. Now I was in the South, land of mac 'n' cheese and fried chicken, so I figured I might as well eat up. I tossed out all the frozen Jenny Craig meals. Not the desserts, though! I was going to be big and hopefully *Pitch Perfect* was going to be BIG too! I just had a vibe it'd be brilliant! Before filming, Tabatha had instead tried to get me to do a "boys" movie I'd been offered that filmed at the exact same time where I'd play the wife of Zach Galifianakis, but *Pitch Perfect* was just my jam. I knew it'd be aca-mazing!

We basically lived as college students at the Homewood Suites. Anna Kendrick got a slightly more luxurious place down the street— she had just been nominated for an Oscar and was the only real "star" in the cast, so she could afford to do that.

I met everyone on the first day of rehearsals and then later that night I went out to dinner with Anna Camp, Skylar Astin and Ben Platt. I just loved them instantly. We were all theater kids. We all loved musicals. There was an instant bond and I respected them all as artists immensely.

We practiced our a cappella harmonies and dance moves during the day at boot camp. The boys' group seemed to be way better than us. They crushed. I think it helped that the arrangers were men, but also an all-female group in general can be limited in a cappella arrangements because of the limited vocal range females have compared to men. We ladies were all underdogs in real life. And that's who we were in the movie too. We weren't polished. We didn't have the best routines. We were a ragtag bunch, but throughout rehearsals high up on the eighth floor of an abandoned building (yes, we seemed to take over a lot of abandoned things), with AJ, our super-cool choreographer, drilling the moves into us every day, we were developing a bond. We were quickly becoming friends.

We'd coordinate to wear the same-colored clothes to our rehearsals—like Brittany Snow or Anna Camp would say, "Okay, today we're all wearing pink or black." We were a team. We'd get really nervous to perform each Friday for the film's creatives. It was called "presentation Fridays," where we'd show everyone what we'd been rehearsing the whole week, and the director, Jason, would make changes accordingly. Elizabeth Banks cried when we first performed the finale into the mirrors of our makeshift rehearsal room.

I invited Mum to visit and she made it in time for our final presentation Friday and full-cast table read. After my role in *Bridesmaids*, Mum's feelings about my acting changed dramatically. She was always supportive of me as a person, she just always wanted the best for me, but now she was coming around (finally!) to the whole idea of my becoming an actress. "It's just, you would've been a great lawyer," she'd always say with a touch of regret—like when you walk out of a cheesecake store with one flavor and you turn back momentarily, thinking, "Should I have bought the other one?"

Adam Devine was cast as Bumper, and I was really excited about that. He was a top-notch improviser and incredibly funny—so I knew that he would be my ally in creating comedy on *Pitch*. There weren't many moments in the script where Bumper and Fat Amy spoke to each other, but as Adam and I were the clear comedians of the cast, we just naturally gravitated toward each other in the scenes. Jason was smart enough to just put the camera on us and let us rip.

My favorite improvised line from the first film is after Bumper says, "I think we should kiss," and I respond: "I sometimes think I can do crystal meth, but then I think: 'Hmmm, better not.'" Like most of my improvised lines, when I see them in the finished movie, I don't remember saying them on the day of filming. It's always a joy to see what the editor and director choose to put in.

Adam and I had great chemistry within the scenes. I thought he was so cute and funny, but off set I thought he'd never go for a girl like me. He started dating Kelley, the quieter, cuter blonde in the Bellas. Funny guys don't wanna sleep with funny girls! I wanted to sleep with funny guys, though. But I was so behind the eight ball on dating and a love life, I just tried to forget my urges. I could barely have a proper off-camera conversation with Adam because I thought he was so cute and I respected his comedy so much.

Mum stayed with me for a week, and we went to a Louisiana State University football game (LSU was the college portrayed as Barden University in the film). We also went on a gator tour in New Orleans. It was so great to have Mum there. She understood more of what I was doing, what I was trying to achieve. She understood after seeing me in *Pitch* how much I loved it.

Liberty later flew in for Thanksgiving and to watch our "Since U Been Gone" audition sequence. During the weekend, as we were driving to and from New Orleans to sightsee, my poor sister had to listen to me try to hit those high notes in the chorus at least one hundred times.

In the film, our girl group was originally called Divisi, based on a real college ensemble, so we used that name throughout the whole rehearsal process. Only at the last minute was our name changed to the Bellas. At the time, we were devastated and thought it was a terrible change that they had to make for legal reasons, but now I guess I don't think of our group as anything but the Bellas. "Bella" means "beautiful" in both Italian and Spanish—and although we were rough around the edges, we were all beautiful in our own ways. Ten girls of different backgrounds, different body types—all beautiful. (PS: Our group chats to this day are still labeled "The Bellas.")

The added pressures of huge success hadn't come yet. We just had fun singing and filming together. We'd rehearse late some nights in the hotel lobby—Kelley was our main a cappella guru and would coach us in our ten-part harmonies. We felt like we weren't as good as the boys and took the responsibility upon ourselves to make ourselves better.

The very first scene I shot for *Pitch* was the one where Bumper throws a soggy burrito out of a bus window and it hits Fat Amy splat in the chest. We were filming in the early morning, and it was freezing outside. When the burrito hit me, the cold burrito juice would seep into my Spanx. Each take, I would change my Bella top, but the juices were all up in my underwear, and being wet made me even colder. But still, they could've thrown a thousand burritos at me and I would've loved it. I just loved every second of being on that set and being around those people. "Ahhh, I've been shot!" I'd say after another burrito hit me in the chest.

It was also insanely cold when we were shooting the singing scenes in the abandoned swimming pool—so much so that we girls would huddle together like little penguins for warmth. I remember walking past the producer's tent and being very jealous of the numerous heaters next to their seats. "One day I'm going to be a producer," I thought. But when that camera was rolling, there we were, living our best lives. I was never cold when the camera was rolling.

I think our cast chemistry is one of the reasons why the film was such a massive success. It was a relatively small film, with a budget of around $15 million. It wasn't the Universal Studios juggernaut that it became . . . it was like a little summer theater camp. It's hard picking my favorite sequence to shoot—I loved the finale, where I would just gush joy from my open singing mouth! But I loved doing the whole thing really. Jason was such a warm director and the kindest guy.

I was again obsessed with all the free on-set catering. Honestly, it was like I'd never seen food before. Because I was playing Fat Amy, I didn't have to watch what I was eating at all. The only person who famously ate more than me on set was Alexis, the hot model of the group. Somehow, she could eat a ton. She'd pile up her plates. And yet she had such an amazing figure! My PCOS body type was NOT like that. I gained that Jenny Craig weight back by the end of the shoot and then some.

On one of the last days, we did a poster shoot, and it was a bit odd to stand next to some of the smaller girls in the film. I think I weighed literally three times more than some of them. You can't NOT notice the difference in size as seven girls are lined up in a row being photographed whilst seventy people sit behind the photographer making comments about us. But I was so confident in my skills as a comedic actress that I was like, "Well, I know logically society wants actresses to be hot and skinny—because look how hard these girls are trying to remain that; they must be getting rewarded for participating in this 'girl game'—but I'm going to peace out and just represent for the big girls. I'm talented. I deserve to be here. I deserve my place in this line. I'm just going to shine."

Our darling costume designer Sal Pérez always made me feel super comfortable in whatever I was wearing. Sometimes that meant that he made small changes to my outfits so that no one would notice that mine were slightly altered compared to the rest of the group's. For example, I rarely wore heels in the routines because at my weight, after a whole day of dancing in heels, I'd be absolutely ruined, whereas the smaller girls could manage the pain better. (And trust me, after dancing for twelve hours, their feet were in a lot of pain.) Occasionally, you'll notice my outfits have sleeves when the other girls' don't. Sal, being a bigger guy himself, just always took care of me, and I always appreciated it. It wasn't always like that. Around that time, I did a magazine photo shoot in a swanky Hollywood house and their internal stylist brought the clothes. But it became clear that literally NONE of the outfits were even close to fitting me. I saw the creatives milling around whispering, "What are we going to do?" Talk about feeling like I wanted to cry. I'm half naked at a photoshoot and there's literally nothing to wear. The fashionista photographer, magazine creative director, and "stylist" decide to literally "throw" a piece of rope around my neck to "see how that looks" and use some piece of fabric to cover my boobs. They made me feel like I was so fucking large that no clothes on the entire planet would fit me—so just give me the rope!! It took everything I had not to cry in front of these people. (Luckily, when I was promoting *Pitch 2*, I started working with one of the world's best stylists, Elizabeth Stewart, who, like Sal, makes women feel comfortable no matter their size. BTW, ALL stylists should be this way!)

During my first few years rising in Hollywood, I recall getting a lot of comments like, "Oh wow, you're so brave!" These remarks were normally meant as "Oh wow, you in your size-twenty body strutting down a red carpet like you're hot . . . That's so brave!" or "Oh wow, you're obese and you still get in front of a camera and smile—that's so brave!" and even "Oh wow, you go on television in your big body and are so positive and confident, gosh, you're brave." "Oh wow, you openly play a character called Fat Amy, bless your brave heart." I was always really put off by these comments, which 99 percent of the time came from other women. People would come up to me on the street and say, "I just want to thank you for being so brave!" Why am I so fucking brave? I'm not going off to fight in a war! I'm not running into a burning building to save kittens. What are people going on about? I'm brave because I'm just ME?? Because I dare to exist as a plus-size woman in Hollywood? But the way women would say this to me also usually had the sense of "I'm glad you're the one out there doing this . . . I wouldn't have the courage to do what you do." They wanted me to represent for women of a different body type, and the way they kept going on about being "brave" made me wonder—gosh, how many negative comments were these women getting about their bodies in their daily life? What was the negative commentary running in their own minds?

I seemingly didn't care about society's pressure to be thin. But that pressure was SO GREAT in women's minds that it was as if I was fighting a war against the patriarchal gaze. Against the corporate spin that wants you to go on that weight-loss program and exercise and hate yourself enough to buy this product. I was Fat Amy leading a rebellion, like what Fat Mandi had done against the fat camp in those sketches years earlier.

If someone wrote on my Facebook, "You're a fat bitch," I'd notice it, but, well, I guess I was just brave enough to keep being me. I was fat. Throw a rope around YOUR neck, losers! I'll just continue my glow-up.

I love all the girls on *Pitch*, but one of the best connections I had on the first movie was with my co-star Ester Dean, who was also a great songwriter who had written huge hits for Beyoncé, Rihanna, Nicki Minaj and Katy Perry. I felt like Ester wrote or co-wrote half the hits we sang in the movie. That's how she got into the movie in the first place—because they wanted to use so many of her songs that she negotiated a role in the film despite not having acted before. Smart woman!

Ester is beyond talented, and sometimes when we were in the van heading to work, she would play us cool demo tracks that she was working on and explain her musical process. I found her fascinating. She wasn't a big girl like me, but she was on the thicker side and proud of it. And normally, while the majority of the cast were partying on the weekends, Ester and I were both in our rooms writing away. Ester was writing music. I was writing a new sitcom I was developing for myself called *Super Fun Night*. Ester has such an incredible work ethic and such fun energy. Her life story is also so full-on that it should be turned into a book or a film. But I'll leave her to do that.

Sometimes in the entertainment industry your workload can be "feast or famine." With the success of *Bridesmaids*, I was in feast mode. This meant that even though I was having the best time performing "oral magic" with my Bellas (of course I'm referring to our gorgeous ten-part harmonies in musical numbers—keep your minds out of the gutter, readers!), in every spare second I had, I was thinking about what was next. I kept in mind some wise words from Amy Poehler, who was gracious enough to have lunch with me months after I arrived in LA. (Tabatha had set this up, as Amy was also her client at the time.) "You must generate your own work. No one's going to just hand you an amazing opportunity. You have to create it for yourself." So, there I was, writing—sometimes I would work a fourteen-hour day on set and come back and write. I wasn't going to the bar and getting smashed with my per diems. I was writing. I was feasting. Food- and work-wise.

My most difficult scene to shoot was the Bellas' regional perfor-mance where Fat Amy breaks out of formation, and I have a "Turn the Beat Around" solo. It was my biggest solo in the film and I was really looking forward to it. Like, I couldn't sleep the night before be-cause I was too excited. However, maybe because of my self-inflicted heavy workload combined with the freezing-cold night shoots, I had developed bronchitis and woke up that morning feeling very sick. Someone from the production office sent a doctor to my trailer. A "production doctor" who is used to visiting actors on set. I'm coughing grossly. I feel like I can't get up. I'm only half dressed in my Bellas uniform because I don't have the energy to get ready. The doctor casually examines me, but he seems to know what I need. He shoots some steroids into my thigh. Twice. I guess just to make sure it works? It gives me enough energy to shoot the scene . . . and then also keeps me awake for the next thirty-six hours!

I thought about all those stories people told of Judy Garland as a child actor, provided with uppers and downers. "It must've been true," I thought as the doctor was injecting me in my trailer so I could get out there and sing and dance. But at least I could do it—with a huge cast, it was hard to get a vocal solo and I wasn't going to give mine up. I'm still the girl who performed in *Fiddler on the Roof* post-fall, with my arm and ribs bandaged. (And to my knowledge, I've never had a sick day off work—even from *Cats*, where one week I had vertigo and bronchitis from the freezing weather and demanding cat movements . . . I was again shot up with steroids to complete my number. Standard.)

Production would prefer to just shoot you up with something to keep you going rather than take a rest day for the cast and crew, which could cost the project hundreds of thousands of dollars. You're given this awful ultimatum: you can shoot the scenes you're supposed to shoot today, orrrr hundreds of people will be sent home and you'll cost the movie hundreds of thousands of dollars. I always wanted to be the good girl, the professional, and shoot the scenes. I hated letting people down. I'd rather have let my own health suffer. I cared about succeeding. I cared about making money. I cared about making a name for myself and being respected as an actress. But my own health was insignificant.

This was true even on *Isn't It Romantic*, when I suffered a concussion after slipping on a grass hill walking to set. I was taken to a hospital in an ambulance, treated for a few hours and then returned to work and filmed a full day. I guess I think, "Well, hundreds of girls would love to be in my position. Hundreds of girls could replace me if I don't perform. So no matter what, I have to perform." If you're sick, if someone just died, if something awful just happened in your personal life, you have to suck it up and work your ass off for the production. The message is very loudly, "Be a team player . . . especially if you're a woman." My inner monologue was, "Come on, body, what the hell is wrong with you, suck up the pain and be strong!"

One night on *Pitch Perfect 3*, it was three a.m. and my back was seizing up during the "Cheap Thrills" routine. It was again freezing (productions often shoot in the off-season months because it's cheaper), and the director, Trish, had made us do take after mindless take, not knowing what angles she wanted. I'd given all I could and was taking a break in my trailer. Trish wanted me to come back out and shoot more, and it was only then, on my FIFTEENTH Hollywood film, that I had enough self-esteem to say, "Nope. I'm going home, I've done enough for today." It took me until I was a thirty-six-year-old woman to stand up for myself on a film set. To know that I could in fact say no when I was in extreme pain and/or extreme conditions. Before that, it had never occurred to me that I could actually say no. Actors normally say YES. I'd done full-out performance after full-out performance in front of hundreds of extras, and it wasn't my fault that the director hadn't captured it yet. Even though I could barely walk, I still felt so guilty for leaving my other Bellas behind that night. "You're pathetic," I told myself. "You can't do the job." I'd given it my all . . . but that night it wasn't enough.

When the first *Pitch Perfect* shoot ended, I returned to my small apartment in Los Angeles, and it was like a depression took me over. I'd had such an absolute blast shooting the movie and made all these incredible new friends, and we were all together in such an intense way, chatting and laughing—and then it just disappeared, overnight. It was suddenly over. Was I even going to see these amazing people ever again? It was the BEST filming experience of my life. In the finale, there's a bit where us girls are all clumped together rotating our bodies like we're a group wheel. If you pause on that bit, you'll see me living my best life. My mouth is open as wide as it can possibly be whilst I'm giving out pure joy.

It sucks coming back to LA. The loneliness is back big-time. I start yet another draft of my sitcom *Super Fun Night*. I order another family-size pizza, even though I know I shouldn't. I discover these amazing ice cream sandwiches in a shop down the road that are made with macaroon-type cookies. I buy them almost every night. Except the nights when I'm "trying to be good" and don't eat junk food . . . only to obsess about the junk food I'm not eating, pretty much sitting on my hands so that I don't raid the fridge. It takes all my energy on the nights when I'm "being good" not to eat the sugar. Especially now that I'm writing. I eat so much that I feel bad about myself, and I promise to work harder and be better the next day.

"Ahhh, I'm Fat Amy now. I can eat this tub of ice cream," the little devil inside me says as I sit on my couch. "They might need you for reshoots, you have to stay fat. You did sixty minutes on the treadmill plus weights today at the gym, you can eat dessert! You deserve it!"

"But I know that this nighttime behavior isn't exactly healthy—like, it's NOT—I feel gross. And maybe if I lost weight, someone might fancy me? I'd love for someone to love me."

"Everybody loves you, stupid! You're Fat Amy now."

"No! No one's going to romantically love me like this! No one's asking me out on a date, are they?!" This seeps into my core, like that burrito juice on day one of filming. I haven't been on a date with anyone since Justin from high school—that's now sixteen years ago!

"REBEL!!" I say to myself. "Shut up and enjoy the feast."

TWENTY-ONE

Sudden International Fame

Pitch Perfect was released September 28, 2012. This was the day my life changed forever. This was the day I instantly became internationally famous. I was thirty-two years old and had finally moved in with my *Bridesmaids* co-star Matt Lucas in a gorgeous and spacious house in West Hollywood. Matt has exquisite interior design taste and it was the first nicely decorated house I'd ever lived in. I remember sticky-taping magazine posters on my wall as a kid—now there was a large two-million-dollar painting hanging in the hallway with a special protective barrier so you couldn't accidentally bump into it.

There was a guesthouse in the back with a projector cinema in it. There was a nice pool that I naturally used for "mermaid time." (For some reason, swimming and doing flips in the water like a mermaid really relaxed me . . . in water I didn't feel my weight. I felt free. I floated so easily.) And for the first time ever I had: a housekeeper!! Someone to cook and clean. Someone to do all the washing. Wow. I would normally spend my Sundays going grocery shopping, cleaning my apartment and doing laundry for the week. But now I could NOT go to the supermarket in my pajamas with my hair thrown up in a messy topknot. Now I was famous. I was so famous that even with a hat and sunglasses on (the classic LA actor disguise), I was recognizable.

I feel sorry for kids who get famous when they're young—because it really is a trip when it happens to you. There are amazing things about it, sure—you get courtside tickets to the Lakers, you get offered free holidays to the Maldives, suddenly the restaurant that's always full will accommodate you. You get invited to parties with other A-list celebrities who seem to know you and say hi. The lovely Julia Roberts is talking to me like it's totally normal. It's surreal. But there's a diffi-cult side too. You lose your anonymity. You can never go to a restaurant again without someone staring at you, someone coming up to you. I've been mid-mammogram, my boob squashed in the machine like it's in a panini press, and had the technician ask, "So what's it like to be in *Pitch Perfect*?" When you lose your privacy, it kinda sucks. But that's just one part of it. The other part is this enormous pressure you suddenly feel. Am I worthy of this success? Am I good enough? Am I deserving of all this acclaim? Then comes the next wave of anxiety: How am I going to keep up this level of success? I don't want to fall off the wave and have to paddle back out. What do I need to do to now hold my position in the industry? Things don't get easier professionally. Things actually get harder. The stakes get higher, and you now have to work even harder to succeed.

Fame chose me the day *Pitch Perfect* was released in cinemas. It found me fast.

Paparazzi swarmed our house in West Hollywood. I couldn't go anywhere. People were hiding in bushes to take my photo. Everybody I ever knew who had my email or phone number called or messaged. "You're on a billboard!" "I just saw you on TV!" "Hi. I'm thinking of coming to LA, can I stay with you? You're the best." (Um, no, seeing as you weren't really my friend, and you now work the reception desk at a brothel . . . I'm not going to reply but I will still feel guilty for saying no.)

The fame wave hits me in the face. And it's sink or swim. It's like that time when Dad took me to Avoca Beach one weekend when I was about fourteen and for a second, I wasn't looking and a big wave smashed my board into my face. BANG! I had braces at the time and the impact mashed my lips into the metal. I had to pull my lips off my braces, which caused blood to now gush out of my mouth in addition to my nose. I came running out of the ocean, blood dripping down my face. "Dad! Look!" I said. "Should we go to the hospital?" "Nah, you'll be right," he said as he passed me one measly napkin to clean up with.

BANG! To deal with my newfound fame, all I could think to do was to sit fully clothed in the bathtub and kind of shake for about thirty minutes. My life was not ever going to be the same again.

Down at WME, my agent Tabatha was now wanting total control. Somehow, I never spoke to my original signing agents or manager anymore. Tabatha wanted to be the gothic gatekeeper for all the opportunities flooding my way. *Pitch Perfect* was one of those rare unicorns, a movie that played in the cinemas for months. People found it and they loved it. Fat Amy was a crowd favorite.

Matt and I were out at Chateau Marmont and a super-hot waiter slipped me his number on a napkin. Matt's like, "You should go for it!" "No!!!" I say. I can't hook up with some random waiter. Apparently when you are famous, this kinda shit just happens. People outright offer to sleep with you (more to cum . . . okay, that's the worst pun in the world).

I threw myself into work like a good little workaholic. *Super Fun Night* was commissioned by ABC. I played Kimmie Boubier, a socially naïve American lawyer who prefers the company of her dorky friends but wants to improve her social and love life. This was very much me at the time: secretly wanting to improve other aspects of my life when my career was going amazingly.

I was happy to get the deal for *Super Fun Night* because I was guaranteed a substantial weekly salary. I was earning around $50,000 USD a week as the show's star, creator and producer. Since I was living at Matt's, I'd save money to buy my first-ever house!

I fly to Australia for a screening of *Pitch* at Castle Hill Greater Union, the very cinema where I used to clean up used tissues and popcorn from under the seats. All of my friends and family are there, and I give a speech before the film. My dad comes too and brings some of his friends, including his best man from my parents' wedding. He is so excited to see me as I come down the aisle looking glam in my new dress (yes, famous me now has a glam team!), shaking everyone's hands and thanking them for coming. I don't give Dad any special treatment. We still have that very strained, almost estranged relationship. I haven't really seen him since moving to America. He looks much older now. But the smile on his face is huge. He's clearly extremely proud of me. I clock that. Mum then ushers me in a different direction because she's promised ALL of the five hundred friends she's invited a photo with me. It takes bloody ages!

"Mum! Did you tell ALL your friends they could get a photo?"

"Yes," she says bluntly. "What's wrong with that?"

Dad now apparently has a new job helping underprivileged youth at the Police Citizens Youth Club (PCYC—a not-for-profit organization to empower young people). I still haven't forgiven him, though. It doesn't make up for what he's done to my mother and our family. I guess I invited him to the *Pitch* screening because it was "the right thing to do." Which is probably the same stupid female rationale my mum used when after the separation she made my younger brother and sister spend weekends with him. "It's the right thing to do," she'd always say. But was it? Anna didn't think so when she was about seven and he locked her in a bathroom once for hours.

There's a game my father used to play with me when I was a very small kid. It was called "Doormat." In the game, the adult would essentially use their feet to apply pressure on the child lying on the ground, as if the kid were a doormat. The adult would apply just enough pressure so as not to hurt them but to make it impossible for them to pry free and get up. The kid (being me or my siblings) would struggle and squirm whilst the adult would gleefully yell, "Doormat! Doormat!" and move their feet back and forth slightly—as if wiping their feet on the doormat—occasionally easing up the pressure just enough to allow the kid to think momentarily that they might escape. Then suddenly more pressure is exerted by the adult and their strength is too much. Eventually the kid gets tired from struggling and submits to being the treaded doormat. Game over.

As a kid, I loved to play this game with my dad. So did my brother and sisters. He'd be sitting on the couch watching TV and we'd lie in front of his feet and beg to play the game. "Doormat! Doormat!" he'd say with his feet on my back as I tried to get up.

But now guess who's really gotten up in real life? Me! Now I'm so much stronger than him—in every single way. He has no pressure to exert anymore. I have the power. And he does know that. Mum's got five hundred friends here—he was allowed five.

After the film, Dad walks out into the aisle and hugs me. It's awkward as I don't think we've hugged in a good decade. He grabs on to me like I'm his precious child. "Just know I love you," he says. I notice he shakes a bit now. Is he nervous around me? It feels like he is just incredibly grateful to be invited after being excluded from my life for basically sixteen years. He's absolutely fucking thrilled that his daughter is SOMEONE. I can see it in his eyes. (Still, I'm not going to invite him to lunch afterward with the rest of the family and pretend that we're all some happy family. That would be awkward city.)

I go back to my luxury hotel room on Sydney Harbour and take out my clipped-in Hollywood hair extensions. I think about seeing my father. He was trying to connect with me at the screening, but I wasn't going to just let him back into my life now. He'd never even said sorry. But is it not the Christian thing to do, to forgive him? Should I start being nicer to him? He's clearly trying . . . but is this because I'm now famous? It feels weird that journalists who get the chance to interview me know more about my life than my father does.

A few months later, Dad and my brother, Ryan, have a trip to Los Angeles planned. They're going to Las Vegas to gamble, as my brother became a professional poker player after high school, but they're flying into LA. I'm really not happy about the gambling. I tried to encourage my brother, who is also super gifted mathematically, to do something else with his skills. But even though I'm incredibly busy with waiters offering to bang me and all, I say I'll make time to catch up . . . you know, I can manage like one meal with them in LA.

My father is a massive Matt Lucas fan and a big lover of British comedy in general. He would've loved to meet Matt and see the nice house where I was living. But I can't stomach it. That would be opening the floodgates for me. I can't go from barely communicating to letting him see my bedroom. It feels like too much, too soon.

So my brother, my father and I meet at this small restaurant in West Hollywood called the Village Idiot near the Groundlings Theatre. I think, "I'll take them to dinner and then, so I don't have to talk too much, I'll take them to the Groundlings to see a comedy show. Dad and my brother would enjoy that, being fans of comedy."

We sit at a long wooden table. My brother sits next to him. I sit on the opposite side. We have a stilted conversation. "When is my hamburger gonna come?" I'm thinking. "I need saving from this awkwardness." Luckily the food arrives pretty quickly. His hands tremble as he cuts into his corncob—is it nerves again? He's trying so hard to be a kind, loving dad. Like he doesn't want to make any more wrong moves. He's being overly effusive about being invited to the *Pitch* screening. He says he's bought twenty tickets since then and taken other friends to see it. I think to myself, "Is now the time I confront him?" But I look down at his shaking hand—I see the fork clutched in it. I remember my dream. "Don't say anything, Rebel."

"So . . . um . . . are you seeing anyone?" he asks.

"No," I say abruptly. I really hate that question—especially because it's coming from him. I'm thinking, "Oh, the nerve of him, asking me if I have a boyfriend! As if I'd want to get into a relationship and, what? End up like him and Mum! No thanks. I'd rather shave down my own teeth with sandpaper. No! Just no!"

I change the subject to work . . . because that's an easier conversa-tion. I tell him about *Super Fun Night* being commissioned and about how I'm getting an office at Warner Bros. studios, right next door to the *Ellen* set. He says he thinks I'll win an Academy Award one day. That's why he gave me that book about the Oscars for my birthday.

"Do you still have it?" he says.

"Yeah," I say. I keep answering him with as few words as possible. Already this is a big step on my end, having dinner with him when it isn't even his birthday OR Christmas.

He talks about working at the PCYC. He seems to really enjoy it but is near retirement. He says that he's just packed up Nanny's house and bought a small apartment in Drummoyne that overlooks Sydney Harbour. I keep looking at the scabs on his forehead and the shaking fork in his hands.

We see the show at the Groundlings Theatre. We laugh together at the sketches. Dad is really enjoying it, really enjoying spending time with me. He beams with pride when other people in the crowd recog-nize me and want photos. Afterward, as we're standing on Melrose Av-enue, there's an awkward hug. I say I have to go home—I don't wanna take any more selfies with people, so I can't linger for too long. I turn away from him as he and my brother walk down Melrose to get to their rental car. I go the other way.

I could turn back and say, "Oh wait! Why don't you just come by the house quickly." I almost do. I almost stop and yell out to them. But I don't.

He disappears into the darkness. And I never see him again alive.

I worked my ass off on *Super Fun Night*, as we were now in pre-production and about to start shooting in a few weeks. The workload was intense. I had a brilliant team of people working on the show. My showrunner was John Riggi, a writer from *30 Rock*, and my writing staff included writer/director Michael Showalter and Brent Forrester, a writer on the US version of *The Office*. I spent weeks trying to communicate my style of comedy to them and sharing life stories in the hope that it'd make good TV. But it wasn't enough time. Prime-time television schedules in America are no joke. There was huge pressure. The great Robin Williams also had a freshman show against us on rival network CBS. And we were to air after *Modern Family*, which was a huge hit for ABC. I wanted the show to be great. To be hilarious and heartfelt. But I was working with a huge team of people who didn't really know me, and at thirty-three, I was a relatively young woman in the industry. My chubby face made me look even younger. It was hard to assert what I wanted. Between the studio, the network and the staff, there were all these people weighing in on my process, trying to tell me what to do. There were too many chefs in the kitchen, and I was too polite to pound anyone with a rolling pin. I'd have to stroke them with a butter brush. And that got exhausting. Women can't be too bold. You get labeled a bitch. Just ask Ellen next door. You have to be diplomatic. I have a heated one-hour "conversation" with the network's legal department as to why my character's Wi-Fi password can't be "tit rhino." Originally, I'd been told by the powers that be, "Rebel, it's your show, you can do whatever you want!" And then you start handing in scripts and you're given back an even longer document listing all the things you can't now do or say.

And then, two weeks before we were to start filming, I got the call that my father, Warwick, had passed away from a heart attack. He was sixty-two. Earlier that day, he hadn't been feeling well and thought he had the flu. My brother picked him up from his new apartment in Sydney and took him to a local medical center. My dad felt chest pain, so he was told to go to the hospital. He told my brother not to wait around as it was getting late, so Ryan went home, thinking Dad just had the flu. Then in the early morning hours my father had a fatal heart attack in the hospital. The doctors tried to revive him, but his arteries were clogged. The nerve damage to his heart, caused by diabetes, masked the symptoms of the heart attack.

"Warwick's dead," Mum said over the phone through tears. Matt comforted me; he was like my wise older brother, just so kind and caring.

I immediately booked a flight to Sydney. I'm the oldest and the most responsible, so I needed to be there. I'd never dealt with something like this before. What are you supposed to do when a parent dies? I told people at the show what had happened and that I'd be gone for a week. It was a critical week of prep but obviously I had to leave.

I met my family at Liberty's apartment. At least her awful husband refrained for one night from saying, "Wifey, get me a beer." Mum, Libby, Ryan and Anna were all there sitting around a table. We were all crying. We were all in shock. We didn't know what to do or say. Even though we had complicated feelings toward my father, it was so tragic. He'd only just moved into that new apartment with a view of Sydney Harbour. He was ready to start a new chapter of his life after Nanny had died the year before. He'd literally just cleaned up his whole life, he was trying, and now he was dead.

I thought about the last emails I'd received from him. I didn't want him to have my American phone number, but email felt like a safe form of communication. He was so proud of me for hosting the MTV Movie Awards, and for his most recent birthday, Libby had given him a framed picture of the four of us kids from that night. He'd watched the show from Australia and said he was cheering me on.

In May I'd wished him a happy birthday and sent him pictures of myself with Whoopi Goldberg, Bette Midler and Tom Hanks in New York. He said Nanny would've been proud of me. He wrote, "Ryan told me that ABC has taken up your TV show for 13 episodes. That's huge. Great work you deserve all the success. Better let you get back to work. All my love Dad xxxx."

On the twenty-ninth of May he'd written:

> Hi Reb
>
> Hope all is well and you are living a balanced life. We have had heavy fog in Sydney the last couple of days but each night there has been a festival resulting in the Harbor Bridge being lit in a different and changing array of colors.

Quite spectacular. One just has to watch to see what combination of colors it is changing to.

Like you I have been bogged down with work and haven't done a great deal. So just wanted to let you know that I was thinking of you . . . Set myself a new goal each change in daylight savings, 1) photocopy contents of my wallet 2) change the batteries in the smoke detector 3) de-clutter my junk.

Best go
Love always Dad xxxx

Not exactly a thrilling email but we were communicating. It was clear that in these past few months we had both been trying to reach out in our own ways. And then we emailed on June 7, 2013, which was the last correspondence I had with him before his death. I'd sent him a copy of my *Glamour UK* magazine cover, and he'd written:

Hi Reb

Just thought I would let you know that you look absolutely glamorous and deserve the front cover of any magazine. Any of my daughters are front cover worthy. Guess I am a very lucky and proud Dad. Congrats also on your latest award. It made the evening news . . . Know I always love you

Dad xxx

And now he's just suddenly dead. Gone. I remember at times, when he was really putting my mum through hell, wishing that he'd just drop dead. We all thought it'd be better if he just disappeared. It'd be easier. But now that it had happened, it was awful.

I'm crying because I wish I could've empathized with him more and tried harder to rebuild our relationship. For all his faults, he was trying. I just always thought that because he was the parent, the onus was on him to mend our fractured bond. But maybe I should've taken the initiative? I hadn't done as much as I could have. He did love me, yeah? He was proud of me. I helped organize the funeral with Mum, my brother and my sisters. After the seven-year separation court battle, Mum had rarely spoken to my father. She'd tried hard to move on and not waste another second on him. And why should she? He was particularly vicious to her. Yet she never legally divorced him, which I found confusing. She always said that she thought deep down he had some weird delusion that our family would all get back together and that if she did divorce him, it would be so final that it'd probably cause him to commit suicide. She believed that despite his awful actions, he loved her and was hoping one day it would all work out and we'd be that family unit again going to Disneyland.

We sit around the table and try to remember some of the "good times," like when Dad would take us to the local theme park, Australia's Wonderland, or to rugby league games. But my younger siblings barely have these memories. Anna barely remembers him period.

I am told by the funeral directors that I'll get to spend some private time with Dad's body right before the funeral, if I want to. Mum doesn't, but I do. I go back to my hotel room and write down all the things I wanted to say to him but never did. I take pictures of the letter because I know that I'm going to put it in his casket and that it's going to get cremated with him. I want to remember my final words to him.

At the end of the week, we hold Dad's funeral and I get to sit with his cold, lifeless body behind a curtain before the crowd arrives. I let my brother and sisters go first, so that then I can be the last one alone with him. I am crying so much I can barely see. I touch his cold chest and I place the letter inside his suit jacket. He looks peaceful. In his suit and tie he looks like a businessman. Like the businessman he always wanted to be.

I tell him that I love him. I love him so much and I wish things had been different. I come out from behind the curtain into the funeral parlor and walk onto a stage I don't want to be on.

When Rebel met Whoopi Goldberg after seeing her perform on Broadway, 2003.

University of New South Wales law school graduation ceremony with Ryan, Anna and Liberty, 2009.

Rebel with co-star Matt Lucas filming
Bridesmaids at Sony Pictures Studios,
Los Angeles, 2010.

Rebel with *Pitch Perfect 2* co-star Hailee
Steinfeld filming the finale sequence,
Baton Rouge, Louisiana, 2014.

Rebel on a rooftop on Sunset Boulevard, Los Angeles, 2015.

Rebel and Brad Pitt at the
92nd Academy Awards, 2020.

Rebel on top of Loser Mountain near Mayrlife Altaussee in Austria after reaching her goal weight of 165 pounds (75 kilos). *Photograph by Mischa Nawrata*

Rebel walking around Lake Altaussee, Austria, near Mayrlife, 2020. *Photograph by Mischa Nawrata*

Rebel Island's eighties-themed pool party. Anna, Rebel, Liberty and niece Sovereign. *Photograph by Laurie Bailey*

"Billionaire's
Swimming Pool,"
The Brando,
French Polynesia,
2021. *Photograph by
Laurie Bailey*

Rebel Island's
mermaid-themed
party, 2021.
*Photograph by
Laurie Bailey*

Filming *Senior Year* in Atlanta, playing the character Stephanie Conway, a cheerleader who wakes up from a twenty-year coma, 2021.

Ramona and Rebel with baby Royce at the Polo Lounge, Beverly Hills, December 2022.

Rebel and baby Royce at their Hollywood Hills home, 2023.

Rebel and Ramona's
engagement photo
from Disneyland,
February 14, 2023.
*Photograph by
Jenna Henderson*

Even though I've given thousands of speeches in my life, I can't speak at Dad's funeral. Libby, Ryan and Anna speak. I don't want to draw attention to myself. Oddly the funeral is mostly attended by police, who I am guessing knew my father from the PCYC. Dad's brother, crazy uncle Robert, arrives late and swans down the aisle like he's drunk and boarding a flight to Bali. We just ignore him. I just cry like I've never cried before. Goodbye, Dad.

We hold a reception at the Parramatta Eels Leagues Club because that was my dad's favorite rugby team. As I wait in line for the buffet of over-fried spring rolls, party pies and mini sausage rolls, I hear Dad's best man talking. "Warwick used to run drugs for Bob Trimbole," he says. Like he's casually remembering the good old times of running drugs for a notorious drug lord. Huh?? What the hell is this?

I know who Bob Trimbole is because I loved watching the Australian crime series *Underbelly*. The second season of that show was all about him and the drug dealings out at Griffith. I don't ask the best man for details. It's been a massive day and this bombshell is a bit hard to process. Did I mention half the people at this wake were police? But of course, I do ask Mum in a quiet moment.

"Mum, ummmm . . . I don't know how to say this . . . but I overheard the best man say that Dad ran drugs for Bob Trimbole. Ummmmm! Is that even true?"

"Well, I don't know anything about that." My mum's the most innocent, law-abiding person in the world and would never have gone along with something like that, but then she adds, "But we did used to go to his farm a lot out at Griffith."

"Oh my God, Mum! To Bob Trimbole's farm? Did you know that he was a notorious drug dealer?"

"I didn't know anything. When we got there the ladies would go into one room and the men would go into another. I don't know what they spoke about."

I guess this is just another one of my dad's mysteries. Is this why he was fired from the bank when I was very young? Was he laundering money for this crime syndicate? Did he run drugs for Bob Trimbole, and if so, in what capacity? I always thought it was odd that Osco Pet Products, which was an import/export business of cheap pet products, was always getting burglarized. I'll never truly know the real story.

(A few years later the best man came to see me, completely out of the blue, in London when I was performing *Guys and Dolls* in the West End. It was like he wanted to tell me something. But by coincidence, my mum had come to see the show on the same night and she exited the stage door with me. He approached me but then saw my mum and instantly readjusted. He just gave me a hug, said that my dad would've been really proud of me and then made a quick exit.)

After the funeral I immediately flew back to LA as I only had one week before we started production on *Super Fun Night*. Now I was working seventeen hours every single day (which was anything BUT super fun!) trying to make people laugh. I ate a whole block of chocolate in bed most nights before going to sleep. It was just how I was dealing with everything. I had one day off (normally I never got a day off, being the star/writer/producer) and was offered a million dollars to shoot a Best Buy commercial on that day, and I literally had to say no—I needed the day off more than the money. I had so much inflammation from my bad eating habits that my back would ache. My feet would ache. I was now at my heaviest, 253 pounds (115 kilos). (You can see it if you ever watch an episode of the show.) This was really big, even for me. My arms and stomach were massive. If I look at pictures of myself from that time, it's like my whole face is engulfed by fat, and my eyes and features are dwarfed by chubbiness. I was so sad about Dad, and I was only dealing with it by eating. I couldn't let anyone see how sad I was. I had to be a leader. There were hundreds of people working on the show. "Wipe those tears away, Rebsie, you have to be hilarious now." Sudden international fame. Dad's sudden death. I walked past the two-million-dollar painting in the hallway. To me it read like the artist had painted a gorgeous day at the beach and then taken a thick black paintbrush and swirled darkness everywhere.

TWENTY-TWO

Letter to My Father

Letter to my father: June 21, 2013

<u>Weight</u>: 115 kg [254 pounds]

<u>Relationship status</u>: Single. Obviously.

<u>Mental attitude</u>: Total sadness.

To dear Dad,

So I am sitting here, looking over the beautiful Sydney Harbour, about to go to your funeral in a few hours. I never thought I'd be writing this letter, saying goodbye to you for the final time. I'm going to see you before the service and say my final goodbye then but in case it is too emotional and I can't find the right words, I wanted to put some down now and give this letter to you.

So where to start? Well, me, Ryan, Lib & Anna have been talking all week about our fond memories of you. I remember you taking us to the races, teaching me about trifectas and quinellas, reading the form guides. I always liked horses who had just come off a spell, I wanted them to get back in the game and win. I wanted that for you too . . . and after the breakdown of our family unit, which was long and hard and for the most part unnecessarily cruel and spiteful—I wanted you to come back from that. We all hoped you would but feared that letting you back in too much into our lives would hurt us even more.

I hope you had a lot of wins in your life.

I think your four kids are probably your biggest achievements and as you always told me that you were proud of me, I think you should be proud of yourself for that. We're four children, all different and special. I'm smashing it overseas in my career and I'm glad that you got to see that.

I've said a lot that you were never really part of my acting career but on reflection you were and are. There's a cheekiness, a dodginess and entrepreneurial-ness, a darkness, a creative-ness, a bravado-ness that comes from you and your side of the family. These things I use as strengths, to entertain people, to make people think and feel—this is my craft, and it is and has been enriched by your influence and so I thank you greatly for that.

I will continue to make you proud and hope that you are with me as I continue in my success as an actress and as a writer.

Thank you for the great education I had at Tara. When I left there, I really did have the world at my feet and by God I've taken that ball and run with it. You were a smart guy; if your early life had been different, it could've been you with the law degree, you being the one who everyone knows your name. But I'm sure you did the best you could. I'm sure you didn't mean to bring so much pain to Mum and us kids, you didn't mean to lose your temper and do spiteful and hateful things. When I was about 13 and we were up at the Entrance and I wanted a Slurpee and you snapped and told me you were going to choke me, that was devastating. The man that was supposed to love and protect me, telling me that was wrong. And I carried that same hate and anger back toward you many times over. Until the point where I pitied you. We all did really. That's the reason why we started letting you back in. You had no one in your life apart from a demented old woman who you stole from and that was just so sad. We couldn't hate you anymore, because you had nobody. You must've felt it, you must've known that this was caused by your actions. Your repeated and continuous actions over many, many years. I hope your soul learns from this and I hope I meet you again in a wiser, kinder version. It must've been hard having a brother like you did, a mother like you did and the tragic early end of your father. So I want you to know that I forgive you. I release you. I thank you for loving me, for being my father, you will always be a part of me and I will try to use all the gifts you gave me in a positive way. I have learnt the value of family and of having strong friendships. I will nurture these relationships. I will strive to find love, I will no longer be afraid of it, I want more love in my life. I will not think that I am not worthy of love anymore, for I am. Even though I had a father who at times did not show me love, I will move past that for I am a daughter, a sister, an individual who is worthy and loving and kind. I could've shown you more kindness and my only regret is that I didn't move past the hurt and anger more quickly. But I leave you knowing that you knew of my successes and for that I am happy. I want you to know that I will provide for the family too. I will be very blessed, I can sense it, and I will pass on what comes to me to all of the family. You did provide very well for me when I was a kid—going to Tara, being able to board, the tennis lessons, the family holidays.

Just now I'm remembering when I was about 12, at Kenthurst, asking you to judge a dance concert between me and Libby. I remember you holding me in the waves at Blue Bay. Having massive sale days at the Easter Show. Sitting in the back of the Mobil gas station eating lollies. Fireworks nights. There's thousands of these little memories—fun times, times where you were a great father to me. Times when I looked up to you and you were there. Please be with all of us and watch down on all of us if you can.

Your book is closed, your race is run. Goodbye, Dad. May

my heart be open as yours clogged and withered. May I take
from you the good and learn from your mistakes. I love you
and I will truly miss you. My eyes sob now as I end this letter.
There's more to write, a lot more, but the time is ending and I
have to move forward. Again, I love you, thank you,

Your daughter,
Rebel xoxo[*]

I'm glad I put this letter in his pocket. I'm glad it was cremated
with him. We spread Dad's ashes at several places that were important
to him—on the King's School oval, at the finish line at Rosehill Racecourse and then up at Blue Bay. When we were on the beach, right
as we were spreading his ashes, we saw dolphins appear in the waves.
In the hundreds of times I had been on that beach, I had never seen
dolphins. Only this time.

After Dad's death, my family became more open and emotionally
honest with one another. Dad's death made us all realize that life is
short. That you can be here one moment and gone the next. Eventually
this tragedy opened us all up. My brother eventually quit poker and
went back to university. He's brilliantly smart and is now headed into
teaching. Liberty eventually left her unhappy marriage and proves every
day to her daughter, Sovereign, how strong she is. My mum eventually
found a loving and kind partner, Pete, who's become a great father figure to Anna. Mum lives her life freely, she has thousands of friends and
travels all around the world as an international dog show judge. Almost
every family phone call between us now ends with "Love you, byeeeeee!"

---

[*] I then drew a simplistic drawing of a horse and wrote, "Gallop off into the
unknown—there's more races for you to win." And then at the very end of
the page, after drawing a star, a flower and a heart, I wrote, "Always look on the
bright side of life." This is from the Monty Python song from 1979 that we
played at Dad's funeral as everyone was walking out of the service.

Sacha Baron Cohen and Other Assholes

Okay, so here's the deal: I rue the day that I met Sacha Baron Cohen. "Never meet your idols," people say. No shit!

I first met the towering presence of SBC through Matt Lucas. They'd been in the same high school class back in the day in London and were still good friends. It was an all-boys school that apparently has a lot of graduates who are now quite high-profile in comedy. I can only imagine the banter that went on at that school playground . . . it was probably a comedy show in itself. Wit can be a great weapon.

Just like how I adored Matt as a comedian and watched the *Little Britain* series religiously, I had loved every episode of *Da Ali G Show*. I was also a huge fan of the *Borat* movie, so much so that even though I was technically a star in Australian comedy, I lined up to attend the *Bruno* premiere in Melbourne and sat in the cinema excitedly just for a glimpse of SBC. He came in before the film to say a few words and there I was, in the twenty-eighth row, quickly licking my fingers of Maltesers chocolate residue, keenly trying to take a cool photo of him, zooming in, trying to cut off the heads of the people in front of me so that it could look like I was closer to my idol. There he was—the hilarious, outrageous SBC.

"I'll never be as funny as him," I thought. "He's a genius."

Matt is a very sociable guy and would often have exciting peo-ple over for dinner and a good chat. One night Russell Brand came over and regaled us with stories of his "interesting" life. The next night it was Boy George, or Tom Felton, who played Draco in *Harry Pot-ter*. Fascinating! And then one night, Matt's like, "I'm going to have a few people around for dinner—Sacha's coming—if you want to join." "Oh my God, Sacha Baron Cohen's coming to the house for dinner!! Geeeez!!!" Often, I was exhausted from working almost every waking hour of the day, but of course I'd make time for a dinner party with SBC. I'd never properly spoken to him—this was a once-in-a-lifetime opportunity.

We were in Matt's expertly renovated kitchen/dining space—and sitting around the table were Matt, SBC, me, Sarah Silverman and someone else—it could've been Jerry Seinfeld, but he left early. Suf-fice it to say, it was a table of comedy heavyweights. I couldn't believe I was having dinner with this group. And I mean, of course the chat was hilarious—and serious and dark—and a tad competitive when it came to talking about our projects. Somehow there's always a slight whiff of competition when a bunch of performers are around each other.

Later that week, I was about to host the 2013 MTV Movie Awards. I'd already shot a fun promo with my celebrity crush Channing Tatum where he'd touched my boobs, so I already felt like a winner. We filmed a little sketch where we were driving at high speed, being chased, and he was looking for his gun and I said innocently, "I think it's down my top," and then he reached in. Channing dug under the bra—I felt his hunky hands on my velvety-soft boobies—and did I really enjoy it? Hell yeah. It was the most action I'd ever had, and it was from Chan-ning "Magic Mike" Tatum. (I still have a photo of that day in my office! #memories)

SBC had hosted the MTV Movie Awards before, so he was keen to give me advice. So, gingerly, I stood up at one end of the table and told the group jokes from my opening monologue. Then: silence. Comedians are the worst audience because they don't usually laugh at jokes. They are often analyzing.

My heart was racing. Joke after joke for my opening monologue was falling flat, and I was really trying to impress them. After about twenty jokes, I gave up and didn't read the rest. SBC looked at me with a solemn face, the kind of face that's about to tell you something terrible, like your arm must be amputated. He said, "You're in trouble."

The others tried to gently reassure me that I still had time, but SBC made me feel like my career was about to be over. Fuck. These comedy geniuses thought I was shit. I wanted to cry. Instead, I messaged Tabatha saying I needed help, and we enlisted five or six stand-up comedians (one of whom was Ali Wong) to urgently write me some more jokes in the few days before the show. I started to really panic. Should I have not accepted this hosting job? SBC had really thrown off my confidence.

I went to Upright Citizens Brigade, a comedy theater in Los Angeles, with my stack of joke palm cards and essentially did the same material I'd tested in Matt's kitchen—along with some of the newer jokes. Surprisingly, the cool kids who came to UCB to see comedy really loved the jokes. "Huh?" I thought. Why did SBC put the fear of God into me? Was I really awful? I just powered through on adrenaline over the next few days, absolutely full of nerves. I made sure to eat only a small vegan, gluten-free meal before going onstage that night—out of literal fear that I might shit myself—but by all accounts, I did CRUSH the MTV Movie Awards. The opening musical number, which had a lot of moving parts, went great, the jokes landed and I won an award for Best Breakthrough Performance as Fat Amy in *Pitch*. My publicist Dan and I high-fived afterward. For a live awards show that involved prerecorded segments, live musical numbers and various "bits" including audience interactions, everything went pretty much according to plan.

While 99 percent of the people I've worked with are professional and lovely, you do get the assholes from time to time. And yes, normally they are men. Sadly, I did have a cliché "hotel room incident" with a top Australian male comedy director. I never thought something like that would happen to a girl like me. I wasn't exactly sexually desirable—I deliberately made myself not so—and this guy was very old. I believed him when he said, "Come back to my hotel room and we can talk more about comedy." He was a nice guy, married. I felt safe when I agreed to go to his hotel.

His wife called on his cell phone and he tried to dismiss her while attempting to ply me with more wine—I'd only taken a minor sip as I don't drink because I drive myself everywhere. Then his wife called the hotel room. The director sensed it was her and didn't pick up the phone. But it was one of those old-school phones where you could hear someone leave a message through the speaker on the console. I sat on the couch and heard the wife's message: "I know what you're doing! You're fucking Rebel Wilson, you piece of shit!" That was the first time that I considered anything other than comedy talk was going to happen in this room. What the hell? This guy was trying to sleep with me? He was soooooooo old! (And also no one ever wanted to sleep with me! So it was a double shock.) I promptly grabbed my hand-bag and headed straight out the door. We then never talked about it at work or addressed the incident. He was embarrassed . . . I think? I was embarrassed. That guy did have an incredible reputation in Australia, so I just brushed it off as maybe a misunderstanding, completed the show with him and never spoke of it.

I also brushed off an incident with a prominent director of pho-tography. I asked him, "Where's my mark?" (a common on-set actor question—a mark is usually a piece of tape placed on the ground so you know where to stand for camera focus). He pulled off two pieces of tape from a roll, made an X-shape and then placed it on my skirt over my vagina. "There's your mark!" he said. (This was so brazen, it was kind of funny . . . the guy would always say that he was married to an actress, so somehow it was acceptable for him to flirt with all the girls on set.)

In movie studio meetings, I've heard male executives talking about women in demeaning ways. "She's hot, I'd wanna bang her." I wanted to be in the room where important decisions were happening . . . because at the end of the day I wanted my film projects to be green-lit. Since these men certainly weren't ever looking at me as a sexual object, it's almost as if they saw me as a buddy and not as a woman. It's not that these men were particularly vile, it's just that this behavior is seen as acceptable and so they do it openly.

I've been at industry parties where it was very clear that powerful men had called in prostitutes during the festivities. That was usually my cue to leave. I'd see, out of the corner of my eye, a Mercedes Sprinter van full of women pulling up: Russian accents, short skirts, designer bags. I'd say to my friend casually, "Ahhh, you know what, it's getting late, you wanna go?" No one wants to talk to me when eight sets of legs topped with tits enter the room. The dogs salivate like it's one of Mum's arranged matings.

Okay, but forget those small freshly bleached assholes. Back to the biggest one: Sacha Baron Cohen. About a year after that MTV Movie Awards debacle, I get a call from him out of the blue. I answer, kind of giddy with excitement but trying to keep cool. It's not every day one of the top guys in comedy is personally calling you. I felt like a cardigan-wearing teenage girl talking to Elvis. "Oh, hiiii . . . yeah . . . I'm good. How are you?" Why is he calling me? Why am I so special?

And then he says it—he's DESPERATE for me to be in his new film, called *The Brothers Grimsby*. He says it's going to be the most hilarious film ever made, "a comedy classic," he keeps saying. He's going to make me shine and guarantees I'll just be so, so funny in the film. I'd play his wife. Would I do it?

"Yeah, sure, Sacha. I'll do it." I feel like Elvis has just shared his giant peanut butter sandwich with me. I'm so excited to work with him.

I'd had the great opportunity of working with some other high-profile men in American comedy—for example, Ben Stiller on *Night at the Museum: Secret of the Tomb*. He was such a total gentleman and allowed me to improvise whatever lines I wanted. Will Ferrell produced *Bachelorette*, and again, he could NOT have been lovelier. Seth Rogen had invited me to a few of his parties and had been very generous sharing his joints (which I didn't smoke, but I was flattered he offered). Jason Segel agreed to sit down with me for lunch at Chateau Marmont when I was fresh off the plane from Australia and gave me advice about the business. Just lovely. I remember doing a kind of gala comedy night with people like Bob Saget and Garry Shandling, and these guys just couldn't have been nicer or more fun to work with.

My most memorable chat with a male comedy great was with the incomparable Robin Williams (although meeting Mel Brooks in London is a close second!). We were on the set of *Night at the Museum* and it was the middle of the night in cold, wintry London. Robin was watching a scene I was filming with Ben and asked if he could chat with me during the break. I was of course down . . . I mean, hello! It's THE LEGEND Robin Williams.

We sat during the "turnaround time" (the time it takes for the camera department to turn the cameras around, which is often thirty minutes) talking about comedy and life in general, both of us wrapped up in blankets. He had the kindest face and the warmest energy on the coldest of nights. He told me that he saw something in my acting that made him think that I'd be excellent at drama as well as comedy. Wow, what a compliment coming from him. I hugged him. I was honored to learn after his passing that he had also told his daughter, Zelda, about the exchange. To get that kind of recognition and encouragement from someone as iconic as Robin was absolutely inspiring. When people who are more senior in the industry take the time to advise and help other performers, without any agenda, it's amazing. Bette Midler had also given me great advice when I'd been to see her on Broadway and I absolutely adore her too. (She'd had a similar experience to mine with network TV and told me not to feel down about it.) I got the same energy from her as I did from Robin, and I left feeling so inspired and enthused. (Okay, but enough name-dropping for the moment, Rebel!)

We had a table read at Paramount for *The Brothers Grimsby*, and—I don't know how SBC managed to do this, he's a very persuasive guy—Brad Pitt (sorry, one more name-drop, I can't help myself) was there sitting RIGHT next to me. Yes, literally, I could have licked his ear if I wanted to—I was that close.

Brad tells me that he's seen *Pitch Perfect* like thirty times because his kids are big fans. I melt with delight, and now that he's facing me, I want to lick his face. He's so amazingly gorgeous. And he's looking into my eyes and smiling. Wow.

SBC is quite an imposing person—he's very tall, I think six foot three, with wiry black hair and dark, almost black eyes. I noticed he always stacked things in his favor. Like at that table read, where movie studio executives were invited, all the other people there were either friends or employees who were instructed to laugh at absolutely everything he said. It was to make him look good and the project look successful. It wasn't a surprise when *The Brothers Grimsby* got the green light and went into production.

Sadly, Brad Pitt didn't end up being in the film (noooooooooooo!!!!), but there was a cast of other stellar stars—like Penélope Cruz, Gabourey Sidibe, Mark Strong and some fantastic British comedic talents. And the director was an incredibly talented man, Louis Leterrier, who had done the magic movie *Now You See Me*, which I really liked. I was excited to get started. We were filming in Cape Town, South Africa!! This was my first time back since I'd been there as an eighteen-year-old youth ambassador. Now I was thirty-four.

SBC had been hounding me to make sure my Northern English accent was perfect and authentic for the film. I spent all of my off-set time watching TV programs with the correct regional accent and trying to perfect it. He'd become almost obsessed with it. Earlier in the year he'd sent me on a research mission to the North of England to hang out with real people and record their voices, so that I could mimic the accent. I socialized with families and went to the pub with them and to their homes and recorded the whole thing for accent research. I didn't mind doing it as an acting exercise, but it wasn't like this was a Martin Scorsese film . . . though the way SBC was behaving, it was as if it was. (Oddly he didn't seem to put much effort into his own accent, which I personally found patchy.)

I guess the first disappointment came on my first day playing husband and wife with SBC. I improvised a joke that got a good laugh from the crew. And you know it's a good joke when even the burly boom operator has a chuckle. Then, in the next take of the scene, SBC took the joke and said it as his character. I was internally like, "Whaaaaaat!" I remember being so shocked, because that had never happened to me before. Then I began to notice that SBC never seemed that quick himself. He always seemed to be relying on his writer buddies to feed him jokes. On the days I was on set, I never saw him improvise anything himself that was "comedy genius."

Then more weirdness. It felt like every time I'd speak to SBC, he'd mention that he wanted me to go naked in a future scene. I'd have to run in the nude across a soccer field in a hooligan crowd scene. I was like, "Ha, I don't do nudity, Sacha. You know that." I was constantly saying no to him, and he didn't like it. Everybody around him was a yes-man. It felt like every day I had contact with him, he'd keep pushing the subject. For the record, it was in NO WAY essential to the plot that my character run naked onto a soccer field. It seemed to me he could see that the notion of this made me uncomfortable, but HE kept pushing for me to do this. Maybe he thought it would legitimately make the film funnier? It was hard to understand his motivations, but, either way, it made me feel uncomfortable.

One day I got ready to film a scene and walked over to set. SBC instantly said that he didn't like my outfit and made me change. From how I perceived it, he wanted me to wear a sleeveless top that showed the chunkiest part of my arms and a much shorter skirt where you could see as much cellulite as possible. I know making yourself unattractive is a device in comedy, but this felt personal—like he just wanted me to look and feel awful. This felt like he and his mates on set wanted to laugh at me, not with me. Fat Amy was different. I was in control of that character. But now everything felt off. It felt to me like a bunch of men were degrading me, making me show off the excessive fat behind my knees, the girth of my belly, my thick upper arms and thighs, because, in my opinion, they thought it was funny to laugh at the fat girl. SBC seemed to get off on the fact that here I was, a powerfully rising female comedy star, and he was yelling off camera, "Do a Sharon Stone and show your vagina," as I'm sitting on the couch. Was all this because I said I wouldn't go naked? He'd said that we should go out on a boat one weekend and take fake paparazzi pictures of us making out because it would bring publicity to the film. I had laughed that off because I knew his wife, Isla Fisher, and really didn't want to be involved in anything like that.

SBC continued giving me gross directions in the scene, all of which I thought were either derogatory to women or to my size. I was just thinking maybe it'd be quicker to do it and not argue. The scene would happen much faster if I just did what he said. I was aware of other incidents in R-rated comedies where men were in control creatively and female co-stars were essentially "booed" in front of the crew if they didn't go along with a tirade of insulting jokes that were thrown their way in a scene, even jokes about rape. I didn't want to be labeled a troublemaker or someone who couldn't "hang with the boys." SBC would laugh when I did the things he asked (although I drew the line at showing my vagina on camera obviously)—and I thought, "Well, maybe he's seeing something I'm not and maybe this is the right way to go comedically?" He made me doubt myself.

When I finished work for the day, I couldn't help feeling like I was being humiliated. "What am I doing here? This isn't me. I'm all about girl power. But SBC is a comedy genius, right?! I just have to go with it," I thought.

The next week we were filming a scene at a soccer stadium in Cape Town and I was sitting in my trailer, waiting to go to set. SBC summoned me via a production assistant saying that I was needed to film an additional scene. What followed was the worst experience of my professional life. An incident that left me feeling bullied, humiliated, and compromised. It can't be printed here due to peculiarities of the law in England and Wales. ██████████████████████

██
██
██
██
██
██
█████████████████████████████████
██
██
██
██
████████████
██
██
██
██
██
██
██
██
██
████████████
███
██
██
██████████████
███
██

██

██

███████████████████████████ As soon as I could, I got out of the room and back to the relative sanctuary of my trailer.

I called Tabatha at WME right away. It was super awkward because at the time she also represented SBC. "Look, you know, some weird shit's been happening with SBC, but just now this really weird thing happened. ███ " She was genuinely sympathetic, but I was also acutely aware that SBC had probably earned the agency way more money to date than I had. It's a tricky situation. It's like you're complaining to somebody at HR, but you know the person you're complaining about is also their superstar. It felt like a conflict of interest. What should have happened is that I should have been put on a flight back to Los Angeles—quit the movie. But I was encouraged to "be professional and finish the film." I said, "Well I wasn't physically attacked, so, you know, maybe I should just stay and finish." Tabatha: "Yesss, actually, maybe you're right. You should just do that. But if anything else like that happens again, then you can go."

My team complained to the movie studio. I was told that I may not have been the only one to have had issue with his behavior. Did he also "love-bomb" others to convince them to be in his films, only to then humiliate them on set?

Are the jokes in *Borat* directed toward women really just his deep-seated misogyny packaged with a comedy bow? (He carefully tried to disarm this image by creating and publicly promoting a great female role in the second *Borat* film after having a clear pattern in all his other work of demeaning female characters. I don't think it's a coincidence that he championed Maria Bakalova so heavily . . . it is my opinion that this was a deliberate strategy to wave a flag saying, "Look how nice I am to females!")

For the hooligan crowd scene in the soccer stadium, he hired a local stripper to be my body double and run naked across the pitch. He made me watch her do it. He was sitting at the monitors watching her boobs and big stomach flopping about as she ran. "Oh, look how good she is. See, Rebel, she's doing it!" By this point I'd become numb to him, to his comments. I stopped reacting. I noticed he had now moved on, trying to get the director, Louis, to show his penis in a scene—so at least other people were now the target of his antics.

I left South Africa a few days later, feeling more than uneasy about the whole thing. While I reported the incident to my agent and had now engaged a lawyer, this was before the #MeToo movement, so I didn't have the strength or know-how to do anything more. SBC was no longer my comedy idol. In my opinion, he was a gross asshole . . . and really had something against women, particularly overweight women. It's like the fourth-grade bully who teases the fat girl on the playground and tries to make her life a living hell.

I later did a radio interview with Kyle and Jackie O (the most popular radio show in Australia) and I made light of the incident ██████ ████████████████████████████. I'm not sure why I did that? I knew how everybody in Australia loved SBC and his outrageous comedy. My way of dealing with it at that point was to try to laugh it off. I often use negative experiences in my life as fodder for jokes.

I was trying to forget about the whole thing, I really was. I was trying to develop more projects for myself, movies that were female driven with empowering messages. Then I got an email saying that SBC wanted me to fly to London for "reshoots." I opened the script attachment and was horrified to see these reshoots were for a graphic sex scene between us for the beginning of the film.

I called my agent immediately. What am I supposed to do about this? Well, I could fly to London, she suggested, and have a face-to-face meeting to tell him what I would and wouldn't be comfortable doing in the scene. That was about as exciting as the prospect of being served a bag of dicks for dinner. But what was my only other option? I could walk away from my role in the film and be labeled "UNPRO-FESSIONAL." (Fun fact: Penélope Cruz refused to do any reshoots, but she was clearly a bigger star than me and I'm not sure of her reasons why. It could've been the classic excuse of "scheduling conflicts.")

In anticipation of this grotty predicament, I asked my lawyer to draw up a letter to be sent to SBC and the writers about the scene itself, stipulating that under no circumstances would I be naked or involved in grotesque stuff with sex toys. I mean . . . NO. At what point does self-deprecating humor become exploitation? I've never, ever done nudity. (Even though it was tempting when Miley Cyrus once asked me to do a nude photo shoot with her when I first got famous . . . THAT I considered for a hot second because I am such a huge Miley fan.)

I flew to London, assured by my agent that all the producers would be at the meeting with SBC, including the one female (who surely would be on my side and sympathetic? Like, surely?!?). Maybe SBC would understand where I was coming from and that some of his actions were not cool toward women? That's what I hoped.

I called the meeting in a conference room at the Corinthia Hotel and sat on one side of the large worktable that took up most of the room. All the other attendees sat on the opposite side. Against me. It was SBC, his writers, and the director, Louis, who didn't know what had occurred at the soccer stadium at that time, nor did he know about my complaint at that point. There was no female producer present. The guys looked annoyed that I'd caused them to take time out of their busy day to deal with this nuisance. I'd flown halfway across the world to help the film, but the attitude I felt from them was: Rebel Wilson is causing an issue. I'm the problem. Why won't I just film the graphic sex scene as written, where because I'm so overweight the bed falls through the floor? Why am I being so annoying?

I was sitting directly opposite SBC and he was staring at me with his black-hole eyes, intimidating me, letting me know that he was personally funding these reshoots and that I should be grateful. Eventually, just like in the unfinished room at the soccer stadium, I agreed to shoot something so I could get the hell out of this awkward room.

Louis and one of the writers were the only sympathetic ears, but it was clear SBC was running this show.

The next day I filmed the scene, after demanding the rewrites complied with my letter, stipulating things like "no dildos" can be used. But I still had to simulate having sex with this guy. I still had to kiss him repeatedly.

A few months later, it really sank in that all this wasn't something that could be laughed off; it felt like SBC had sexually harassed me on the set of *Grimsby*. So, for the first time in my career, I relayed to the producers via Tabatha that I would not be doing any promotion for the film. That was really the only power I had left in this situation. To be honest, I wish that WME had parted ways with SBC when they heard of my experiences with him. At the time, it felt like a conflict of interest for them to be representing us both. However, I'm sure being a high-powered woman in Hollywood herself, Tabatha had dealt with many unfair things in her career too, which I came to realize was probably why she often behaved the way she did in situations. Perhaps this is why she often behaved like a shark? Perhaps this is why she had to. She had to cope in an industry that for decades was male dominated and often wasn't kind to smart women who spoke their mind. Sometime later I was happy to hear that WME and SBC had gone separate ways. I don't know why it happened—it could have been SBC's choice—and I don't blame them for keeping him on after my complaint. That was commonplace before #MeToo, which hadn't happened yet, so I don't feel like anyone should be held accountable for that.

A few days later I got an unexpected phone call from someone I'm just going to refer to as "The Weasel," who was very unhappy I wasn't going to publicly support the film. "You know there's only really five big movie studios in Hollywood, and we can ruin your reputation with all of them," he said. My heart was pumping like I was about to be physically attacked. What? Was SBC also on the call? Was he directing this guy to say this? I didn't know. "The Weasel" was talking in such a dark, ominous tone. I felt threatened. I felt scared. My career was everything to me and now it felt like these assholes were trying to take it away because I wasn't doing what they wanted.

In my mind, this alleged threat was probably worse than the incident in South Africa itself. I sat in my home office, looking over at the Hollywood sign, feeling petrified. Again, I reported it to my lawyer.

I didn't promote *Grimsby*. I couldn't. I never went to the premiere. The movie bombed, which to me was karma enough. I'm not about canceling anybody and that's not my motivation for sharing this story. My goal is to tell you, dear reader, about an experience that was HARD. That made me feel like rubbish. It made me feel completely disrespected, which led to me treating myself with even more disrespect by eating in an extremely unhealthy way. When the #MeToo movement came around in 2017, I shared a small Twitter-size version of my story but didn't mention SBC by name. I was worried. At the time he had far more financial resources than me. I'm sharing my story now because the more women talk about things like this, hopefully the less it happens. And hopefully fewer women have to work harder just to respect themselves.

Who knows what those assholes said about me in high-level meetings with the studios? Did they try to ruin my reputation? I don't know. I'm bloody glad I never ███████████████████, though. But every time I drive past his house in LA, I do wind down the window of my G-wagon and stick my middle finger right up at him.

TWENTY-FOUR

Letter to Myself, 2015

October 2015: At the top of a sheet of Biggest Loser Resort letterhead, it says: "I can. I will. I did. I do."

(This was an exercise they gave all the participants at BLR—to write a letter to themselves encouraging their new healthy lifestyle that would be mailed to them a month later.)

> Keep up the good work, the exercise and the healthy eating. Fuel your body with goodness and love. You deserve health. You will be healthy, wealthy and wise.
>
> I'm proud of you for all you have achieved. But as you move forward on this wonderful roller coaster of a life, I want you to be free of pain and burden. And the way to do this is to keep healthy, to keep my body and mind right, respect it, so that it can work and continue to do even more amazing things.
>
> I love you. Keep going, you legend!
> *Rx*

It's weird to read this letter from back in 2015, around the time when I was my absolute heaviest. I'd gone to a health retreat in Palm Desert called the Biggest Loser Resort. It was kind of like the TV show. You'd do eight hours of exercise a day, eat healthily and be encouraged and supported by great staff. I'd chat with the other folks there. Great people. Pretty much all of them were like me . . . apart from one skinny lady whose face was shaped like a bird's and who seemed to be an excessive exerciser (I always think it's weird when people say they're fat and are NOT AT ALL FAT). But the rest of us were big. Jolly. Fun. One guy was about to play the Genie on Broadway in *Aladdin*. There was a real camaraderie as we were all trying to better our lives and get healthier. We supported each other as we did three-minute wall squats under the blazing sun, push-ups and planks and then a mile run . . . and that was just hour one. We all had the best of intentions and thought this extreme amount of exercise would shock us into being healthy. We all got good results at the end-of-the-week weigh-in (I'd typically lose six to eight pounds in a week). And then most of us would return home to the "real world" and end up coming back again. What was making us do this to ourselves? Why did I seem to have so much willpower, so much desire to get healthier, and then, like a dementia patient, forget it all the next day?

At one point I brought family members with me. It seemed like every female member of my family was struggling with her weight. We were all the same. Mother and daughters. A motivational letter like this wasn't enough to save me. I'd have one stressful day at work and then go right back to eating a pint of Ben & Jerry's ice cream after dinner. I'd go right back to treating my body like shit. Feeling like shit. I could never sustain a weight-loss regimen. I'd think: "Rebel, you can achieve other things, but you can never achieve permanently losing weight. Accept it. You're just going to be this fatty forever."

There's a huge contradiction when you say, "I'm just going to love myself and accept myself the way I am," but then you know, deep down, that you're engaging in very destructive behaviors. Because are you supposed to love that? Isn't that like loving and accepting a domestic abuser? That IS hurting you.

But then beating yourself up doesn't help either. You do have to love and be kind to yourself, but I think you can still do that whilst trying to be a healthier version of yourself—not some perfect version, not a skinny version, just a healthier one. I think that's why I liked the people I met at BLR so much. Most of them were like that.

But back then, I wasn't as evolved as I am now. I was beating myself up—"Why can't I stick to a weight-loss regimen? Why can't I exercise super hard every day? Why am I eating junk after paying to do a program to lose weight? This is a failure, Rebel. You're a failure!" The voice was coming at me like a director yelling "CUT!" loudly on a megaphone. I hated that critical voice. It was driving me nuts. So I freaked out and said, "Well, screw it. Screw weight-loss programs. I'm never going to WIN! I can't really love myself like this, so I'm going to find someone to love me. Their love is going to radiate onto me and then I'll love myself more and quiet that critical voice. And if I love myself more, then I won't wanna eat shit as much, and then I will get healthier. Love is the answer. Surely if the blind six-hundred-pound balding woman on that reality show can find a husband, so can I."

My new boyfriend would fix everything. Because if someone else loved me, then I would therefore be lovable, wouldn't I?

Forget the battle of the bulge, Rebs, and grab some guy's bulge. Let's get a boyfriend, babe.

TWENTY-FIVE

Late Bloomer

This is going to be a heaps-embarrassing headline. "Rebel declares: 'I didn't lose my virginity until I was thirty-five years old.'"

Ugh. Okay, there, I've said it. At least now it's out there. And please believe me when I say that absolutely nobody, until now, knows this about me. It's like this shameful little secret I've kept. A friend told me recently how she lost her virginity at twenty-three, and how much of a loser she thought she was, waiting so long. Wellll, great! Imagine how I'm going to look now that everyone knows I was cherry-popped at the ripe old age of thirty-five.

Yes, I know. That's late. I'm a LATE BLOOMER. Is there something very wrong with me? And did I watch *The 40-Year-Old Virgin*? Yes, I watched that movie extremely carefully and thought, "Well, as long as I can do it before forty, then at least I'll be cooler than Steve Carell." Although in real life Steve probably lost his virginity like most humans say they did, as a teen.

On the plus side of being a good Christian girl: I'd never had a sexually transmitted disease. I'd never had an unwanted pregnancy. And if guys really were into girls who have a low number of sexual partners, then I was as clean as they come. On the negative: I had zero sexual experience. If I did find a boyfriend, what was I going to say when I clearly didn't know how to have sex? Was I going to tell them that they were my first? Were they then going to sell the story to TMZ or something? I'd kissed people, yes. But not one blowie or any other sort of sexual or naked experience with another person until my mid-thirties.

There were times when I thought maybe it was never going to happen. Maybe I'd live my whole life as a virgin like Queen Elizabeth I. I knew I wasn't asexual, as I'd wanted to have sex, but I was either so innocent, in my teens, or so busy making myself look grotesquely unattractive for comedic purposes, in my twenties and thirties, that no romantic opportunity ever presented itself. Seriously, if I'd been a participant on *Married at First Sight: Australia*, I'd have been the virgin girl who's never had love but instead had a good career. I would've hoped then that "the experts" would pair me with a guy who was very sexually confident. Because that's what a girl like me needed. When it came to physical intimacy, I was terrified. I'd kissed more people on-screen than I'd ever kissed in real life. And seeing as I'd waited this long, I wanted to really love the person I was going to sleep with. So, I wasn't going to let some random at a bar pick me up. I'm too heavy to pick up anyway!

At odds with my deep, dark secret was that I often played characters who were very sexually confident. Fat Amy is über-confident and has had "so many boyfriends," she has to swat them away. I always liked improvising jokes like this because if people had known the truth, they'd have known that my personal life was the opposite. My vagina was as dry as a burnt piece of toast. (Sorry, reader, didn't mean to spring that image on you!)

And now it's May 2015 and I've just started work on the comedy film *How to Be Single* opposite Dakota Johnson and Leslie Mann. I play Robin, a single girl living in New York City who ironically must show the stunningly gorgeous Dakota how to slut it up all over town. I've got my tits half hanging out, and according to some of my character's lines, my vag is as well, because I'm just sooooo sexual.

Now that I was doing well in Hollywood, I did start to get some limited attention from men despite my weight. The fatness invisibility cloak that I wore for many years would occasionally be dissolved by my new "look at me" fame caftan.

And I feel like these potential suitors were confused when they met me in real life, because after a one-on-one interaction, they quickly understood that I was quite shy and reserved. I wasn't as sexually confident as Fat Amy and Robin. I could be mega confident in my skills and abilities at work—but in the bedroom, ummmmm, I had nothing. No game. I went out on a date to the Polo Lounge in Beverly Hills with a guy whom I quite fancied. He was an attractive Hollywood producer. I really liked him, but I had no idea how to initiate physical contact and he was a bit shy in that area as well. So, we just chatted for hours at the restaurant, and the only orgasm we had was enjoying the incredible chocolate soufflé. "Oh yeah!" I said as I swirled my tongue around a spoonful. Other girls would've known how to "jump him"—to me, just giving him a hug at the end of the date was such a big deal that it was awkward.

It was like I couldn't get over myself—I couldn't initiate sexual contact with someone because I was too naïve or too scared. When the cameras were rolling, it was fun to play a sexually confident woman, but when it was just me, in real life, I was . . . almost frozen. I really wanted to have sex. It's a huge part of being an adult, but it's just like opening that giant flat pack from IKEA: I didn't even know where to begin. Where's the Allen wrench to open my sexuality?

So only now, armed with the personal confidence of being a successful movie star, did I think I could tackle finding a boyfriend and actually having a sexual encounter. (Maybe it's just because of decades of receiving the message from society that big women aren't as hot, aren't as sexually desirable, that I never mustered up this confidence before. I didn't rate myself at all regarding attractiveness, but now that I was successful, could I score?) I was now softly "putting it out there." I was at least trying to attract someone. I'd get my nails done and blow out my hair regularly. I experimented with hair-removal cream in the bathroom . . . to remove the overgrown bush. Ouch.

Yet any intimate interaction—and by this I basically mean one-on-one time with a guy when it was just us—felt like I was about to bungee-jump backward off the Sydney Harbour Bridge. Like my newly bald beav, I felt so exposed. Was this guy going to ridicule me? Because let's face it—I now only vaguely recalled our one class in the ninth grade where Miss Dykstra asked us to put a condom on a banana.

I got thrown a last-minute invite to a tech billionaire's party—the guy who invited me, who's like fifteenth or twentieth in line to the British throne, had said to my male friend, "We need more girls." What a perfect opportunity to find a boyfriend, I thought.

The tech billionaire had rented a huge ranch just outside of LA. It had a medieval theme and guests had to come dressed up, so I rented a buxom damsel outfit complete with cone hat. It was a vibe. I was the image of a virginal yet fun gal with childbearing hips and enough fat to last me through any winter famine.

The party was insane. Men were jousting on horses in a field, girls dressed as mermaids were in the pool (not exactly medieval, buuuuut . . .), Cirque du Soleil types mingled with the crowd and performed little routines. The property was massive, and because it was quite a drive, people had been assigned rooms to sleep there overnight.

I walk up to the tech billionaire, swatting the veil flowing from the top of my cone hat that keeps annoyingly getting stuck on my lip gloss. "Hi, thank you so much for inviting me!" (PS: I love how I'm a complete virgin and yet I still shoot my shot with a tech billionaire.) He doesn't even look me in the eyes. I mean, why would he when there are hot mermaids in the pool? I shuffle back toward the crowd, re-flicking my veil, as if the whole interaction never happened. It's all very Bridget Jones.

I watch the British royal flounder around whilst I continuously hike up my boobs. They are my best physical asset, I think (well, along with my soft lips and long eyelashes and classic English-rose skin tone). I talk to a cute British guy who is a wannabe screenwriter. There's a huge private fireworks display and then all of a sudden, it's two a.m.

and a guy comes out with a large tray piled with what looks like a ton of candy. I'm like, "Ooooh, is that candy?" and the guy holding the tray says, "No, this is the molly," and I turn to the screenwriter I've been talking with, confused. He says, "Oh, it's for the orgy . . . it's about to start . . . the orgies normally start at these things about this time."

"Whaaaaaaaaaaaatttttt!" I scream silently to myself. "Orgy!!!" You could've stabbed me with my conical hat, and I was in such shock I wouldn't have noticed. Now the comment by the Windsor about needing more girls started to make a lot more sense. They weren't talking about a boy-girl ratio like it was a year-eight disco. They were talking about an ORGY!

So I'm like two minutes away from being in an orgy . . . for my first sexual experience!!! I look around for help. I can't find the male friend who scored me the invite. I don't wanna run to my designated room—because maybe that's where the orgy happens? I don't know. Maybe it happens around this giant outdoor firepit surrounded by large rectangular cushions that's in front of me. I also get this weird feeling that maybe all this is being filmed by hidden cameras—but that's just a gut instinct. Needless to say, I hike up my damsel dress and run out of there as fast as I can—not looking back for fear I'll witness some insane centipede of tech guys and Hollywood wispies around the fire pit.

Some of my friends have subsequently told me that I should've just tried the orgy. But that would've been like going from zero to a thousand. Around this time, in 2014, I was also offered $2 million to spend a weekend with some Jordanian prince. As part of the deal, you were allowed to bring your own security, as if your own security was going to have any power in their Middle Eastern country! I asked around the industry about this kind of offer; people implied that if you went—and some big female stars did apparently do things like this—the expectation was that you would at some point sleep with the prince. I was actually flattered by the offer but turned it down. Again, my first sexual experience wasn't going to be a "pay for play," although that would've been an interesting story. Some of those princes are quite ripped actually!

Okay, so how did I lose my virginity, you're probably asking. I'm close (pun intended).

You know that Justin Bieber song "Lonely," where you're back in a hotel room after a big night and you've got nobody to call and "that's just fucking lonely"? Despite the occasionally colorful Hollywood party, my life was very much like that. Lonely. On my thirty-fifth birthday, I get an early morning phone call from my mother. I think she's obviously calling to wish me a happy birthday. Instead, I instantly sense that she's crying.

"Mum? What's wrong?"

"I have breast cancer," she says through the tears.

Breast cancer!? Oh no. I mean, the moment you hear that, you instantly think the worst. Not cancer. My father's dead and now—no—this can't be happening to my mum. I jump on a flight later that day to be with her and help her through her surgeries later that month. Life is short, I keep saying to myself. Here is another huge reminder of that.

My mother is exceptionally strong, and after two surgeries followed by radiation treatment, she was cancer-free. But the whole thing was terrifying.

Life IS short. I didn't want to live my life without experiencing sex. Experiencing love. I put it out into the universe that I was finally ready. I was going to feel the fear and just do it. I was going to get over myself, get over my complete awkwardness when it came to intimacy and just go for it. I was going to slut it up with the next guy that came along—who also seemed like a suitable marriage candidate.

And then, almost like magic, the moment I opened myself up to the real possibility of sex, the moment I returned to LA after Mum's breast cancer, someone "came" into my life (pun intended again . . . ha ha).

The guy: Mickey. (And, Micks, I know this might be news to you if you are reading this, but yes, I lost my virginity to you.) First, I loved his name because of loving Mickey Mouse and all things Disney. Tick. Our first date was at Mickey's Malibu mansion. Second, I loved that he had his own mansion. Tick. It had a gorgeous pool overlooking the ocean, a squash court, a steam room—even a batting cage. My friend Hana Mae Lee from *Pitch* had introduced us and set up the first date—and naturally, I made her come with me. Mickey barbecued for me, which I found very sexy. So many ticks. More ticks than a bush rat. "He's the one," I thought.

Mickey was not afraid to be sexual. He was so confident and so handsome. At the end of that first date, as Hana was not-so-subtly angling to leave by walking to my G-wagon and standing by the passenger door, he kissed me. I leaned back on my car as our lips moved in sync, his fingers trying to get in places they were not going to go whilst I had my clothes on and whilst Hana was awkwardly trying not to look. What I do like about most American guys that I've encountered is that it's very clear when they want to sleep with you. And as someone who was inexperienced in this area, I really appreciated it. Mickey just went for it. It was hot.

Mickey pursued me. He was sexy and passionate and had money, so he could chase me around the world.

He'd take me to the nicest restaurants, and for the *Pitch Perfect 2* premiere he got us a hotel room, but we only cuddled before I said I had to drive myself home. He must've thought I was playing hard to get but I just was really innocent. I'm sure he could see it in my eyes when we made out. The make-outs would build in intimacy each time. But it hadn't led to sex yet.

I then started filming *How to Be Single* in New York and had a gorgeous hotel room. Mickey flew in that weekend to see me, and I decided that this was going to be it—he could stay the night. An overnight stay in a swanky hotel room was surely going to lead to sex.

He comes enthusiastically to my hotel room grinning and full of positive energy. "Hey, Micks," I say. "Hey," he says like he already knows it's on. I'm always amazed when people are so confident with their bodies because I sure as hell was not. The fact that I know I'm about to get naked with someone for the first time is so scary. Mickey quickly takes his clothes off and jumps on the bed. I like him so much and we've been dating for over a month now. He's from a good family. He's hilarious. He's chiseled, with gorgeous blue eyes.

We make out on the bed. It's going to happen. It HAS to happen now. I watched some porn movies the night before on the hotel TV (never actually watched porn before) and tried a vibrator in preparation. I wanted to have some "skills" and put in some studious research before the big night.

And then it just happens. I finally have sex. And I guess I get those lovely sex chemicals into my body for the first time ever, which really bonds me to him. I'm at almost my highest weight, but this great guy finds me desirable. It feels amazing. Part of the reason I waited so long to have sex is because I felt that as a big girl, no one would ever truly find me sexually attractive.

And I know there's a lot of people out there who put off sex and relationships until they lose weight—"I'll lose ten pounds and THEN I'll look for love in summer"—but I think that desirability has nothing to do with size or weight and everything to do with the confidence you project. I was now giving out a confident vibe. And here was a hot guy, wanting to touch my body. I had used my weight as an excuse to avoid intimacy for so many years and now I wished I hadn't. If someone's into you, then they're into you. You're a whole package—not just a number on a scale. At least I had now learned that lesson.

I go to the bathroom and high-five myself. So happy I've finally had sex—and with someone I really like and feel safe with at the lovely Greenwich Hotel. (Fun fact: this hotel is owned by Robert De Niro.)

Later I talk with Micks as I hold his sexy chest in bed. I notice some scars on his body. He tells me that he had some issues with drugs and alcohol in the past and that he's been to rehab a few times. "Rehab? How was that?" I ask. I'm amazed at how open Mickey is, with his feelings and his life. At the time rehab sounds like a glamorous thing that all rich kids do at one point or another. I hold him tight, just blissed up by the connection we have sexually and emotionally. He may have a past, but I'm so into him. And of course, now that we've had sex once, now that I've broken the seal, I pretty much am into having sex all the time. I'm a late starter and now I want to be MVP. Mickey makes me feel loved and desired. Little does he know he's helped me reach a huge personal milestone.

Mickey and I date for the next six months. We have so much fun together, and we both love sports and entertainment, but on our first big trip away together it becomes clear that, sadly, our relationship isn't going to work out.

We're going to Dubai; my whole family is flying to an amazing resort. They're ready to meet this guy that I talk so highly of. I stupidly don't realize that it's a terrible idea to holiday in Dubai in July as it's boiling hot (Dubai is a travel stop for Australians on the way back from London, so that's why I chose it). Rookie mistake. But at least that means Mickey and I can have lots of great sex in the air-conditioned villa room. I still high-five myself after great sex and smile in the bathroom mirror. I look at my freshly ravished hair. I like my new wild sexual self. I love that she now gets to come out and play. I used to live so much in my mind only—I'd imagine having sex and being in love and everything would always be in my head. Now I'm someone who lives much more in my body. And I'm loving it. Now I actually have a boyfriend, and he's handsome and rich to boot.

It's such a long flight to Dubai and I brought some sleeping tablets with me. "I'm taking a temazepam, do you want one?" I say to Micks on the plane. He nods and takes one out of my little pill container. I don't really think anything of it and bliss out for the rest of the flight.

When we get to Dubai, my family is all very keen to meet Mickey. Basically because he's the first guy I've ever brought to meet my family. Now I have a very eligible bachelor by my side and am excited to show him off.

We shower and all go out to dinner at the hotel. Mickey starts downing Red Bulls like he's dying of thirst and only Red Bulls can save him. It's a bit odd. I've never seen him like this before. My family quite likes him, though—he's a lovely guy, and I think Mum's just excited I've found someone at thirty-five. There's hope now for grandchildren. We all swim together and go to a water park, and then the family leaves and Mickey and I travel to Spain. First stop, Ibiza; second stop, Barcelona (it's a celeb freebie trip in exchange for an Instagram post).

When we get to the Hard Rock Hotel in Ibiza, it's a blazing party scene. Mickey had said he'd been sober since rehab and I didn't realize that where we were going is such a party place. It'd be like putting me in Willy Wonka's chocolate factory and not expecting me to drink out of the chocolate river. Mickey starts saying he's tired and retreating to the room. By the end of the trip in Barcelona, he just seems to want to sleep all day. He doesn't want to see the sights or go out anywhere. He seems just to lie in bed. "Is everything okay, Micks?" I ask. "Are you depressed?" It's a huge change in behavior. If I were more adept at dealing with addicts, I'd pick up on the fact that he's relapsed, but I've never met anyone who's recovering from drug and alcohol addiction, so I don't know what to look for. It's later clear, though, that he relapsed at some point on that trip. Maybe I should never have offered him that sleeping tablet? I feel like maybe this is all my fault?

When we fly back to LA, he comes over and just lies like a lump on my couch. This isn't the vibrant, positive go-getter guy I've been dating. This is like a completely different person. I keep asking what's wrong, but he won't tell me. A few weeks later I know instinctively that I have to dump him. This really isn't right.

Micks later tells me that he'd been to rehab seventeen times. That his addiction struggles were more than he'd initially let on. He said he would get help. I said I would support him. I actually waited a whole year to see if he would clean up so we could get back together. Being a role model to young people, I couldn't date someone who was an active drug and alcohol addict. But I adored Mickey and I wanted him to be well. I wanted him to be the fun Mickey I had fallen for. He had such massive potential. I could see myself marrying him . . . if he was sober.

I would swing from being angry with him to feeling sorry for him. He was a straight, good-looking, rich white guy—he had a Malibu mansion—and now he was fucking it all up? I kept waiting . . . waiting to see whether he'd return to being the guy I knew. Eventually, after it became clear from Instagram that he was sleeping with some Hollywood ho, I stopped waiting. In many ways, I understand how hard it would be to change. If someone told me, "Rebel, you've got a disease now and you can never, ever eat chocolate or processed sugar for the rest of your life," I wouldn't be able to do it. One hundred percent, I would NOT be able to do it. I have so much sympathy for him; I get the firm grip of addiction. It can have a hold on me too, just in a different way. Eventually I worked out that no matter how much love or attention I gave him, I was never going to "fix" him. I still had some of his trucker hats that he'd left at my house when we were dating. I guess I was holding on to them for sentimental reasons. I took the hats back to him at his Malibu mansion. I sat and chatted with his lovely mum, who was living with him. I really felt for her. She was lovely. I wished things had gone differently with Micks; I cared about him greatly. I will always have a soft spot in my heart for him. We hugged it out before I left. He called me his "angel." To me, he is my first shag, and a bloody good one at that!

TWENTY-SIX

In Atlanta I'm a 10

Two thousand sixteen was quiet on all fronts. I had no boyfriend after I broke up with Mickey, and now seemingly no big career opportunities (which I believed was fallout from the negative Bauer Media articles in 2015). So now I was treading the boards eight shows a week in London's West End in the musical *Guys and Dolls* for the summer. Live theater was where I'd started my career—it really is my first love, but boy, is it a next-level grind.

I'd get so nervous before each and every live performance. Unlike in films, you can't just do another take. I feel the pressure and responsibility of the fact that someone has come to see me live, and I always want to give my best. It takes an incredible amount of energy.

Back in the day, one of my first acting teachers at the Australian Theatre for Young People had sensed how nervous I would get and gave me a little pep talk. "Whenever you perform," he said, "you only really have two choices! You can IMPLODE—just be shit and fuck it all up. Or you can EXPLODE and be brilliant and shine and show everyone what you're made of." So every night when I walked out of my small dressing room and down the stairs toward the stage, I would just make a simple choice. I'd just decide to explode rather than implode.

I would also then imagine a staircase, something that Australian acting legend Ruth Cracknell said to me as I was driving her home one night after a theater performance. When I asked her if she got nervous to perform, she said that each thing she'd done in her career was like a brick and as the years pile up, so do the bricks, until they form a solid staircase. "I go out there onto that stage knowing that I have that whole staircase supporting me, so I can't fall down." This was a powerful metaphor—I'd been pushed down by the defamatory Bauer articles, but I had to believe that all those career building blocks that I'd worked so hard to achieve were now going to somehow hold me up. I'd imagine being supported by my now eighteen years of professional experience as an actress as I walked out onto that stage . . . ready to explode.

It's funny. Sometimes you've got the spotlight in your career and sometimes you're struggling to find the light. Two thousand sixteen was one of those tough years. This is where it helps to be a multi-hyphenate . . . to have so many bricks in your staircase. The depression caused by the court case and the negative media attention (since this was a case against a media organization, the media tended to cover me unfavorably for fear that my case would set a precedent that might put their companies in legal hot water) almost made me quit acting altogether. The pressure was so much. The attacks were so hurtful. But I'd sit in the dingy dressing room and inhale steam (a common vocal warm-up for live performers) and try to just breathe. Try to feel that even though it felt like I had nothing, I had my own staircase that I was climbing and that was supporting me. Every bit of effort I'd put into my career—every performance, every rehearsal, every hour spent writing, every lonely night when I'd sacrificed—it all had to come good, hadn't it?

On "two-show days" (Wednesdays and Saturdays), in between the matinee and the evening performance, I'd climb up onto the roof of the Phoenix Theatre on this very precarious old ladder and sit by myself on a beach towel and eat Chipotle. I'd look up into the sky thinking, "Should I move back to Australia and just be a lawyer, get out of the limelight?" But then I'd get out onto that stage and hear the audience laugh. I'd see the young people after the show at the stage door who looked up to me. I remembered how when I'd written, produced and starred in my first play, *The Westie Monologues*, at twenty-two, a lady wrote me a heartfelt letter. She said that she'd taken her thirteen-year-old niece to watch my play because a few weeks earlier her mother had died. At my play, her niece, for the first time since her mother's death, actually cracked a smile. For a few moments, despite the recent tragedy, she was enjoying herself. The auntie said that this meant more to their family than I would ever know.

Even though at times my work might seem frivolous or superficial, sometimes it can make a huge impact on people's lives. So NO! I wasn't going to quit just because I'd come upon hard times. I was going to put my head down and work even harder. Develop. Make connections. True grinding is sometimes the only way to make more progress in your career. I was putting my energy into a film project I was producing called *Isn't It Romantic*, where I would play, as a plus-sized actress, the lead in a romantic comedy. This was very important to me because traditionally the plus-size girl in rom-coms was always the "funny best friend" to the attractive lead girl. But now I was going to develop a film where the big girl was the attractive lead girl and had a guy like Liam Hemsworth fawning over her. The movie also had a powerful message about loving yourself . . . doesn't everybody need a reminder? I know I did.

The following year, 2017, was the biggest professional year of my life to date. I won the defamation case against billionaire bullies Bauer Media, my reputation was restored and I filmed three movies back-to-back—*Pitch Perfect 3*, *Isn't It Romantic* and *The Hustle*—for a whopping twenty million US dollars in acting salary total. I also produced *The Hustle* and *Isn't It Romantic*, which made me even more money. It was the most money I'd ever seen in my life. (Of course, I lost almost 50 percent to taxes, 10 percent to agents and 5 percent to my lawyer, and had other costs like a publicist, business manager and assistant, but I still netted what to me was an absolute fortune.) What did I do with the money? Well, I certainly wasn't snorting cocaine off strippers' asses. I purchased a second home in Los Angeles, one in Sydney and an apartment in glorious New York. I love buying property; it reminds me of how little Rebel would strategize whilst playing Monopoly—"Buy, buy, buy!" was always my motto. Property was something tangible I could touch and feel. It was literal bricks that could support me if I needed them to.

I helped family members with housing and bought my brother a car. I sent my grandparents on the *Queen Mary 2*, which was always their dream, and they had an exceptional time having high tea on the high seas. I donated more money to the School of St. Jude in Tanzania. I bought them a school bus that they painted koalas on and later helped them build a special girls' secondary boarding campus. I donated back my original Nicole Kidman scholarship money to the Australian Theatre for Young People and started a scholarship there of my own for creative young people. This led to me to donate money toward their new theater at the Wharf in Sydney, now named the Rebel Theatre. (If you want to see the next generation of amazing Aussie performers, check out a show there when you're next in Sydney!) The Rebel Theatre now gives thousands of young Australians each year the chance to shine in the creative arts. ATYP is a not-for-profit company and does incredible work with Indigenous Australians and young people living in rural areas. There are so many studies that show how important creative arts are for young people's confidence and self-esteem. So, I'm happy that through my support, so many young Australians are finding their voice.

For *Pitch 1* I was paid SAG minimum scale, which was $65,000 USD . . . and now I was earning $10 million USD for this third installment. Pretty big pay raise, right? Well, there's a reason for that. At the very end of filming *Pitch 2*, the producers told the older girls, like me, Anna Camp, Anna Kendrick and Brittany Snow, that we would not feature in the third movie. They were going to replace us all with younger actresses, led by Hailee Steinfeld, whose character was introduced in

Pitch 2. This seemed like a pretty nasty and unnecessary thing to say to us hardworking gals right at the end of filming *Pitch* 2. They had us film a scene handing over the reins of the franchise to Hailee. It was like a kick in the face to us original girls. I love Hailee, don't get me wrong, she's a stellar performer, but she had only joined us in the second film as the newbie and wasn't part of the original DNA of the franchise. None of us original Bellas were happy about this . . . but as the lawyer in the group, I knew that this could help us.

Since the studio didn't think they needed us and deemed us too "old," they never signed up any of us for a third-picture deal like they did with some of the newer cast members. When *Pitch* 2 became the highest-grossing musical comedy film of ALL TIME, we totally had the leverage. Oooh, as a law graduate, I love having leverage. Then, in a random fortuitous coincidence, my housekeeper's niece was part of a market research group for Universal where they polled people as to the most important parts of the franchise. One of the questions was: "What actor would you MOST want to see in *Pitch Perfect* 3?" Then "Which actor could you NOT LOSE out of the cast for *Pitch Perfect* 3?" I ranked as number one. This info was sweet harmonic music to my ears and is why I believe I was subsequently the highest-paid person on *Pitch* 3. (I did ask some of the other girls to negotiate as a team with me, like what the cast of *Friends* did, but there were too many agents and reps involved, so that never happened. I assume that everybody received significant pay raises, and rightfully so.)

Cue the big bucks. Cue us girls now living it up in a high-rise building in downtown Atlanta, dancing behind the huge floor-to-ceiling glass windows, loving life. Loving each other. People talk about shattering glass ceilings, but sexy dancing along glass windows was our way of doing it. Girl power!

The day I signed that ten-million-dollar deal, I thought of all the hard work I had put into my career every day since I got out of the hospital after I recovered from malaria. Although the fame had come at thirty-two, now, at thirty-seven, I had the full financial reward. I thought about that hard slog of putting myself through law school and acting school at the same time. Of acting, writing and producing on Sydney's stages—where I could barely afford petrol for my shit secondhand car. I thought of all those times as a kid when I was going through the rubbish bins at dog shows fishing for aluminum cans—and spending my school holidays packaging birdseed for $5 a box. I thought about all the friendships I had to sacrifice because I simply didn't have time for them. I thought about all the times I didn't go out, I didn't get drunk, I didn't stay out late, because I had to work the next day. I always had to write and create. I always had to work. I hate it when people say that my career has come easy, because they didn't see the incredible amount of work, effort and focus it took. The enormous sacrifices. The Herculean effort. It was one of the reasons why those defamatory articles were so devastating. If I had been their sister, or their daughter, and they had seen how I'd worked my ass off to have this career, they would have thought twice about carelessly setting a torch to something I'd worked brick by brick to build.

Pitch 3 started shooting in Atlanta. We'd been warned by production that men in this area could be particularly aggressive in picking up women that they fancied. We all laughed this off. What? Were they just going to jump out from behind a wall and ask us out? Yes. This is what actually happened. And it wasn't necessarily because we were movie stars . . . it's just that we were all put-together women. In terms of looks, in LA, gosh, I was probably a 5, but in Atlanta, I was suddenly a 10.

Guys would drive past me, wind down their window and ask me out. I had to stop going to one Whole Foods store because a guy there was obsessed with me. Men would offer me free drugs, free drinks, free ice cream. What was this place, where suddenly I was popular with the opposite sex? People had often said I had a pretty face, but I sure as hell wasn't "hot." But in Atlanta, where there were a lot of amazing big girls, suddenly I felt desirable for the first time in my life. It's funny, 'cause in HOTLANTA I was now suddenly seen as hot.

We'd have plenty of fun on the set too, just us girls. Anna Camp and I would scream, "I love acting!" before every take. Anna Kendrick and I held hands as we jumped off an exploding yacht together—we did a free fall off the side of the fake yacht built inside a huge soundstage until the ropes stopped us from hitting the crash mats below. It was a stunt that I never could've done without Anna holding my hand and singing to me to relax me (I'm deathly afraid of heights). In other scenes, Brittany would do something cute, Hana Mae would come up with some zany funny thing, Chrissie would just be an all-around supportive rock star. Hailee was effortlessly excellent; Ester was always just cool AF. Kelley and Shelley are just the best girls to be around, and a whole other movie could've been made with just their characters— the Rosencrantz and Guildenstern of the Bellas. It's honestly not even acting when you're around these great girls—it's just fun.

And then off set I was very busy having a very steamy love affair with a stuntman. He was so strong he could lift me up with one hand. He wasn't appropriate to date properly, but the sex was fun. I really loved spending time in Atlanta. I liked feeling desirable after never really being looked at in that way most of my life.

As we sang George Michael's "Freedom!" at the end of *Pitch 3*, we all cried. None of us wanted it to end. *Pitch* was such a gift to me in so many ways and now, after working with this crew for so long, we were like a family. I sprang for a luxury vacation for all of us Bellas in Cabo San Lucas, Mexico, straight after the film wrapped. It was the least I could do to show how much I loved and respected these girls and how grateful I was for our teamwork.

I return to New York, to my brand-new apartment that Fredrik Eklund from *Million Dollar Listing New York* helped me get for a great price. (Side note: Jeff Lewis from Bravo's *Flipping Out* designed my two LA houses.) It's summer in New York, and I am now starring in my first-ever lead role, as Natalie in *Isn't It Romantic*. Natalie, who is very cynical about love, hits her head in a subway and wakes up trapped inside a romantic comedy. My character has to learn to love herself first before she can have love in her life. And I feel like you can tell from reading this book that I very much related to the plot. I was a producer alongside a team of great people, including powerhouse Gina Matthews and producer extraordinaire Todd Garner. We had a truly talented cast: Adam Devine (my now work husband), Liam Hemsworth, Betty Gilpin, Brandon Scott Jones and Priyanka Chopra.

New York is a dream to film in and we shot in all my favorite parts of the city. My trailer on some days was positioned smack-bang in Central Park—not a bad day at the office. Filming in Times Square— also so incredible. The one issue with this shoot was that it was in the heat of summer and the sequence where I hit my head was filmed in a subway station where it was literally 110 degrees. At times I was being dragged along the subway floor by my hair, watching the rats scurry as I lay on the ground, rendered motionless by the heat. It was so hot, Gina got an air-conditioned Mercedes van nicknamed "Mercedes Island" for me to lie down in between scenes so I didn't overheat.

Then, ironically, playing a girl who hits her head, I got a real concussion.

I slipped down a grass hill while walking to set to rehearse a scene. I was taken by ambulance to the hospital, was treated and returned to film for sixteen hours until we had captured the scenes scheduled for the day. I had a massive headache for days after that.

I wasn't sure if it was the heat, or my excessive weight, or the super-long days of filming, but it took every ounce of strength I had to shoot *Isn't It Romantic*. It was so, so hard to get out of bed every morning. Months later, when I actually had a day off, I went to a doctor, and after analyzing my bloodwork, he told me that I had had mono, which can make you feel super lethargic. At least I wasn't crazy—I knew something was wrong with me during that shoot, I just hadn't had the time to do anything about it. I'm not sure which of the three men I had kissed recently gave me mono—but somehow, I'd gotten it.

The scene where I got to kiss Liam Hemsworth very passionately was a total delight. (I hope it wasn't from that! I don't think it was!) I was not feeling pretty in any way as earlier in the day I'd had to superglue my own toenail onto my foot. It had just broken off because sometimes when you constantly must use gel polish on your nails for work it can make the nail bed very thin. So embarrassing. There's a shirtless Liam looking so hot and fit, and there's me gluing on my toenail like a cartoon leper.

Liam was a total stud, just totally one of the hottest (and nicest) guys you will ever meet. I felt like in real life a girl like me would never kiss Liam Hemsworth. But when that camera rolls, you just have to go for it. So, I did. And that scene was the quickest to shoot in the whole bloody film! Every other scene seemed to take half a day. Kissing Liam was over in twenty minutes! Our director, Todd Strauss-Schulson, did such a beautiful job crafting the film, and the message—that you really need to love yourself to bring love into your life—was a message I needed to hear more than anyone. Even though professionally I was back in top gear, there were still voices inside my head telling me that I wasn't good enough. I think it's why I pushed my body to the absolute extreme with exhaustion. It was like I was a working mule, and I would kick myself to keep going, to keep climbing. Every morning I'd get up at five a.m. to exercise and then work a sixteen-hour day on set. "Come on! Stop being lazy! Get up and work!" When you're overweight there's always that stereotype that you're lazy. I know logically that I have a very strong work ethic, but sometimes you think, "Nah, I am lazy. Look at me walking to Mercedes Island to take a break. I could be writing more jokes, I could be dancing better, I could be taking care of my crew more."

Only three days after wrapping *Isn't It Romantic*, I flew to London to star in and produce *The Hustle*, which was a female remake of *Dirty Rotten Scoundrels*. Three days in between major Hollywood films is an insanely tight turnaround. Nobody in their right mind would do this. But the opportunity was there, and like the hot sex in Atlanta, I really wanted to take advantage of it.

I'd cast myself opposite Anne Hathaway, and I was really excited to work with her. I remember when I had to call her up as producer and ask if she wanted to be in the movie. "Hey, how's it going?" I love how I'm trying to be so chill but on the inside I'm like, "Oh my God, I'm calling up Anne Hathaway! Oscar winner!" I was so happy when she said yes.

Every scene felt easy opposite Annie, and we shot first on sets in London and then in beautiful Majorca for the exteriors, which was just WOW! Day after day, I'd shoot and try to be hilarious. At night, I'd plop into my hotel room bed, eat a dessert and wake up the next morning ready to do it all again. I was now in a film grind, and because I'd shot three movies back-to-back, with a high-profile defamation court case in between, this was actually worse than the theater grind.

On an eight-week comedy shoot for a film, you can afford to have one "off day," but that's it. Every day you need to deliver. You need to bring your A game. You need to know your lines and also improvise like a beast. You need to have tons of energy to do the physical comedy take after take. You need to be aware that people are watching you, filming you, photographing you constantly. You need to be on your best behavior. You need to be nice to everyone, even when they're not nice to you. Everybody wants something from you, and you have to give it to them.

This was the second movie I had produced, and each time I was learning more and participating more in the important decisions. One of my biggest wins as producer on this project was successfully appearing before the Motion Picture Association of America (MPAA) on behalf of the movie after they'd given it an R rating (which would've severely limited our potential box office). I persuaded them to give us a PG-13 rating, without making changes to the completed film. It was a coup. Lawyer Rebel kicked it into gear. The original version of the film, starring two men, was rated PG-13, so in my oral address to the MPAA, I argued that it would be sexist NOT to give us a PG-13 rating. I said:

It would be unfair to harshly require lines of dialogue from *The Hustle* to be removed in order for the film to be granted a PG-13 rating when the exact same words and similar jokes are

used in male-driven PG comedies. For example, the biggest comedy film of last year, *Jumanji*, starring Dwayne Johnson, Kevin
Hart and Jack Black, has seven jokes pertaining to asses. [We only
had two.] . . . The Austin Powers franchise films starring Mike
Meyers, that are ALL rated PG-13, literally contain hundreds of
rude words or double-entendre jokes PER FILM. These films are
all about sex, every line is literally a pun on intercourse, there
are character names such as Felicity Shagwell, Fook Mi, Fook Yu,
Ivana Humpalot—at one point a character drinks a cup of excre-
ment. *Austin Powers: The Spy Who Shagged Me* literally contains a
sexual reference in the title that was on show for anyone of any age
entering a cinema or seeing a public poster or billboard. There's a
whole sequence in this film based on penis euphemisms. So how
can a film with about 80 percent of its content being adult in nature be rated PG-13, and yet *The Hustle*, which has 3.75 percent,
be given an R rating? Any average American parent could say that
comparatively, *The Hustle* is more suitable for a fifteen-year-old
than any of the Austin Powers comedies.

After my passionate speech, the jury deliberated for less than fifteen minutes and agreed to change our rating back to PG-13. As far as
I'm aware, not since *Mean Girls* had a film successfully had its rating
changed in this way, with no alterations to the film itself. It was the
right decision and I thank the MPAA for making it so decisively. I
loved how I ended my speech too; I felt like a Hollywood suffragette
as I powerfully said the following:

We ask you to value the importance of context when considering the cumulative effect of language or humor in this
film. And while you may personally find a line or two from
this movie to be in a gray area, please consider that this film
is about two confident, intelligent women who are only con-
ning men because they deserve it—because they are cheaters,

racists, highly superficial, misogynists etc. These women are, at the end of the day, empowered. Their type of humor should be protected rather than cut, for it is much better for teenagers to view this kind of content rather than content that promotes women as victims of violence and sexual assault. Nothing in this film objectifies girls or women, turns them into commodities, or employs them as mere props in a comedy as so many male-driven comedies do. If a parent can take their fourteen-year-old girl to watch a movie where there are severed limbs, attempted rapes or decapitations, but they can't take that same fourteen-year-old girl to a comedy starring two confident women cheekily remarking about sex six times, then that is a serious problem in our society.

To say that a female remake of *Dirty Rotten Scoundrels* deserves an R rating is ludicrous and would be a decision open to criticism of overt sexism. It would be as ludicrous as saying that sexual jokes made by a woman are dangerous but sexism itself is fine.

I walked out of the MPAA offices in Sherman Oaks with my colleague Jon Glickman (who at the time was head of production at MGM) feeling like I was so in my element. Like I'd just won a war.

By the end of 2017, though, I was drop-dead exhausted. I hadn't felt this burned out since I worked on *Super Fun Night*. I found myself on an expensive doctor's premises getting an IV vitamin drip . . . opposite the biggest music artist in the world. There we both were. In sweats. Both exhausted. Both depleted. I know we are different types of entertainers, but as we talked, I realized that there were so many similarities. When we went out on our stages, we were literally giving our all. And even though we were earning millions of dollars, even though she's fierce as hell, that level of work comes with a price—the price being your health. Despite having just earned all that money, I was personally spent.

TWENTY-SEVEN

The Year of Fun/ The Year of Love

Okay, this is the part of the book where I'm finally off the struggle bus and riding on a Jet Ski at full speed off Bora Bora. Girls just wanna have fun, isn't that right, Cyndi Lauper?

Every year since I was fifteen, I'd written out my New Year's Eve resolutions. Usually, I jotted down about ten things that I wanted to accomplish. Always somewhere on that list was to lose a certain amount of weight—whether it was four and a half pounds (two kilos) when I was a teenager or seventy-seven pounds (thirty-five kilos) when I was an adult. But the idea of theming my years came in 2018—when I decided to spend the year focused on one area of my life. (I had been inspired by reading Shonda Rhimes's book *Year of Yes*.) So, 2018 was going to be an easy one: the Year of Fun. My only goal for the whole year was literally to enjoy myself.

I started throwing dinner parties at my house for friends and going out to Rams football games—these were things that I had wanted to do but just never had the time for. I would see Snoop Dogg at the games, and he'd be like, "What up, Rebbieshizzle? You want some weed?" I felt so cool but didn't take him up on the offer. I started playing tennis again, which I loved, but again, before I'd never had the time. I'm lucky that from time to time some famous Aussie greats, like Lleyton Hewitt, Rennae Stubbs, Todd Woodbridge and more recently Alex de Minaur, would have a hit with me. (This year I even got to play tennis on the prestigious grass Wimbledon courts through my friend and former player Matt Reid, which was incredible!) Here I was doing things that had absolutely no association with advancing my career—it was just pure pleasure.

I joined Club 33 at Disneyland, a secret and exclusive club that Walt started, and I went to the parks more with friends and family. Being a Club 33 member means I don't have to wait in lines for the rides, so one time, I went on so many rides so quickly that I had to go to the Disneyland hospital and lie down for an hour due to motion sickness. But before you think I'm too much of a diva, that day I was escorting some high-achieving students from the School of St. Jude that I had brought to LA from Tanzania to give them a fun break from their studies.

I had become friends with an outgoing Scottish girl, Carly Steel, whom I'd met when she was a reporter on *Entertainment Tonight*. She had come to the sets of *Isn't It Romantic* and then *The Hustle* in London to do a piece on the films. Like me, she had graduated law school but decided to pursue a career in entertainment. Carly was more worldly than I was. She'd been to lots of great places that I'd never even heard of, like Saint-Tropez, Monaco, Cannes, Portofino and Saint Bart's. The places where rich celebs hang out on yachts and have parties. How did you even get invited on a yacht? I didn't know. But Carly did. We were both single gals and didn't have anything tying us down, so we decided to go on some adventures together. The first up was a private island near Bora Bora. Carly was great at getting free hotel rooms and scored us two overwater villas. We went to this coral reef where the tidal patterns are supposed to float you naturally over beautiful coral and you can look at all the fish below through your face mask. However, we didn't realize that you weren't supposed to go there at low tide. We started floating face down with the current, and pretty quickly I got marooned on a huge piece of coral, my stomach caught on it. I tried to suck it in, but I couldn't move without cutting myself. Carly saw me flailing and swam against the current to rescue me, cutting up her legs in the process.

"Ahhhhhh!" we both screamed in pain as a hotel worker squirted lime juice on our coral cuts.

The actress Anna Faris was there with a new fella, and she was like, "Why are two single girls on a romantic island together?" "Well, why not?" we thought. Then a giant typhoon hit the small island. I escaped to my villa, only to have the night from hell. The rain was so strong that water was coming into the room and hitting me from all angles. I put my laptop in a plastic shopping bag to save it, but everything else I owned got soaking wet. We had to fly out the next day on a small plane to get back to Tahiti, and it felt like we were going to die. The typhoon was still raging, and Carly cried as we sat in the back of the plane, hoping we wouldn't crash. So that was "fun" adventure number one.

I then flew to meet my sister Liberty in New Zealand and we did zip-lining—which was NOT fun for me as I'm terrified of heights (yes, sometimes the fun missions ended up being disastrous, but at least I tried). We went up in a helicopter and visited some amazing wineries and had some quality "sister time."

I bought a boat in Sydney so that the family and I could go on some fun adventures together. This is probably the stupidest of all my "fun" ideas. I didn't have time to get my boat license myself, but my mum and sister Anna got theirs. Turns out, though, we were all pretty shit about parking the boat behind my new Sydney house on the harbor and we had two minor crashes. One time we also had to be rescued by Maritime Rescue. They thought we were total wankers. But it's amazing to drive your boat under the Harbour Bridge and take a spin around the Opera House—whilst you're barbecuing a burger on the grill in the back. Sydney is such a pretty city. The boat was fun while it lasted but definitely not my smartest of ideas. I felt a huge relief when I sold it a few years later.

Carly and I went to a Taylor Swift concert and danced our hearts out with Julia Roberts, actor Miles Teller, quarterback Jared Goff, Kobe Bryant and his daughter, and a bunch of other cool people who all just happened to be in the VIP tent that night. I went on a private jet to Vegas with Derek Hough, Tyra Banks and Justin Hartley for a music awards show where I met the South Korean boy band BTS. Awards shows are super fun purely in that you are in such close proximity to soooo many super-famous people and it's always interesting.

I performed at the Hollywood Bowl in Disney's live *Beauty and the Beast*. I played LeFou. The best part about this was that the night before the concerts, we did a run-through where the only person in the Bowl's audience was genius composer Alan Menken. And to see Alan dancing while I performed one of his songs onstage was just a highlight of my life.

Although I didn't want to focus too much on work, I did shoot the Academy Award nominee for Best Picture *Jojo Rabbit* opposite Scarlett Johansson and Sam Rockwell, which was directed by my friend Taika Waititi. That was a relatively small job, but it meant I got to stay at the Four Seasons in Prague for a month, which was a cool experience. Cue me ordering room service in a fluffy robe like a boss bitch. "Yes hello . . . I'm wondering what ice cream flavors you have?" I say in my very professional room-service-ordering voice. Taika is like the king of fun. I would watch him and wonder, "How does he have the energy to have fun every single night and then get up and be a brilliant director and leader by day?" "Chilling" didn't actually come naturally to me. Before 2018 I never truly let loose. I never gave myself permission to enjoy myself. I was always thinking of what was next. I was so focused.

Maybe I thought I couldn't be successful and have fun at the same time. Almost like I didn't deserve the fun, like I wasn't worthy. I always believed that in order to be successful, you have to sacrifice and be disciplined. Like a little worker mouse, running on a wheel, hoping for that pellet of success. But here was Taika, right in front of me, working hard of course, but also seemingly having the MOST fun.

I went to New York and saw terrific Broadway shows with Zahra, my high school friend from Tara, and one of my besties, Sam Kennedy. When I was working so hard, we lost touch for a few years, but then during my trial, Sam was there for me literally every day. He's such a sweetheart and has a sweet six-pack to match.

Sam and I then went with my dear friends Nicole, her now husband Josh, and Snickers to Iceland. I stayed at this incredible hotel, the Retreat at Blue Lagoon. They have these natural volcanic hot springs that are a vibrant light blue color where you can swim, and you can also get massages whilst lying on a floating mat. Can you imagine? Lying on a floating mat in volcanic loveliness whilst some hot Icelandic person massages you. It's heaven. Absolute heaven.

We visited waterfalls and took in some of the natural beauty of the country. Sam and I helicoptered to a glacier, where we rode snowmobiles. Driving out there, we listened to musical soundtracks. Then our whole group rode quad bikes along the volcanic terrain. It was the best holiday I had ever been on up until that point. I was surrounded by loving friends, and we could just be ourselves and have a good time. I will never forget that trip.

I even took up golf lessons in Palm Desert and started going to some Hollywood parties that I never would've thought to attend before. And then, using my newfound status, I went to the US Open, and I sat courtside at a Lakers game next to their bench and got a selfie with LeBron James (whom I also later went to Iceland with in 2022!). I went to polo matches. I just tried lots of new things where the only purpose was to enjoy myself.

At the end of the year, I celebrated Christmas at Disneyland with my pal Hugh Sheridan and my sister Anna. For New Year's Eve, I took a special trip with Carly to Aspen—which included partying with Mariah Carey and spraying champagne-filled guns at fellow partiers at a place called Cloud Nine. Picture half-naked rich skiers indulging and spraying each other with champagne whilst club music plays.

We get on the chair lift and go up into the Aspen Highlands—as we're going higher and higher up the mountain, I'm starting to freak out. "How am I supposed to ski down this, Carly?!?" This is clearly an intermediate run, and I'm not very good. When we get off the chair lift, Carly is worried about losing our reservation at Cloud Nine if we don't arrive by two p.m., so she effortlessly skis off to the chalet like an ice princess. I, however, spend the next forty-five minutes sliding down the hill on my ass because I think it's too steep to safely ski. Piglet, our ski instructor, looks on, trying to be encouraging.

I finally slide into Cloud Nine, late, and the atmosphere is absolutely insane. There are girls with their tops off. Everybody's dancing and drunk! Paris Hilton is there, giving me a friendly hug. What is this secret place in the middle of the mountain? Personally, I'm looking forward to some fondue—but everyone else is getting wasted. Carly spots a group of fun-looking guys at the table next to us. I pay $500 to rent this ridiculous golden gun that sprays out champagne. I load up the gun and fire away. I spray the guys next to us. I feel cool as fuck for sixty seconds. I turn to Carly, loving it. She's not loving it, though, because as I turn I spray her right in the face and the champagne stings so bad that she can't see for a few minutes. Ooops. But because I have the massive golden gun, all eyes are on me. It must be the same feeling when people order obnoxiously large bottles at VIP sections in nightclubs and the other partygoers look to see who's such a big spender. I was the dumbass who literally paid $500 to spray randoms with champagne for a minute. It did feel cool, though.

When Carly can see again, she thinks she recognizes one of the guys at the table next to us and approaches. He's tall, handsome, dripping in champagne. "Are you so-and-so's brother?" she says to him.

He takes off his sunglasses; it's not him. But whoever he is, he's super cute. "I don't think so. Hi, I'm Jacob. I'm here with my buddies from Snapchat." This guy seems nice and grounded amongst this wild chaos. Carly's quick to get his number. "Always ask for their number!" Carly always says. And she knows what she's talking about, because prior to this she was dating arguably the biggest male movie star in the world. Later that night we catch up with these guys in a nightclub. I'm really not the nightclub type but Carly forces me to go.

The Snapchat boys agree to take us on a group date the next day— the odds are good for Carly and me as there are five of them and only two of us. The boys organize a snowmobile outing that can only be described as a *Bachelorette*-type group date in extreme snow and cold. Because we're such "fun" girls, we bring an inflatable to tie onto the back of one of the snowmobiles for some people to ride. A lot of girls would chicken out considering the blizzardy conditions, but not Carly and me. We're both dedicated to adventure and finding dates, and she has her eyes firmly on the alpha of the Snapchat pack, Jacob. I like this other guy whom I'm going to call the Swedish Teddy Bear.

Carly and I get back to the hotel and we talk about our wish list for a partner. I've never quite thought about what I want in a significant other. Back when I met Mickey, I was just desperate for a boyfriend. If anyone showed romantic interest in me at that point, I was extremely grateful. But now, for the first time, I think, "What do I want in a part-ner?" Carly writes down her list and finds every single thing in Jacob (whom she later marries).

I was probably going to have to kiss a lot of frogs to find my prince. I still felt very naïve when it came to love and dating. Yes, I'd had that relationship with Mickey and some other dalliances. But not many compared to a regular thirty-eight-year-old. I felt behind the eight ball. But I was willing to put love first, now that I'd let go of a lot of stress and had enjoyed myself. My New Year's resolution was to spend the next year trying to find love. Two thousand nineteen was going to be themed my Year of Love.

My main rule was that if anyone asked me out, I was forced to say yes. Except, of course, if they were a criminal in prison who DM'd me for a date (that has happened many times). I obviously wouldn't advertise that this was a little experiment I was doing. I was just going to be open to finding love. Carly was all for it.

I wrote a list of things that I wanted in a partner—as if to manifest them out of the blizzard. I stuck this piece of paper in my wallet to carry around with me. I wanted someone kind and loyal. I wanted someone who had a job and passions of their own. I wanted to have a mutual physical attraction.

I decided to take the massive step of joining the dating app Raya—which was probably the only dating app that celebrities could use—and ticked that I was a woman interested in meeting men age thirty to forty-five. Tap, tap, select a hot profile picture. And boom, I was live on the app. I was officially on the market.

I was also going to do things in real life to meet single guys. For New Year's Eve, Carly invited Jacob and I invited the Swedish Teddy Bear as our dates to Kate Hudson and Goldie Hawn's Aspen party. It was as raging as the big bonfire outside in their backyard. It was nearing midnight, nearing the first day of my Year of Love. What was going to happen? Despite some epic fails, I'd definitely succeeded in my Year of Fun. If I dedicated a whole year now to finding love, could I manifest it?

We all gathered around the bonfire a few minutes before midnight, and everyone was asked to write something on a piece of paper and throw it into the fire. It was supposed to be symbolic of something that you wanted to shed before going into the new year. I wrote, "Not feeling worthy of love," and I threw it into the flames whilst Orlando Bloom and Katy Perry started dancing and making out behind me.

I wanted to be worthy of love. There was nothing hideously wrong with me, was there? I knew I was overweight, that I was "medically obese" or whatever, but fatphobia is wrong, and as a whole package I had a lot to offer. I am like a "family meal deal" that comes with a free bottle of successful-career soda and a large well-educated, well-traveled garlic bread. I had so much love to give and I wanted to give it to someone. The right person. And then it was midnight. The Year of Love had officially begun. There wasn't a second to waste. Carly kissed Jacob by the bonfire and I kissed the Swedish Teddy Bear. We were two women on the rise. Trying to have it all. Careers, fun, love. (It then took us hours to leave the party as our Escalades got stuck in snowbanks.)

On the first day of the Year of Love, I actually went out on three dates in Aspen: the Swedish Teddy Bear 'til three a.m., Mickey (who had flown into Aspen knowing I would be there, so following my rules, I had to accept his invitation for a small date) and then there was one mystery man whom we just referred to as "Mexican Aquaman"—he literally looked like a Mexican Jason Momoa. I kissed him of course. A topless girl from Cloud Nine had also texted me asking me out, but I just ignored that one. The Year of Love rules only applied to guys, obviously.

I was on fire. It was like a revolving door of men that day. Carly joked that the hotel staff saw a parade of dudes coming in and out of our apartment and had nicknamed us "the Infamous Wilson Party." But I never slept with them. I do want to make that clear. In all of 2019 I went on dates with about fifty different men, but I only slept with two. Some of them were billionaires and some had nothing—one guy lived next door to a strip joint with two roommates. I gave everyone a fair shot. I really spent time on each date investing in getting to know the other person. (And for all my single readers out there dating—I really know the effort that dating takes! It's werk!)

I'd started listening to these podcasts about love and dating, which led me to one where these girls talk about orgasms. I was fascinated. I'd never really learned about orgasms. I wasn't the type of girl who, as a teenager, stumbled upon the fact that her electric toothbrush could make her feel something downstairs. I didn't have an electric toothbrush. When I'd had sex over the past few years, I'd never re-ally thought about MY pleasure. It was more about the guy climaxing, and then pretty quickly sex was over. And while I had experienced pleasure, I don't think at this point I'd truly had an orgasm. I might've thought I had—but after listening to this podcast series and later buying some sex toys online, I truly experienced an orgasm for the first time at thirty-nine . . . just by myself. "Huh," I thought, holding this suction product called the Womanizer. "Is this what I was missing out on?" But now my research for my Year of Love taught me that there was so much more to sex than just the guy getting off. I should have been orgasming too. That should have been a priority. No one had ever taught me about that—I had to learn it from a podcast.

I invited the Swedish Teddy Bear to my *Isn't It Romantic* premiere in February. I quite fancied him, but whilst I was doing press on the red carpet, he apparently had a panic attack. He said that he couldn't possibly date me because I was in the public eye and that caused him anxiety. It was the first time a guy had turned me down because of my public profile—normally guys liked the attention that brought. The rejection stung. But I guess that's part of the dating game, isn't it? You're going to get rejected. You're going to waste your precious time on people and that's going to get annoying. I don't think it's easy finding love. But I'd literally seen Carly manifest it firsthand with Jacob. So, I knew it was possible.

I'd spend my nights now trolling through hot surfers/models/DJs on Raya. "Hey, how are you?" they'd text. "Ugh," I'd think. "Now it's thirty minutes of texting back and forth with a stranger to ascertain whether they're sane enough to meet up with IRL." As long as they weren't a psycho and didn't seem like a predator, if they asked me out, I'd go out with them.

One guy I met on Raya, who worked in the "space industry," I'm sure just wanted to say he'd been out on a date with me. At the end of our lunch, he asked me to take a photo with him clenching a rose in my mouth as he dipped me. For some dumb reason I did it and took the photo. And I never saw him again.

The great thing about the Year of Love, though, was that I got really comfortable going on first dates and having an interaction with someone that was potentially romantic. By this point in my life, I had learned to be great at meeting someone new in a business environment—but now I was actually getting good at dating. I listened to a lot more dating podcasts and read a lot of books. Steve Harvey actually had some great advice in the love department! So did my soon-to-be friend Matthew Hussey. By going on so many dates in one year, I saw things in guys I liked: stability, a job, manners. I saw things I didn't like: drug and alcohol addictions, criminal history, smoking.

Carly set me up with a new guy: Jacob Busch. I didn't know this at first, but the Busch family is one of the richest families in America. You know, Budweiser beer? That's them. I wasn't aware of this family, but Carly was quick to tell me as if she was the Wikipedia of rich eligible bachelors. I just knew, when I first laid eyes on Jacob B. at the dinner party Carly had set up at San Vicente Bungalows, that he was super hot. Like Liam Hemsworth super hot! It was like the fantasy of *Isn't It Romantic* was becoming my real life. Jacob's childhood was fascinating and almost the complete opposite of mine. He had a zoo on his family's estate, for God's sake! As a kid he went to theme parks actually owned by their family—Busch Gardens! Jacob told me on our first date his hobbies were "perfumery and gemology." I mean, talk about bougie. He dressed impeccably. He had great manners and style.

Aaaand, let me tell you, he knew how to please a woman in the bedroom! I thought, "Who is this Disney prince? He's absolutely perfect."

I also liked that Jacob B. was financially secure. I had dated guys whose flights I'd paid for if we traveled, or I'd paid for expensive restaurants if I had chosen to go there with them. It was all right at first, but when it turned into a pattern, either I'd start feeling used or they'd start feeling emasculated. There was a slight difference in that I had made my millions and Jacob had essentially been given his. But I wasn't going to hold this against him. For now, I was going to hold my ample bosom against his hot bod.

I was classy, though . . . and waited 'til our second date to have sex. We started by getting naked and making out in the shower. Jacob's body was just glowing, looking ripped AF under the warm water, and he said to me, "I'm sorry, I'm not looking my best right now. I've put on a few pounds." First, he was HOT AF. I didn't understand what on earth he was talking about. He wasn't fat in any way. Second, I was like, "He does know I'm fat, right? And he's making out with me?" Then I just got too turned on to ponder all of this and shut my mind off. I wanted to fully concentrate on this beautiful man whom I was about to make love with.

After, I almost couldn't believe I'd had sex with someone who was so good-looking. Like the whole thing was too good to be true. Some kind of *Isn't It Romantic* fantasy sequence where I'd just been sliding my tongue down this super hot guy's ripped abs like I'm in a "desperate desert" and the only hydration I can get is from his chest sweat. However, a few dates later, the "mirage" started to wear off pretty quick. Despite Jacob being so very nice, we didn't really have that much in common. For example, I barely drank, but Jacob liked to drink. I guess that's a thing when you come from a family famous for alcohol? I worked really, really hard. He had inherited his wealth—not saying that's not "hard," though—I mean, I've watched *Succession*, it's just very different to how I grew up.

I broke up with Jacob over the phone. He seemed to be in total shock and really upset. But I couldn't be with him. I had to see who else was out there. Carly thought I was crazy for letting this prize catch go, but she hadn't been on the dates. On paper Jacob B. looked perfect, but I knew in my gut it wasn't going to work.

When dude after dude didn't work out, I'd have to keep telling myself that I was a valuable package. It's very easy to fall into a wombat hole of "I'm not good enough and I'm never going to find love." I had to just keep reminding myself of my attributes—I was smart, loyal, kind, funny, well educated, financially secure, owned my own houses . . . there were all sorts of great things I could bring to a partnership. But being a big person, you also must face the fact that when it comes to dating, first impressions matter. And even though your larger size itself may not make a bad first impression, what you might be giving out to people are impressions like "I don't look after myself," "I don't care about my body," "I treat myself badly," "I can't cope with life and so I overeat." There are a multitude of things you could be saying, almost instantly, just with how you present on that first date. I know it sucks—but it is the world we live in. It's society. And I was living in LA, which does have ridiculous beauty standards. I had people who instantly rejected me because of my size. I would have loved to have been born in the seventeenth or eighteenth century, where my plump, Rubenesque features were seen as a sign of wealth and nobility. But back then, women had no rights—no vote, no ability to own property and basically no career opportunities—so I guess if I did have to choose what century I'd like to live in, it would be now.

Everyone has pros and cons. I knew my con was being overweight—not necessarily because of the number on the scale or my actual size, but because being overweight was a barrier preventing me from truly being intimate with people. If I was "dating" someone, I'd only really let them hang out with me twice a week and rarely allow them to sleep over. I still wanted my own space. I wanted love badly, but I still might not have been ready for deep intimacy with another person. But maybe this was because I hadn't met the right person yet?

Of course, I couldn't articulate this at the time. Back then, I'd truly accepted my size and weight and thought, "I'm going to be like this forever and anyone who's not into it is just a superficial dum-dum. If they can't look past my body and see my interesting mind, my kind soul, then screw them." But the problem with that way of thinking is that I was ignoring the fact that I was mistreating my body. It's like my not wanting to date someone once I knew they had substance abuse issues—because they weren't treating their body or themselves with respect. I was doing the same thing, just in a different way, with bad eating. This was a con to potential romantic partners. If I had been healthier, then maybe these people would've been interested in me.

Now, of course this doesn't mean I'm advocating that you must be skinny to find love. Not at all. You have to be happy in yourself. And I truly was, for the most part. Which is why it sounds contradictory. It wasn't really the weight I was rallying against; it was those unhealthy eating patterns and behaviors that were keeping me isolated, keeping me lonely, keeping me feeling guilty. That's what was keeping me single. At the time, I just associated it with my weight.

Eventually I needed a break from the constant dating, so I went with Carly to an amazing health retreat in Austria called Vivamayr Altaussee (now rebranded to Mayrlife). Carly somehow managed to get the nearly $50,000 stay for free in exchange for my posting about it. Apparently, a lot of successful people had been there. It's a chance to reset your body and whole digestive system. I met Dr. Schubert, and every day throughout the program whilst he checked in on my progress and we had a chat, he massaged my belly. The first time he did it, I had to hold back the giggles. Here was a grown man tenderly massaging my big belly, the thing I always tried to hide with high-waisted leggings. He would massage with kindness and care. It was the opposite of my approach to my body, which was normally "You better hike up this hill, bitch!"

Altaussee is like a little paradise. I had my first-ever colonic there—which, yes, was so embarrassing, an Austrian woman sticking a tube up your butthole is not fun, but, I guess, it was a release! I did a water shiatsu massage where you float in a private pool whilst a woman moves you around as she sings Austrian folk songs. It was a cool experience. Everything was designed to relax, recharge, rejuvenate. With the bland, easily digestible foods, I was being kind to my digestive system for once. When we left after two and a half weeks, I felt amazing.

Still, I wasn't mentally ready to shed all my weight. Even though I thought it was my biggest barrier to finding love, I was holding on to it like it was the doona I brought with me to America. This weight was mine. I wasn't going to give it up so easily. It had served me well. Maybe the only reason I was a successful movie star was because of my weight? It was what I knew. I knew how to be fat. It's who I was.

But going to Mayrlife was a big step in truly positively overhauling my life. It seeded an idea in me, that it was possible to feel physically better. Just like in *Isn't It Romantic*, I was definitely learning to love myself more, and the more I did that, the less I wanted to eat the bad foods. Originally this Year of Love had been about nabbing some eligible husband before I turned forty—but it was now morphing into something way bigger than that. Maybe what I needed was more self-love.

I sat in the restaurant of Mayrlife looking out at the gorgeous Alps and the magical lake outside. It's stunningly beautiful, which helps when you're only eating about six hundred calories a day. I saw all these successful entrepreneurs and CEOs at the other tables. They were all incredibly busy people, almost obsessed with their health. "Hmmm," I thought. "These are really smart people and they're really treating their bodies with kindness and love. They realize that health is actually wealth." I decided at this point that the next year, 2020, would be my Year of Health.

I would speak to my new doctor, Dr. Habib Sadeghi (famous for being Gwyneth Paltrow's doctor), on the phone every two weeks to discuss my emotions and how they might have been affecting me. Dr. Sadeghi really believes in the body-mind connection. It had never even occurred to me that what's happening in your brain, your thoughts, could affect your body. But after working with Dr. Sadeghi, I realized there really was something there. I was holding on to all sorts of negative thoughts and emotions, which led to bad patterns of behavior that kept me physically feeling like shit.

He believes in cleansing yourself of your emotions, and one of the great things he taught me is called Purge Emotional Writing. You set a timer for twelve minutes and handwrite all your emotions on paper, ending with the things you are grateful for—so that you end on a positive note. You then destroy the piece of paper—you get rid of it by burning it or ripping it up into tiny pieces, which is symbolic of the emotions inside you leaving your body. Just like you'd go to the toilet to get rid of unwanted waste in your body, this is a method to get rid of unwanted emotions.

The fat I was carrying around was symbolic of all the emotions I was holding on to. Every time I spoke with Dr. Sadeghi, I was slowly uncovering things I'd suppressed. I hadn't dealt with or even spoken about many mini traumas in my life. It was like I was carrying them all around with me, like a woman coming out of a grocery store walking to her car with twenty heavy bags. It was why I was always exhausted. Imagine carrying those bags not just from the supermarket to your car but every single minute of your life.

At first, I felt a bit like my chats with Dr. Sadeghi were making me more emotional, more confused. But after a few months, things started to click, and I started to process my emotions in a healthier way. I slowly started to release the barriers I was carrying around with me. I started saying, "You know what, that particular heavy bag of guilt or shame, I don't feel like I want to carry that anymore. I want to put that down." And it felt weird—being so vulnerable, like that feeling you get on a first date. You're putting yourself out there and it's scary. But I did notice that mentally I was feeling better and I was dealing with life better. I didn't need food as a crutch as much. I'd unwound a bit with my Year of Fun. I'd now been so much more open with my Year of Love. And right then I was hit with a curveball that I never saw coming.

TWENTY-EIGHT

The Tennis Player

It's the hottest day at the 2019 Wimbledon, and I'm watching her play with grace and style. I want her to win more than anything. I am so nervous, as if it's me out there on the court. My friend Marissa is looking at me like, "Why on earth are we out here watching this girl play when we could be living it up getting the free drinks in the sponsor suite or watching Roger Federer right now on center court?" But I can't take my eyes off her. She's fucking amazing. She's fighting so hard to win her match. It's exactly how I fought to have a career in entertainment. I feel her.

Sweat's dripping down the back of my legs, but I'm glued to her. I feel something. I don't even know how to describe it. What is this? I think I'm majorly attracted to this girl but no, I can't be. I clearly find men attractive. I date men. I have sex with men. So, what the hell is this? It hits me like an ace hits the line of the service box. POW.

We text after the match, but I can't meet up with her. High-class celebrity problems. I'm flying to France the next day for a holiday with friends, including Carly; her boyfriend, Jacob A.; and the one and only Barbra Streisand. And I'm so hot and sweaty after watching her in the direct sun; I don't want her to see me like this. Also, I have so many complicated emotions going on that I'm sure I'd sound like an idiot if I actually spoke to her. What on earth am I going to say? "You played so well!" Ugh.

We met in person a year earlier and had dinner in New York after the US Open. She'd won a big match and I'd seen in the press that she was a big fan of mine. I DM'd her on Twitter, I think . . . which is very random as I don't think I'd ever done that before. I said congrats on the win, which started a little chat. I offered to take her to dinner as I was a big tennis fan and she apparently loved *Pitch Perfect*. It definitely, 100 percent wasn't a date. That thought wouldn't have even crossed my mind. It was just a nice dinner with a great tennis player who liked my movies. I didn't think anything of it . . . until I saw her play at Wimbledon on that very hot, hot day. And whoa. Is my Year of Love about to have a mega plot twist?

I try to forget about these new feelings whilst I talk to the iconic Babs in the swimming pool of our shared villa in Saint-Tropez. (By the way, I loved listening to anything she said, especially her stories about how hard it was to be a female film director and what she's overcome in her iconic career . . . I think about her as I'm now directing my first feature, *The Deb*.) When I return to America, I try to forget about the Tennis Player and her cute American accent, the cute way she said the word "good"—"Ahh, it was probably nothing," I think. "Just forget about it, Rebsie." It kind of freaked me out, to be honest. Sure, deep down inside I never thought I was 100 percent straight. But I never knew what to call that. I just ignored the not-straight part of me. That became that one random M&M that fell down the back of my love seat and sat there in the dark near the springs, collecting a bit of dust over the years.

I'd liked watching movies and TV shows that had small lesbian moments in them, but I never thought I'd fancy a woman in real life, or, if I did, that I'd ever act upon it. Not that I thought there was anything wrong with being gay—most of my besties were gay guys. It's just that I didn't think I was gay. At one point while I was using Raya, I clicked on the "Interested in Women" button because some of the *Pitch* girls told me they did that on their profiles to "check out the competition." Seeing all the hot women in their bikinis walking tiny dogs as small as their waists made me depressed, so I unclicked this option pretty quickly.

Now these feelings for the Tennis Player are so strong and they aren't going away. I'm compelled to follow them. Like someone put a Harry Potter magic spell on me, and I'm sliding toward the next massive Grand Slam event with no grip on my shoes and nothing I can do about it.

The US Open comes around again, and I fly to New York. I say I'm there for work, which might be partially true, but really, I'm there for her. We meet for lunch. And let me tell you, it's awkward as all hell. Because now I am aware that I have a huge crush on her, but I don't even know if she is into girls romantically. How do you even tell? I had no idea.

The Tennis Player doesn't even eat anything. We're at Cipriani next to Central Park, one of my favorite lunch spots, and I'm chowing down, but she's on a strict diet plan with the tournament coming up. Later that night, she says, she'll eat some plain chicken breast, rice and broccoli. I get the check and then I walk her back to her hotel. When we're one block away, she tells me to go. What I would come to understand is that the tennis world is very small, and all the players normally stay in the same hotel. So, if you walk into the lobby with someone, the tennis gossip wheel is going to be on fire.

She really doesn't even want people to know we're hanging out. What does this mean? Will people think we were on a date? Were we even on a date? She's a bit cagey and mysterious. But God, is she beautiful and talented.

I go to the US Open the next day and watch her match. Then later that night she texts me. It's like ten p.m. and she wants "to go somewhere." Oh shit. Is this now a date? I think this is a date. I quickly text Brittany Snow: "Hey, I have a date. Where's somewhere cool I can take a tennis player late at night with zero notice?" Brittany hooks me up with this cool club in the East Village. We go, but it's really noisy and we can't talk. Also, it's very public and I'm very recognizable. We only stay for a little bit and then she says she has to leave.

Later that week, I take her to a Broadway show, my absolute favorite thing to do in New York. Then the next day, once she's finished at the "tourney," we go out for a nice dinner and talk. As we walk back to my Tribeca apartment, we literally pass two other girls on the street holding hands. Is it a sign? And now she's sitting on my couch. After a week of interaction we're alone. We're so close and it's just the two of us.

When I'm on a date with a guy, it's now very obvious to me if he's into me sexually. But what am I supposed to do here? I'm on a date with a woman. I'm making small talk from the other end of the couch at a million miles an hour. "And then I was in a novice all-styles martial arts fighting tournament!" Blah, blah, blah. I can't shut up, I'm so nervous. I just wanna ask her, "Are you into women?" But I can't.

I want to impress her. I want to be around her. I think I want to make out with her, but I really do not know how to make the first move.

"I don't mean to offend you," I say, my heart racing ten million miles an hour, "but are you into women?"

She's hard to read, because on the court she plays emotionless for the most part—which I think is deliberate. It's how Roger Federer plays, and a lot of younger players have adopted this approach. Always look like you're in control. Always. But now this is making it hard for me to read her. Finally, she answers.

"Yeah," she says with this sly smile.

My expressive John McEnroe face probably gives my game away. I am fucking delighted by this.

"Oh!" I say. "So, you've, like, been out with a woman?"

"Yeah, I've dated guys, but I have been with a woman . . . it was only a short thing."

"Oh!" I say again like it's the only fucking word I know. But then I ascertain that she has actually slept with one woman before and then—shit—I've been talking for so long she now has to go, and so I walk her out to the Uber. I don't want to walk her out. I want to kiss her. I'm just wayyy too shy. So I just hug her goodbye. Ugh, a hug. "Rebel, you're such a loser," I think. "She just admitted she's into women and you don't do anything." I should've told her I fancied her, but it was scary. These feelings and the strength of them terrify me. It's like I'm on a roller coaster and someone cut the track, and so I'm just sailing through the air, potentially about to fall to my death. It doesn't matter if I hold on; I have no control over what is going to happen.

I don't have the courage to say anything to her face about how I feel. I'm flying to LA the next day, and she's flying home too. It's midnight now and she's back at her hotel room, and I text her.

"Hey, I don't know what this is, but I feel this deep connection with you."

The agonizing one-minute wait for her to text back . . .

"Yeah, I feel it too."

Holy shit. She feels it too!! This is now looking fucking good.

By "fucking good," I mean I don't sleep the rest of the night. I can't sleep. I'm too excited. I get up at five thirty a.m. and walk around Tribeca. I sit staring at the Statue of Liberty, deep in thought, so much so that a squirrel steals my croissant right out of my hand. Fuck you, squirrel. But I'm feeling so pumped. This is something I've never felt before. The wayward roller-coaster car has landed safely on a cloud of rainbows.

I didn't even touch her, though. We haven't kissed. But I think I'm already in love with her. I know that sounds mental. But I'm lovestruck. And now, sadly, she's overseas . . . for like, forever!! Professional tennis players have the worst schedule, worse than actors. They're in a different country basically every two weeks. They're lucky if they have a few weeks' holiday a year.

This led to what I like to call a "complicated long-distance thing." Maybe the kids would say a "situationship." I'd offer to fly to see her; she wouldn't commit to a plan; I'd get majorly frustrated and cut off all communication, which would last for like a whole minute; and then I'd really want to talk to her again. We'd both flirt. It was sometimes hundreds of texts in a day.

"Sweet dreams. 😴"

We text this every night when we end a chat. Basically, I text her about everything. We encourage and support each other, and that part is nice. But from my end, it's at times painful. I'm frustrated that I can't be physically close to her. I want her. I text her that I'd really like to sleep with her. There's no beating around the bush when it comes to my texting.

I'm probably a bit too full-on in my messages. But I can't be near her, and she isn't someone who FaceTimes or talks on the phone, so texting is all I have. I place emojis like I'm composing a sonnet. In my mind, the Year of Love is now a complete success. These feelings are so real. So visceral. Experiment successful. Conclusion: Maybe I'm not totally straight, but I have found someone to love. I just have to see if they love me back.

Now it's clicked over to the new year: 2020, the Year of Health, the year I'm turning forty, although right now it feels more like the Year of Getting Together with the Tennis Player. It's the Australian Open in Melbourne and we've planned to spend time together. Sadly, she loses way too early in the tournament. She's pissed. She texts that she's already booked a flight home and is leaving in two days.

"Can't you stay longer?" I beg. I'm still up in Sydney after spending time with my family. "I thought we were going to spend a whole week together."

"I can't," she says coldly. "My team's booked the flight already."

I get on a flight the next day and aim to see her in Melbourne that night. I have less than forty-eight hours before she jets away again. My heart is beating out of my chest. I am so nervous. All our texting has built up the sexual tension big-time.

She rocks up to my two-story hotel suite and she's actually a few minutes early. The hotel manager lets her into my room. There's a piano on the entry level. I'm upstairs still getting ready, madly trying to put on some makeup, heart literally beating out of my chest. I'm so nervous.

I get myself together and walk down the stairs to see her tinkering on the piano—of course she's good at a multitude of things beyond tennis. I take her to get Grill'd hamburgers (my favorite from when I lived in Melbourne) and then to my former local beach in Elwood to eat them. I was so quick to race out of the hotel room that I forgot towels or a blanket to sit on at the beach. She offers me her jacket for us to sit on together. There's only moonlight on our faces. It's very low-key but romantic. I try to eat my juicy burger but I'm not very hungry. I'm only hungry for her. And then as the waves crash in front of us and the moonlight shines and shimmers off the ocean, she looks at me . . . she looks deep into my eyes . . . and . . .

"I can't have a relationship with you," she says. "I need to focus on my tennis."

Oh my fucking God!!! Are you serious??? With this one sentence, my heart is completely crushed. We're finally alone again. We're finally together after almost five months of flirting and texting. What has happened? I'm devo'd. (That's Australian for "devastated.") I'm completely devo'd. I'm the MOST devo'd a person can be. I try extremely hard not to cry—like I'm holding my own heart tight and won't allow it to flood me with emotions whilst I'm sitting next to her.

What did I do wrong? I feel like a complete idiot. Does she not like me because I'm overweight and she's a super-fit athlete? Is my texting too much? Or does she just not like my movie *Cats*? (Just joking.)

I offer to drive her back to her hotel. I'm so upset that I get lost and I'm driving a bit in circles. Eventually she can see her hotel out the window and just gets out of my car. It's still a few blocks away and she has to cross a busy six-lane road, but she prefers to jump out of my car and run through traffic rather than spend five more minutes with me. I don't get it. How did I fuck this up so royally?

I cry when I get back to the hotel room. The ugly cry. I go to the cinema by myself the next day and eat a whole large box of popcorn and a large packet of Maltesers. I text her that I can't talk to her ever again. And then, like a psycho, I reach out again two weeks later begging to have our friendship back. Can we PLEASE be friends? I guess it's better than nothing. I can't lose this person from my life who cracked my heart open like it was a fresh can of tennis balls. So even though she rejected me, the one positive is that my passion for her makes me feel alive. Even though right now it's painful and torturous, I was so open to love, so into someone other than myself. And that was good.

I reconnected with hottie Jacob Busch. I met with him to go hiking in Malibu. He looked hotter than ever. We started a proper relationship as I tried to ignore the previous incompatibilities I'd tallied up from before. Maybe I had been too judgmental? Unlike the Tennis Player, he wanted to be with me, and it felt great. We went on glamorous trips to Monaco and Cabo and had sex everywhere. Could I marry him? We started to talk about it.

I got the feeling he was thinking of proposing. He made a few obvious comments about gems (his favorite topic). And rings. Yep, it was pretty obvious. But I wasn't sure how I felt about this. There was a part of my sexuality I hadn't actually explored and that might have been important for me to address. I returned to the Austrian health retreat Mayrlife by myself, to think. I was in a conundrum. "Do I just marry this guy? He's great on paper. Nope. No, I can't. I can't in good conscience marry him. I can't see us together long-term." So, as I was cleansing my system of toxins and losing the last few kilos on my Year of Health journey, I was cleansing myself of him too. I was realizing that yes, even though he's an incredible catch—it doesn't feel right in my heart.

I'm one of those people who absolutely agonize about dumping someone. I still do it when I have to, but I hate upsetting people. I didn't quite know how to tell Jacob and it was tearing me up inside. I was dreading it. He had been nothing but nice and kind to me. He just wasn't the one. It'd been a fun six months, but it wasn't going farther.

After months of silence, I told the Tennis Player I was in Austria. She was also in Europe at the time. She decided to drive five hours each way to visit me for just a few hours. "Hmm," I thought, "what does this mean?" It was a big effort from someone who'd shown little effort to see me in the past.

I had hit my weight-loss goal of weighing 165 pounds (75 kilos)—
which I'll get into in the next chapters—so I was feeling utterly healthy
and vibrant. You have a glow about you when you finish two weeks at
Mayrlife. I was 55 pounds (25 kilos) lighter than when she'd last seen
me in Melbourne. I was clearly different now.

She arrives looking absolutely stunning. I take her for a walk
around the gorgeous lake. Then we hang out in my chalet, eat strudel
(yes, I snuck in strudel from the local shack because I'm a naughty
girl), talk and laugh. I want to kiss her. She's driven five hours each
way to see me. But I'm technically still in a relationship with Jacob. So
here's me, the good girl, not doing anything. I can't do that to Jacob.
I'm not a cheater. As much as I want to, I morally can't. Absolutely
nothing physical happens. It's just a friendly hang, but later, as she's
got five hours to kill in the car, my confident texting fingers get me
back in the game:

"I wish I'd kissed you."

She writes, "Yeah, I mean, I could have made a move too, but I
didn't."

Why didn't she?

Neither one of us is making any moves. It's like a grade-seven
school dance. Soon after, I break it off with Jacob. I shoot a drama
film in the north of England called *The Almond and the Seahorse*,
co-starring with iconic French-British actress Charlotte Gainsbourg.
In the movie, both our partners have brain injuries, and we bond
through the shared trauma and end up having a small affair. There's a
scene where I have to kiss Charlotte. "Oh my God," I'm thinking. "I've
never kissed a woman before and now the first woman I will ever kiss
is Charlotte Gainsbourg." She's so cool, so French. Such a stunning
award-winning actress. Of course, I'm nervous to do the scene, but
I'm professional. Afterward I'm like, "Hmmmm . . . it wasn't that big
of a deal kissing a woman." It felt pretty much the same as kissing a
guy, except that a woman's skin is usually softer, so there's no risk of
pash rash. I feel like I was meant to do this small movie, if only for that

opportunity to kiss Charlotte and realize that kissing a woman is not THAT big of a deal. I wish I'd done it earlier in my life!

And then it's the US Open 2021, three years since the Tennis Player and I first met. I now look radically different. I weigh about 143 pounds (65 kilos). I look, I think, the best I've ever looked in my entire life. All those thirst traps I posted once I'd lost weight, probably annoying everyone on social media, they were usually trying to get her attention. I only cared about her likes. I fly to New York, but again, WE HAVE STILL NEVER EVEN KISSED.

"Don't you ever get lonely? I realize you don't want a relationship, but don't you want to, like . . . make out?"

I text this, clearly shooting my wad. I've already embarrassed my-self like forty times with this girl. What's one more time, hey?

She texts back that she'd be into it, and I'm shocked.

"I have a friend staying with me in my apartment. Otherwise, I'd invite you here, right now," I reply.

"Damn, that'd be hot," she writes.

"Let me get a hotel room for tomorrow night. Come meet me. Let's do it."

Again, my heart's pumping out of my chest. Why does this girl have this power over me? It's thrilling but torturous. Now we're meet-ing at a secret hotel room and no one will know where either of us is. No issues about others finding out. Totally confidential.

She knocks on the hotel door. I light a scented candle and put on some music. We like the same types of pop music. We sit on the couch together, but this time I'm not gonna chicken out. She's so gorgeous. Her eyes melt me. I touch her leg, like how guys flirt with me, and we talk in depth. We catch up on life.

But enough talking. After three whole years, I have to act.

"Can I kiss you?"

She gives me her sly kind of smile. And she says yes.

Now my whole mouth has gone pretty dry. Full nerves. The last time this happened was when I was singing at the Hollywood Bowl opposite Sara Bareilles in a live version of Disney's *The Little Mermaid*. Full pressure! But I kiss her. I kiss her A LOT. We take it to the bedroom and sleep together. It's amazingly sensual. I stare into her eyes. I just love being close to her. I love that she let her guard down. Just for this one night.

Of course, I think to myself, "Okay, well maybe now that we've slept together, things will be different." Surely, she has to feel things after that. Surely, I made her feel good. Surely, having sex now changes things. Aaaaand then . . . nothing. She texts that she can't meet up with me again. She has to focus on her tennis.

"Can I just come and see you for like thirty minutes?" No. The answer is a hard no.

When I got rejected from NIDA five years in a row, it was such a kick to the gut. But this was a different kind of awful rejection. This hurt my heart so much more. I guess you might be reading this and say, "Well, she told you, Rebel, that she didn't want a relationship and then you just kept hoping things would change!" Yep, guilty. I couldn't let go of her. I kept hanging in there—like a koala clinging every day to a eucalyptus tree.

We see each other at the US Open for like two minutes . . . because, lezbihonest, I knew she'd be training at a particular court, and I went there like a bit of a stalker. Her team walks past me with attitude—do they know? We talk for only two minutes. She treats me like a fan and sort of pats me on the shoulder as she leaves. She says something like, "I gotta go take a shower, but thanks for saying hi." My heart is crushed. It's like I've just lost a Grand Slam final. At least this is now some official closure of sorts. I lost seventy-seven pounds (thirty-five kilos), we slept together and it hasn't made a difference. She still doesn't want to be with me.

TWENTY-NINE

Letter to My Body, 2020

Letter to my body: January 1, 2020

<u>Weight</u>: 102 kilos (225 pounds)

<u>Relationship status</u>: Technically single but texting someone every day like a desperate maniac and thinking it's going to work out.

<u>Mental attitude</u>: Time for change. PLEASE. This year it's time to change for REALZ! Don't use the word REALZ, Rebel. I just mean I'm serious this time about changing.

Body,

We've come so far together and I'm so proud of you—you've helped to give me a distinctive career—you've helped make me relatable to so many people—you've protected me from people who'd want to just use me for my flesh & allowed people to like me for my personality.

I'm so grateful to you, body. We've gone all around the world together—we've played sports, danced, sung, done live theater, hiked, walked, run[*], had great sex, swum, slept, hoped, wished, dreamed, achieved together. But now it is time for me to say goodbye to parts of you—the parts that no longer serve me as I move into my next phase, Rebel 4.0. I am so grateful to you. You carried me this far—and I'm a fucking success.

But now the unwanted weight & fat storage, unwanted toxins, will go—please leave me—it's time. I thank you but I don't need you anymore. I love you. But it's time to say our goodbyes and release you.

Rebel xoxo

---

[*] "run"—who am I kidding? That's clearly an exaggeration—I hate running. I don't remember running more than five minutes at a time EVER in the past twenty years, so technically I should've written: "had light jogs that are slower than most people's walk." Also, even though I thought I'd had great sex, even better was to come! Okay, I'll stop criticizing my own dramatic letter now, just had to say that.

THIRTY

The Year of Health

In my very first week at Tara, part of the curriculum was to make all the girls participate in a "lifesaving" course. One of the challenges we had to complete was to jump into the deep end of the school pool, fully clothed. Shoes, socks, underwear, T-shirt, tracksuit and sweater. Then you had to tread water, keeping your head above the water for at least five minutes. It was meant to simulate a situation like being thrown overboard from a boat fully clothed.

When you first jump in the water, you get a slight air pocket in some of your clothes and for the first few seconds you're momentarily buoyant. "This is easy!" you think. "I can do this, no problem." But as your legs eggbeater around, the weight of your body starts to feel heavier and heavier—until you're using all your might just to keep your head above water.

Despite all the fun and acclaim I'd now had in my first thirty-nine years of life, despite learning to love myself more, I felt like this tween girl in the Tara pool moving my legs furiously under the surface whilst trying to remain calm above. Like a duck—from above they can look graceful as they float by, but the view underneath would reveal intense paddling. As a big girl, I didn't let anyone see my "work" under the surface . . . because that was at odds with the fun, vibrant personality I projected. Don't let them see you having an Epsom salt bath at night to

soak your tired feet and legs. Only let them see you strut on a red carpet with that smile on your face. Don't let them see you eating a lot of
ice cream at night followed by two hours in the gym the next morning
in an attempt to burn it off—only to repeat the same cycle that night.
I would always keep people at a distance.

It was more exhausting for me just to show up and work a long
day on a movie set than it was for an actor who was not overweight. If
you're in the swimming pool next to me wearing a regular swimsuit,
then you're going to be keeping your head above water with far less
energy than what I'm using fully clothed. But I was still holding on to
those extra layers even though I knew by now that my comfort-eating
was a form of self-harm. I was still doing it, pretty much every day.
Could I really change as I approached my fortieth birthday?

I did a body scan at Mayrlife and I was carrying, at minimum, fifty-
five pounds (twenty-five kilos) of excess body fat. I was challenging
myself every day to stay afloat whilst carrying that extra weight. And
not just for five or ten minutes like in that lifesaving exercise, but for
every minute of every day. Was the day going to come when my body
broke down and I sank to the bottom? Even though I hadn't been diagnosed with any serious illnesses, at some point, things were going to
give out. That's just logically what was going to happen. Genetically, I
was prone to developing diabetes and heart disease. I couldn't ignore
that. So, starting THIS January 1, 2020, this was going to be my YEAR
OF HEALTH.

"You're turning forty, Rebel! You have to get healthier."

I knew I wanted to freeze my eggs, and after meeting with the
fertility doctor, I knew I'd have a much better chance of getting quality eggs if I was healthier. So that was motivating factor number one.
Even though I wasn't in a relationship, I wanted to have a child so
badly, and this whole year was going to be in service of that. To get
my body in the healthiest shape possible so that those microscopic
eggs could be needled out in a small surgery, strong and genetically
normal. But also, being completely honest, meeting the Tennis

Player really motivated me as well. Because even though it was scary to feel such deep emotions, it was exhilarating. Even if the Tennis Player didn't want something with me, maybe I could find someone else who'd make me feel this way. A healthier version of myself would also probably be a hotter version of myself . . . so once she told me on that Elwood beach that she didn't want a relationship, after a bit of shameful binge eating, part of me was like, "No, wait! I'm going to go all Khloé Kardashian and get a revenge body!" (As you read, it didn't seem to make a difference in the end, but throughout 2020 I still had hope that she'd change her mind after I shed the excess weight.)

Could Fat Amy become Fit Amy?

It's January 1, 2020. Yes, come on. New year, new me. I'm on the beach. I got up early because I didn't really drink the night before—I wrote a letter to myself about being healthy. I've rented a beach house at Palm Beach in Sydney, and I brought some friends with me from America, including Carly, who is deathly afraid that she's going to be bitten by a killer spider. She made Jacob A., her now husband, tape cling wrap over every single air-conditioning vent on the property so that no spiders can get in.

Meanwhile, I'm out on the beach by myself. Looking out at the water, contemplating. After all those emotional chats with Dr. Sadeghi, after working on so many other things in my life—my shyness, my workaholism, my love life—now I'm gonna do it. I'm going to lose weight. There's a voice inside my head that says, "Yeah, right!! Haven't you said this every year since you were like sixteen? That's been one of your New Year's resolutions like twenty-three times!" I've literally defied all odds by becoming a successful actress—first in Australia, then in Hollywood. I've got two degrees from one of the best universities in the world. I've done incredible things in my life—and yet, I've never been able to successfully lose weight.

But now I'm turning forty. This is a big year for me. This is when you're supposedly at the top of the hill. It's all downhill after this, isn't it? So, yeah, I better do it this year. I decide to make my declaration public by putting it on Instagram. This way I'll have accountability. My eleven million followers will see it . . . which is a huge difference from just me writing in my private diary.

I hire a trainer whose superb Colombian ass looks like it's eating his shorts. I've had a number of trainers throughout the years, because I do generally enjoy working out. A lot of the trainers have almost been like father figures to me, like Tony and Gunnar in LA. I know I'm there to work out, but I end up telling them absolutely everything that's going on in my life during the one-hour sessions. I'll be doing leg presses whilst asking their advice about cars and home security. But this time I'm going to work out with the added advantage of having "worked out" emotionally why I was overeating. That part I really do think is the key to my being able to lose the excess pounds.

The waters have always been murky up until now, muddy like the ocean after a big storm. But now things, mentally, are clearing up. The waters are becoming still and I can almost see through to the sand beneath.

I don't plan to work as much in 2020 because I know that work usually causes stress, which will make my health goals more challenging. But there are still a few obligations on my calendar. I fly to London to present the director category at the British Academy of Film and Television Arts awards. Award shows are like the best but also the most stressful audition you could imagine—you go up onstage in front of everyone who's powerful in the industry that year, which can be an amazing calling card. As Snickers would say cheekily, "Don't fuck it up!" Still to this day, Snickers is usually the only person I run my jokes by to see what he thinks. He has a really good gauge of what a general audience will find funny.

I crush at the BAFTAs . . . the irony being that I'm so lovesick that week after being dumped by the Tennis Player. Sometimes, when you're feeling so shit, you are actually at your funniest. I try to remember that on movie sets if I'm having a bad day in my personal life. The turmoil can make you funnier.

Then I fly back to LA, as I get to attend the actual Oscars for the first time EVER! (I was lucky enough to be accepted as a member of the Academy two years earlier, after Anna Kendrick and John Lithgow both nominated me for inclusion.) My buddy James Corden, whom I co-starred with in *Cats*, asked me if I wanted to present with him, and I just adore him, so of course I said yes. Everyone in the world seems to be making fun of our movie, which was released a few months earlier, so, being the self-deprecating comedians that we are, we were like, "Why don't we hit the Oscars stage dressed as cats and make a joke about the film?" I actually quite like the film and think the artistry is incredible—Tom Hooper's an exceptional director—but you can't deny that people seemed to be weirded out by the cat special effects, in particular making jokes about whether our cats had buttholes.

So, I was to attend my first Oscars as a presenter, which was added motivation to keep on my healthy regimen. On a typical day, I made sure to get eight hours of sleep, then exercise for about two hours— one hour with a trainer focusing on strength and conditioning, and one hour doing my own cardio (which was usually walking). I wore a Fitbit to count how many calories I burned and used the app to track how many calories I was eating. My target deficit was about fifteen hundred a day. I tried to concentrate on eating protein with every meal (breakfast, lunch and dinner) and hydrating with water between meals. I needed a thirty-five-hundred-calorie deficit in order to lose a pound of body fat a week, which was my goal. Slow and steady. It's not rocket science. There was no magic pill or some exact diet program to follow—so please don't get suckered into the diet industry's fads. It was simply following common sense and making healthy changes to my lifestyle as a whole. I couldn't eliminate sugar, but I'd try to eat only small amounts and avoid it late at night. Then on the mental health side, I was doing my twelve minutes a day of Purge Emotional Writing and if I started to lose my way, lose my focus and fall back into a day of unhealthy eating, I'd look at a picture of myself from when I was young, like five years old. I'd look at that sweet little girl's face and think, "If I was her parent, would I feed her a dinner of ice cream and cookies? Nope. There's no way I'd do that to that innocent girl. I'd want to feed her healthy, nutritious meals." I was trying to re-parent myself to get healthier so that hopefully I could become an actual parent in real life.

Things were going well with the weight loss—it's always easiest at the start of the journey. I'd quite quickly lost almost twenty-two pounds (ten kilos) without doing anything too extreme, just sticking to the above. I'd done some crazy things at weight-loss camps before— like put a wheatgrass enema up my ass, gone into a hyperbaric oxygen chamber and, at the Biggest Loser Resort, doing eight hours of exercise a day. I'd even tried some machines that freeze or melt your fat, and a laser liposuction-type procedure on my upper arms and thighs, which I think didn't work at all, only damaged my skin. So I wasn't going to do anything extreme as part of my Year of Health. It was going to be gradual.

And then, ten green juices later, I was suddenly at the Oscars. It was like my malaria hallucination was coming true. Though I wasn't a nominee, I was in a movie nominated for Best Picture, *Jojo Rabbit*, which was close enough!

I didn't have a romantic date to take, so I asked Carly to come with me at the last minute because she's someone who can easily pull a dress together and was used to going to the Oscars when she worked at *Entertainment Tonight*. The Oscars red carpet really is something else. Hundreds of photographers and all sorts of TV crews are shooting your dress and makeup and hair from every angle possible. With women, it really is all about how you look. You are judged. There are millions of people watching this on TV at home. On the telecast I got positive comments for how good I was looking in my champagne-colored custom Jason Wu gown. It was nice motivation to keep going. Positive reinforcement. It was the public start of people taking notice of my weight loss—and boy, do they love to comment about it. You normally get paid to wear jewelry to these kinds of events, via your stylist, so I was sponsored by the Italian jewelry company Pomellato and wore one of their amazing necklaces. I felt like a queen as I swanned down the red carpet surrounded by every superstar on the planet. It's surreal. Like there's so much to look at you almost can't take it in.

We get ushered into the Dolby Theatre and take our seats in the second row. I get to watch the opening number and first few awards before I am taken backstage for my transformation into a cat. I have about thirty minutes to go from fabulous to feline. We practiced this change the night before.

Brad Pitt has just won his Oscar for *Once Upon a Time in Hollywood*. And so I'm walking backstage as he's exiting. There's Brad looking drop-dead gorgeous, clutching his gleaming golden Oscar. I know I only have thirty minutes to change, but I have to go up to him. I congratulate him and then, like the massive fangirl that I am, ask to take a photo. "Yeah, sure," he says in his deep raspy voice. I clutch him like I'm holding an Oscar. Would it be too much to touch his ass? Yeah, probably.

Then Timothée Chalamet comes up and says, "Hi, Rebel! Thanks so much for letting me have a shower in your house." Long story. But a few months earlier, my sister had let him into the office house to shower before he had to jump on a flight out of LAX. But just the way he approached me and said that so casually made me look gangster AF.

There's me—the girl from the bush, the former snaggletooth-wielding shy girl whom no one would've picked to become an actress, posing next to Brad Pitt and Timothée Chalamet. I really am on the top of the hill.

I shamelessly flirt with Brad, ending my interaction with, "Okay, Bradski. Now I've got to get dressed up as a cat." Then he smiles and says, "Well, let me walk you to your dressing room." And at this point, I'm a little more than wet in my Spanx.

I think he isn't quite ready to go off to the media room, where the winners are sent. He needs a moment. And he is now going to spend that moment escorting ME! He grabs my arm and links it around his, because I walk like a teetering moose in heels, and it's the most gentlemanly thing I've ever experienced. I never felt like I really truly belonged in Hollywood. But wow, right now I feel like I am exactly where I should be. And it feels incredible.

Brad drops me off at my dressing room door like a Southern gentleman helping a woman out of a carriage, and my stylist, Elizabeth Stewart, and glam team just stare at us with their mouths open. They weren't expecting me to be arm in arm with the biggest movie star in the world. "I'll see you later," I say to Brad as he heads back to the media room. Oh, he's just amazing!

And then it's all hands on deck to help turn me into a ginger cat. Cat suit. Tick. Full face of cat makeup. Tick. James and I emerge from our separate dressing rooms fully cat-ified. We wait backstage for our cat-egory to present. Is this the right approach to take, to make fun of *Cats*? No backing out now, 'cause we're here and we're covered in fur. We're told off by security for having fun and touching the Oscars backstage. James gets up in this guy's face and has some strong words with him. Which is extra hilarious because we are dressed as cats.

Then we walk out onto the stage and try to do a little comedy bit. We do our best and are a bit silly, but the Oscars crowd is notoriously hard to play to. Everybody's hungry at this point after being seated for hours. And some people in the crowd aren't feeling well. Apparently, there's a bad virus going around.

After the bit, I go back to the dressing room and have another thirty minutes to get changed back into my glamorous champagne dress. Then I'm seated in the audience right before the Best Picture announcement. Could *Jojo Rabbit* cause an upset? No. A movie called *Parasite* wins. It's an exquisite film too and deserves it. Everyone gets to their feet and applauds director Bong Joon Ho and producer Miky Lee. We are then ushered out the exits behind Leonardo DiCaprio and his hot model date. Joaquin Phoenix comes up to me, after also just winning for *The Joker*, and says he loves my work. I'm shocked he even knows who I am and am honored he would say that.

Carly and I hit up the *Vanity Fair* party. At one point Brad comes over, touches my arm suggestively and says goodbye. Comedian Chelsea Handler quips, "How long have you been fucking Brad Pitt?" The smile on my face is so massive at the thought that anyone would ever suggest I would have anything going with Brad Pitt. I eat an In-N-Out burger, which is tradition at *VF*, and then we hit the after-after-party at the home of Guy Oseary, a talent manager whose clients include Madonna. This party is even more exclusive and photos are prohibited. Adele is bitchy when Carly and I walk up to say hello but everyone seems to be in great spirits, dancing and drinking. I seek out some cupcakes in Guy's kitchen. That's my poison. Literally everybody who's anybody is packed into this one house partying. We get a free Gucci clutch as a parting gift.

It's around three a.m. and I go home alone. I struggle taking off the expensive necklace and dress by myself. I have a bath with Epsom salts. I'm lying in the bath after such an amazing, eventful night. I think to myself, "I've made it. I really have made it." And then the thoughts creep in. "Maybe I should just stay the fat Rebel Wilson that everyone knows and loves." Now that the Oscars are over, can I keep up this healthy regime? What if I have to shoot a movie? It'll be impossible to keep up this discipline. My agent Tabatha's comments about losing weight still play heavily in my mind. What if my weight loss costs me my career? I've lost enough for people to notice a change, but not enough to change the way I look. If I lose a full fifty-five pounds (twenty-five kilos), which is the tangible goal I set myself for the year, will I lose everything? Will I not be funny anymore? Will people not like me? Is being fat a crucial part of what makes me successful?

I'm wobbling in my willpower, like I'm in the highest of high heels.

I'm going to Disneyland for my actual fortieth birthday on March 2, because Disney CEO Bob Iger granted me the extreme privilege of sleeping over inside Disneyland in a special two-bedroom residence that sits above the Pirates of the Caribbean ride. Walt Disney designed it for himself and his wife, Lillian, but it was only built after his death. It used to be called the Disney Dream Suite but lately it has been called the Residence. In true Disney style, there are buttons that you can press in each room and something magical happens. In the Adventureland bedroom, when you press the button, a train comes out near the ceiling and goes all around the room, complete with sound effects. In the main bedroom, the lights dim and holographic mermaids are projected onto the painting above the bed. In the main bathroom, lights start to twinkle above the bathtub and one configuration creates the rarest of hidden Mickeys.

I'm allowed to invite twelve friends for dinner (in the dining room that has a magic mirror where Tinkerbell sometimes appears), only four of whom can sleep over. We eat a ten-course degustation-style menu especially crafted for my birthday. I get carried away and eat way too much. It's lavish. I feel full, but I keep eating anyway. Holy crap, I'm turning forty. I'm so old!! This is kinda a big deal.

After midnight, Carly, Jacob A., Marissa and I get four mobility scooters and cruise around the empty park. It's weird to be the only people there. We shoot videos of ourselves in matching Disney tracksuits doing formations down Main Street on the scooters. It's so much fun, such a spectacular way to spend a birthday. I'm like a kid again.

I wake up early because the excitement is pulsating through me— and there's a stack of Mickey Mouse pancakes and waffles that the chef has prepared. I keep indulging like I did the night before, unable to stop eating the sweet treats. "It's my birthday!" I keep thinking. "I'm allowed to get off my regimen for a bit."

Then, three pancakes in, I start to feel this sharp pain in my chest. It's like the universe tapping on my left side just under my boob. Am I actually having a heart attack? Should I go to a hospital? No, it must just be really bad indigestion because of the huge amount of food I've consumed in the past twenty-four hours. Surely? And I have to fly to London. My speech at the BAFTAs garnered a lot of positive attention, so my UK agents set up some meetings for several projects. Plus, Mum is there, as she's now a top international dog show judge and gets flown around the world all the time.

I fight through the pain and fly straight to London. I arrive at the

Corinthia Hotel to a plethora of sweets and cake in my penthouse room. Mum and I have lunch together before she flies back to Australia, and she gives me presents from the family that she's carefully carried all this way in her hand luggage. Sometimes my family doesn't know what to give me, because I have so many things now, so they gift me small things with koalas or kangaroos on them. Things that are very Australiana. I think they hope that I will miss Australia so much that I'll eventually return there to live. I know my mum thinks that.

The stabbing pains subside a bit but then I start to feel sick. Then all of a sudden, the hotel starts to shut down—first one floor, then another the next day. Everyone's talking on the news about something called the coronavirus. I cancel the rest of my meetings and fly back to LA. Everybody seems to be panicked, going to the grocery store to stock up on supplies. Is the whole world about to shut down?

I go to the grocery store by myself, and some annoying woman is harassing me for a selfie. "Don't come near me," I say. "I'm sick." Instead, she calls the paparazzi. I try to get a COVID test but no one has them quite yet, so I'm not sure if I'm just run-down or if I do in fact have an early case of COVID. Apart from the grocery store mission, I isolate in my Hollywood home. I watch the news reports about this rampant virus that started in China and apparently could kill people. Australia announces that they're going to be shutting their borders in a few days. I don't want to be stuck in some global pandemic half a world away from my family, so now that I've recovered, I fly back to Sydney right before the borders close. I isolate in my place there for two weeks, spending most days on the couch watching the news. New York looks to be in terrible shape. There are so many deaths. People, particularly those who are unhealthy and overweight, are dying of this virus. I've never seen anything like it. People are all shuttered inside their homes. The entertainment industry completely shuts down and now it seems like the whole world has just stopped. The world is in a health crisis. "I should concentrate on my health," I think. "I'll just finish this one last pint of ice cream on the couch."

The stabbing pain returns with full force and I have emergency surgery to remove my gallbladder—turns out I had a ton of gallstones, and considering my family history of this affliction, the doctors thought that the best option for me was to remove my gallbladder completely. Once I recover from that, I know I have to get back to my disciplined heath plan. But the gyms are closed.

My trainer devises a series of outdoor workouts. Since there are no tourists around, one of them is to run up and down the stairs of the Sydney Opera House. One day we go to a zoo, closed to the public because of COVID restrictions, and I do squats whilst holding a wombat as my weight. It's like the apocalypse. COVID is a huge world tragedy. So many people are losing their lives, and so many are losing their jobs or their income. All the people seem to have just disappeared. People aren't going anywhere; no one is rushing about. The pollution in the air diminishes because of very limited car travel. I watch as Sydney Harbour becomes clearer and clearer near my house without the huge cruise ships entering the ports. The environment is flourishing because of this human stoppage. I can see so many fish in the harbor.

I get outside and go on walks. As absolutely nothing is happening work-wise, I can cook my own healthy meals at home. My favorite is tacos with ground beef. I make healthy protein shakes in the morning with berries and almond milk. I go to bed early, because there really is nothing else to do apart from watching *Tiger King* on Netflix.

I work on developing some projects, like an exciting new Australian musical that came out of my scholarship program at ATYP, called *The Deb*. It's about a teen girl who goes to her debutante ball in a small country town. I feel like it could be a really good film, uplifting. I drink more water—two to three liters a day. I go out for yet another walk and marvel at how the environment really is thriving without all this human activity. But the lack of human interaction is also isolating.

My sisters, Liberty and Anna, decide that they also want to get in on this Year of Health. My discipline has inspired them. So we all meet up at the oval and encourage and support each other. The three of us, in leggings, walk in circles as the sun sets on another day of the global pandemic. I feel lucky to be in Australia at this time. Lucky to be close to my family. I feel protected.

After a few months, I start itching to get back to Los Angeles. People know more about COVID-19 now and things aren't as scary as they were in the first few months. Despite my wobble in March, I've now lost another eleven pounds (five kilos) and am starting to feel really good in my body. Really confident, actually. Like buy-myself-a-bikini confident.

I fly back to LA, and this is when I rekindle things with Jacob Busch. I'm really yearning for connection. It's so nice to date Jacob, to hold somebody.

It's getting toward the end of the year, and I've kept up my healthy lifestyle about 95 percent of the time. Yes, there was the odd Caramello Koala or scoop of Ben & Jerry's . . . but it wasn't the whole pint like before. It was two slices of pizza if I really felt like it, rather than the whole pie. I'm noticing, though, that my body isn't getting the results I initially had in terms of weight loss. I've hit the "plateau." I go a few weeks doing the same things I've been doing, but now the scale isn't budging. I still have a few kilos to lose to hit my goal, so I decide to go back to Mayrlife, the luxury health retreat in Austria. The daily cryotherapy and massages and the stricter diet help me hit my goal in just two weeks. That was the extra push I needed. I step on the scales in Dr. Schubert's office, and for the first time in almost twenty years, it says 165 pounds (75 kilos)! I've done it! In eleven months, I achieved my goal.

I do a photo shoot in the snow on the nearby mountain (ironically called Loser Mountain) to celebrate. I guess you can't really see the full extent of my weight loss because it's so cold that I have to wear many layers, but just looking at my face, you can tell that I am glowing. That I am the healthiest I've ever been in my adult life.

I'm on top of the mountain. Literally and metaphorically. Dressed in traditional Austrian gear like an extra in *The Sound of Music*.

"Yeah," I say to myself. "I have lost all that weight. It's gone. It's gone for good. And now that I've made so many lifestyle changes, now that I've kept it off for months and months, I don't think it's ever going to come back on." What I thought would be impossible was possible. I had jumped over a huge personal hurdle.

I return to LA triumphant. I post a hot picture on Instagram showing some cleave, and a top studio executive calls me back, after I've been waiting for months for his call. You never know who you might catch in a thirst trap. And then I notice just a ton of positive reinforcement coming my way. It feels like everyone I've ever known is commenting on my weight-loss success. Everyone wants to know my "secrets." Out of all the things I've achieved in my life, losing weight seems to garner the most attention. Men start holding doors open for me. Employees in the grocery store offer to carry my bags to the car for me. Wow. Is this what hot women have experienced all along? Even though I was visible as an actress, I was often invisible in my daily life if I was dressed down and out of context. Now it's like everyone sees me . . . or at least, doesn't ignore me. All this attention makes me want to lose more weight. I feel so great about myself, mainly because everyone in my life is saying, "Wow, you must feel so great!"

I feel freer. I'm the healthiest I've ever been in my adult life, both physically and mentally.

I've slowly taken off the three layers of wet clothes surrounding my body over the course of the year. Layer one: the excess weight that I was carrying on my frame. Layer two: All the emotional baggage I was holding on to. Things about my father, all those mini traumas that stick to you like burrs do when you're walking through the bush. And layer three: the protective barrier I built over the years—the one that truly prevented me from letting anyone in. All these layers had their purpose. In a Marie Kondo kind of way, I thank the layers for their years of service. I gracefully retire them. They served their purpose. They're like friends whom I've just outgrown now.

I still wonder whether I'm going to be as good an actress, as good a comedienne, as before. I have a great glossy cheerleading comedy called *Senior Year* that I'll shoot the following year, so I guess I'll see how people respond to that movie. (Eighty-nine million unique Netflix accounts watch it within the first ten days of release. It's a global hit! I think I'm fine.) But for now, even though I'm getting so much positive attention for losing weight and becoming healthier, I still wonder, am I going to be less interesting? Before, I was a multilayered trifle cake like my auntie Sandra would create . . . and now that I've lost the layers, am I unique enough? Now that I'm not plus-size anymore (I'm not skinny either, mind you; I'm in this middle area), do I have to feed from the main trough that all the actresses are eating out of?

But for now, I've passed the ultimate lifesaving test. I'm not getting some small certificate like in high school; I'm now at less of a risk of diabetes and heart disease, the two-pronged death fork that took my father. For the few haters out there trying to troll me, saying things like "Ah, now that she's not big, she's not relatable anymore," or "Now she's not funny anymore," or various permutations of "She's changed and how dare she change and we hate her now," I guess I say: I can't hear your voices 'cause they're muffled under the water while my head remains above it all. I haven't abandoned my fan base. I haven't been hypocritical. I still think beauty is in every shape and size. I still love the bigger version of me. I've changed and I'm now a healthier person. Who am I hurting? No one. I'm saving my own life.

THIRTY-ONE

Rebel 4.0

Now it's time to make a baby!

I choose a different, female fertility doctor who's beyond caring with her patients, and with my new healthy body, I do three rounds of egg harvesting to try to have as many eggs "in the bank" as possible. My kitchen counter looks like a medical facility with all my instructions and medications laid out methodically. Each round takes about a month—the hormone shots in the stomach for two weeks, the outpatient surgery under anesthesia to retrieve the eggs, and then the recovery. Your body bloats up with the stimulation and then has to shrink down. I'm encouraged to do acupuncture, go only on light walks for exercise and eat certain foods, like salmon and avocado. After the shots, each night as I lie alone in my big California king bed, I try to manifest healthy eggs whilst holding this silver crystal that my lovely doctor has given me for "good vibes." She's so caring and seems just as invested in helping me become a mother as I am. "Come on, little eggs, come out strong and healthy." I put it out in the universe, like that time when I was kid wishing to win the Easter egg raffle. But this time it's real eggs I'm praying for.

I guess like dating, fertility can be a numbers game. After three rounds, I have eighteen eggs in the bank. "Okay, eighteen sounds like a really good number, yeah?" I haven't found a serious partner, so after

I talk with my doctor and fertility lawyer, I decide to purchase some sperm to fertilize the eggs and create embryos. When you're younger it's great to freeze your eggs. But what I was soon to discover is that unfertilized eggs really could mean nothing. A healthy embryo has a 70 percent chance of creating a baby . . . but any egg by itself is a wild card. Now it was time to see what my carefully collected eggs were capable of.

How do you find a sperm donor? I first thought it would be hilarious to put out a tweet. "Heyyyy, any hot NBA or NFL players out there wanna be my sperm donor?" I was seconds away from hitting SEND on that tweet before my friends talked me out of it.

Instead, I hired a "sperm concierge." I gave her a shopping list of what I was looking for—I actually had slightly different lists: one that I hoped would create female embryos and the other for males. Since I'd lost weight and had been eating less sugar, the main "addiction transfer" I had noticed was online shopping. My housekeeper could not believe how many Victoria's Secret bras I would buy. If I put all the padded push-up bras in a pile, I could probably jump off my roof onto them and be totally fine. (I think this stems back to when I was a teenager and only got one bra a year.) So anyway, I could write out a shopping list of traits and pursue the sperm donor profiles like I was on Net-a-Porter looking at the new resort collection. Intelligence. Tick. Athletic and/or creative skills. Tick. And then I would read the profiles for some other X factor that I'd emotionally connect with. One said in his audio recording that his favorite films were Disney ones. Tick. One seemed like he was very caring. You see their whole family medical history, and also, potential donors' genetics were screened with my genetics to make sure that there were no recessive genes on each side that could combine to create a baby with any known diseases or disorders. I saw pictures of the donors, usually baby pictures but occasionally adult photos of the men as well. For some, you can listen to audio recordings of the men talking about themselves. I liked one who sounded like an American Chris Hemsworth.

I could've asked a friend to donate sperm—but legally that can create a lot of potential land mines down the track, so I was advised not to do it. Anonymous sperm donation was the cleanest way to go . . . and it turns out that sperm is not really that expensive when you think about it. On average about $3,000 USD a vial. I buy multiple vials from two different sperm donors and store them with my eggs in the bank (the freezing facility that works with my fertility clinic . . . it's like your super-cold baby-storage rental unit).

And now it's time to make embryos. "Out of eighteen eggs, I should get some embryos, right? That's eighteen chances. That seems good, doesn't it?"

My doctor calls me from the lab on day one. Sadly only nine of the eighteen survived the thaw. Half of my eggs, so preciously collected, are now gone. The news hits me in the gut. But there are still nine that can be fertilized. There's still hope. Two days later the news is, "Five seem to have been fertilized." The others are discarded. Then two days later, "Only three are growing, but they've got to grow to one hundred cells within a week to be viable for freezing." And then I wait. I've had a massive week—I've just kissed Charlotte Gainsbourg at work. I'm up in the frigid North of England finishing filming *The Almond and the Seahorse.* Then I get the phone call that gives me even more of a chill:

"I'm so sorry, Rebel, none of the eggs seem to be growing properly. The cells don't appear strong enough. We can keep them over the weekend, just in case a miracle happens, but I'm so, so sorry to tell you this. I'm just so sorry."

I'm in my hotel room with thick socks on, in a tracksuit, and I have the heat blasting, but I'm just eternally cold.

So out of eighteen eggs, I'm now left with: nothing?! I have easily spent over $100,000 USD and no result, no embryos, no options. I feel like I've failed in an epic way. My cells just aren't good enough? I don't know what's happened. The sperm I chose just wasn't a good mix? Apparently sometimes that can happen. Or am I just unlucky? Apparently at my age, which I wish I'd known earlier, statistically you'd need eighteen eggs to create one healthy embryo. I've fallen below the average and I hate that. I've failed.

I question whether this is God's will, whether this whole thing is just unnatural. Does the universe not want me to have a baby? Or just not in this modern way? I feel such sadness. I'm so alone and so sad that I don't know what to do. I share a post on Instagram expressing my sorrow. It helps to share how sad I am with millions of people. They reply with positive messages of encouragement. At first, I felt ashamed of my failure, but sharing it publicly helped me feel less alone.

Then a week later I get another call from my doctor: "Ummm, I don't know how to say this . . . and we can't quite believe this has happened, so we wanted to test it before we called you—but one of those three embryos did keep growing over the weekend, and even though it was slow to grow, we tested it and it did test as genetically normal. Soooo, congratulations, you have a male embryo!"

I think I almost dropped my phone in the toilet! How does this happen? One of the embryos essentially came back to life in the lab and now I have one embryo that's genetically normal! Wow!! I really can't believe it. Now I have one option. The doctor advises me that the smart thing to do would be to harvest more eggs, which we'll try to immediately fertilize rather than just freezing unfertilized eggs. I go through another cycle but sadly none of those are successful. I only have the one miraculous male embryo.

Because of COVID restrictions, I delayed my big fortieth-birthday bash until September 2021. So finally, almost a year and a half later, my family and friends can now gather at my destination celebration. This is the biggest personal event in my life—because who knows whether I'll ever have a wedding or a baby shower? So this is me going all out for my fortieth.

We all head to what will be called Rebel Island but is really Marlon Brando's private island near Bora Bora—an incredible eco-friendly luxury resort. I've rented the whole island exclusively and invited about fifty people. (Yes, Kim Kardashian also did this for her fortieth birthday, but I was technically the first to book the entire island for a week . . . I just delayed my party longer due to COVID, so mine took place after hers. I did use the same party planners and they'd learned from their mistakes at Kim's party, so I feel like Rebel Island was wayyyy better. No offense, Kim.)

Yeah, it cost a small fortune. But this island is one of the most beautiful places on the planet. Other than that Sweet Sixteen that went awry, I'd never had a big birthday celebration. On my twenty-first I just went with a few relatives to a matinee magic show at the casino (told you I was a dork). On my actual thirtieth, I went to a café with the one Australian friend I knew in LA at the time, Jason Gann from *The Wedge*. I hadn't ever truly celebrated myself, my journey, my rise.

Now that I had the means, I was just going to celebrate myself. I was going to put the thought and love into a party for me. Why the hell not?

I invited a guy I had met on Raya earlier in the year so that I'd have a date. We stayed in separate villas because we were only casually dating, but it was really fucking fantastic to have some wild sexy time with him on the island . . . in between doing all the fun things with my nearest and dearest.

The week was planned with half chill time (the spa was sick!) and half fun activities that all meant something to me. We had beach picnics with all my favorite foods and swam in the lagoons. We had a movie night on the beach and played the original *Willy Wonka and the Chocolate Factory* film (one of my favorite movies as a kid). We had an eighties-themed pool party where the whole group surprised me with a dance flash mob. And we had a mixed-doubles tennis tournament called Rebeldon with rotating partners. For my "official" birthday party night, friends gave speeches, and Mum and Liberty spoke on behalf of the family. I then spoke and got super emotional in front of everyone. It was overwhelming, looking out at all the people from every part of my life. Dione Bell, representing my childhood friends the Bell family. Zahra, from my tight-knit high school group. Snickers and Lorelei, fellow youth ambassadors. The *Pitch* girls Anna Kendrick, Brittany Snow, Chrissie Fit and Shelley Regner, who are just THE BEST. Bellas 4 life. Nicole Leal and my awesome American friends from the past decade.

Matthew Hussey gave me some love advice on the island about the Tennis Player: "Rebel, you did the right thing. You just did it to the wrong person." That made me feel better. It made me feel like love was still a possibility. I just had to find the ONE. But on that island, I was surrounded by the most LOVE I could ever imagine from friends and family, and it brought me to tears on several occasions. It was so positively overwhelming that I could barely sleep all week.

I might've been a late bloomer in many respects, but I HAD bloomed. I was and am so grateful to every single person who's been a part of my journey.

I finished the Rebel Island week with . . . wait for it . . . a mermaid-themed party on the final night. Everyone hilariously dressed as a mermaid or merman. I wore a crown of seashells on my head. This party was symbolic of my finding my inner siren. At forty-one, I'd finally found her. And she was swimming beautifully free in the ocean. There were so many times when I didn't think I was worth celebrating, when I'd tell myself horrible things and put myself down. But those thoughts were now minimal. Everything might not have been perfect, but I was so happy, so—in Oprah's words—"living my best life!" Everyone has an inner siren that sometimes just needs to be shown the light. (And, dear reader, I hope that if you haven't already, you find yours.)

My shell crown gets too heavy and so I take it off. I take off my high-heeled wedges too, and dance barefoot in the sand with everyone. Feeling myself. Feeling the fresh air on my skin. Feeling healthy. Feeling absolutely radiant.

The next month I do yet another round of egg harvesting. This fifth cycle creates one perfect female embryo. So now I have two in the bank. And soon, I'll finally find the love of my life.

THIRTY-TWO

My Disney Princess

I'm in LA, sitting in my G-wagon on the side of the road on a street just behind the famous Chateau Marmont. Ramona's in the passenger seat, looking stylish as always in a blue and beige silk pajama ensemble, which, if I wore it, would look like I was actually wearing pajamas! Her blond hair is tied back into a neat ponytail. I don't know how she always looks so put together, she just has that skill . . . along with speaking five languages, which is so European of her. We're a few minutes early for a dinner party with friends, so I quickly check my emails. I guess I'm like most people nowadays, addicted to my phone like a slot machine junkie, hoping for a new unread message. Most emails are something cool—a film offer, an invitation, an interior design plan for my new London apartment.

But now, something alarming is in my inbox. It's an email from my publicist, Marcy Engelman, who is awesome and stays on top of everything publicity-wise. She only has two celebrity clients, Julia Roberts and me, which makes me feel quite special. It's very late in New York, where Marcy lives, so something might be wrong. "We need to talk," she writes. Then she forwards an email from a journalist with the *Sydney Morning Herald*, who says that they're intending to publish details of my same-sex relationship with Ramona and would I like to comment. "My deadline is Friday, 1 pm Sydney time," he writes. That's less than forty-eight hours away. It's worded carefully, but in my view it's a threat. I recognize the name of the journalist: Andrew Hornery. Why? Because he's written things about me in the past. He's clearly not a fan. And now he's trying to out me publicly. Who would do that in 2022? I don't know. I'm clearly pro-LGBTQ+, and HE'S apparently gay. How is this happening? I turn to Ramona. "Ummmm, babe, I'm going to have to call Marcy. This is a situation." I speak with Marcy through the car sound system, and the moment Ramona figures out that we're about to be outed, I see panic start to rise through her body. How do you say in five languages "Oh fuck!"?

Six months earlier, in November 2021, I was introduced to Ramona via text by our mutual friend Hugh Sheridan—the most talented triple threat you'll ever meet—an Australian cross between Ryan Gosling and Hugh Jackman. I'd just been in New York with Hugh, and on the way back from seeing *Hamilton* (yet again), we talked about how it never quite seemed to work out with me and these "dudes." I was convinced that my date from Rebel Island was a player—and another guy I was keen on still lived with his parents. "Why don't you just date a woman?" Hugh quipped as we were in the back of a taxicab headed to my Tribeca apartment. "Naaaaaah," I said. "I don't even know any women to date."

Hugh knew about my entanglement with the Tennis Player. I guess I was open to dating women after that encounter, but the experience had also been a bit gut-wrenching—so much expectation that just led nowhere. And I thought that maybe the connection with the Tennis Player could've been just a one-off.

"Let me connect you with my friend Ramona," Hugh said. "She's got a law degree like you and she's gorgeous. I think you two might really hit it off." We then got back to critiquing the cast of *Hamilton* and trying to think of what musical we should perform in together. Later that night, I told Hugh that I was worried that I'd never find deep, meaningful love. The type of love artists write passionate songs or poems about. Real love. I was forty-one and it just hadn't happened. I was almost resigned to the fact that my career would be my love . . . and I was making plans to hire a surrogate to have a baby by myself.

Turns out Ramona had had similar deep and meaningful chats with Hugh when they'd hung out together in LA. A month passed before Hugh remembered to connect us. I was in Fiji filming a tourism campaign on the remote, gorgeous Vomo Island. There I was, in a distressed gold dress, bobbing around on a small boat, lost in the ocean. (Ironically the campaign was called "Open for Happiness," which was exactly my state of mind.) And Hugh sent the text introduction, which went something like: "Rebel, meet Ramona, Ramona, meet Rebel. You're both gorgeous and talented and smart and I feel like you two would get along. Okay, I'll leave it to you two to get on with it from here."

Ramona and I exchanged messages as I finished my day of saying "Bula" (a greeting that means "life" and "good health" in stunning Fiji) one hundred times. I changed and walked down to the beach on the other side of the island for one last photo shoot in a glamorous red gown. As I was walking, our texts progressed from typed messages to voice texts. I heard Ramona's voice for the first time. "OMG," I thought when I listened to her message, "she sounds so sexy." Can you be attracted to someone's voice? I think I was. I crushed the photo shoot thinking about who this mysterious girl on the other side was (fun fact: the cover photo of this book was taken at this shoot). I saw a picture of her. "Geeeeeeeeeeez," I thought. "She looks stunning." Like an old-school movie star like Kim Novak.

After the campaign in Fiji, I had to fly to Australia to get my US Permanent Resident Card (green card). So Ramona and I started Face-Timing and talking on the phone—just really getting to know each other the old-fashioned way. I know it sounds cliché, but I started feeling things that I'd never felt before. I would sit in front of my fireplace in Sydney looking over the harbor and would chat with Ramona for hours on the phone. It was so romantic . . . and quickly progressed to also being incredibly cheeky.

I asked about her first-ever sexual experience with a woman. I wanted to know everything. She'd only been in relationships with men but had had what she called "affairs" with women. It was intriguing. There was the sensible part of me that didn't want to have full-on conversations with someone I'd never met, but I was compelled to talk to her. She was so open and I wanted to tell her everything about me. I just felt like I could be completely honest with her right from the get-go. She sent me a giant bouquet of lip-shaped helium balloons. My sister came over. "What's that?" she said. "Oh, nothing." I pushed the balloons into the corner trying to hide them, which was impossible because they kept bouncing back into the room, and then I covered up the Amazon box that had just been delivered—a book called *Girl Sex 101*.

I was supposed to stay in Australia through the holidays, awaiting my permanent residency from America. But there was about a week before my interview at the US embassy and I thought, "This connection seems so special and so strong." So, in true Hollywood rom-com style, I jumped on a plane to fly halfway around the world to LA to meet Ramona face-to-her-gorgeous-face. I couldn't endure another situation with months of flirting on the phone that didn't lead anywhere. I had to see for myself NOW if this was real.

Ramona sets up our first date for a few hours after I land: lunch at the Hotel Bel-Air. I quickly shower when I make it home, trying to scrub off the jet lag. My friend Nicole gives me a quick blowout and then I drive to the hotel. I'm so nervous. "Oh my God, what if I meet this girl and there's no attraction in real life? What if she's not attracted to ME in real life? I mean, she's pretty hot. I've now seen a swimsuit photo of her in a red one-piece. *Baywatch* style! I may not be on her level."

I'm also worried that if Ramona and I do hit it off, like we did on the phone, I don't have much sexual experience with a woman. And I've only had time to read half of the *Girl Sex 101* book. My heart is pumping so hard, but I try to breathe from deep in my stomach. I rock up to the Hotel Bel-Air, trying to look cool. I've actually never even been there before. There are swans in the little lake as I walk over the small bridge to get to the hotel. Swans! So romantic. Ramona is already at the restaurant. The German side of her means she's always punctual. She's organized a private table tucked in the back away from everybody's line of sight.

The hostess points me toward the table. I walk up and there she is—sitting, looking nervous but oh so very cute and cozy in her oversized cardigan and cool ripped jeans. I walk up to her with the biggest smile on my face. "Hi, I'm Rebel." And she's like, "Hi, I'm Ramona." We're both just smiling at each other. I'm jet-lagged AF, but I don't care. The adrenaline of the situation is lifting me.

Ramona asks me to hold her hand because she's so nervous, and I do. We both order food and we try to eat, but we can't really eat anything. And so . . . well . . . I don't want to embarrass Ramona, but . . . I have to be honest . . . we instead opt to go to the bathroom and make out. Intensely. It's so hot. We joked on the phone that our sexual tension was so strong that we would sneak into the hotel bathroom and have our first kiss. And that is EXACTLY what happens. It's ON. It's so sexy.

"I think you need to come back to my house," I say. I've never just invited someone straight back home, but I'm only in LA for the week and I just want to get to know her.

I show Ramona into my Hollywood Hills home. I start to give her an MTV *Cribs*–type tour, but at the second stop, my home cinema, Ramona's top is suddenly off. We make out and I take her to my bedroom. We just . . . connect. Yes, I'm nervous, but it doesn't feel weird. It just feels beautiful.

That night we meet at the Sunset Tower for dinner. Hugh comes with us, arriving in a full black-tie suit with bow tie, looking every inch a crooner Cupid. He's brought each of us a little Tiffany heart charm, which is the cutest thing ever. He's so excited for both of us.

What follows is a whirlwind week of romantic bliss with Ramona, including hot dates all over LA. Then I pull out my dating trump card—a VIP visit to Disneyland! Turns out Ramona also LOVES Disney!! Wow—yet another thing we have in common. We walk around Disneyland holding hands. We're both too scared to go on the *Guardians of the Galaxy* ride. Instead, we just hold each other and look into each other's eyes whilst our friends go on the ride. I start feeling cold as the sun sets, and she offers me her cardigan. She insists I wear it. This is real. I know this is real. She's so thoughtful. I purchase a churro which we share and this seems to make everything even more perfect.

I return to Australia at the end of a magical week . . . and find myself getting rubella shots and touching my toes in front of a doctor in my underwear as part of a weird physical you must have to qualify for a green card. I hope that everything can be done in a week and I can get back to LA, back to Ramona. It ends up taking seven excruciating weeks over the holidays to get my passport returned because of COVID backlog. During that time, Ramona and I speak every day. I can't wait to see her. And once I do, we jump straight into a serious relationship. We're both just . . . ready. And so into each other.

Valentine's Day comes around. I'm now almost forty-two and have never had a real valentine. A couple of times I bought myself flowers and chocolates. But that day, February 14, always made me feel acutely aware that I didn't have a romantic partner.

Ramona drives over and tells me that I MUST lock myself away in the cinema room. She's being mysterious, but I do what I'm told. You don't need to tell me twice to go into a room and watch Bravo! I can vaguely hear noises and can tell that she's making several trips to the car. What's going on? I won't spoil the surprise. It now feels like hours.

"Babe, can I come out now?"

"Not yet, a few more minutes."

When I'm finally allowed out, I see that Ramona has decorated the whole house. There are candles and rose petals everywhere! And giant white teddy bears. Because I've never had a Valentine's Day with a partner, she wanted to give me all the cliché things I missed out on with one epic celebration. She's printed out a "menu of activities." Eating chocolate-covered strawberries together, taking a bubble bath . . . and then more sexy things that I'll keep private (wink, wink). She gives me a Tiffany bracelet with two hearts—symbolizing her heart and mine. It's the most romantic thing anyone has ever done for me.

I've been wanting to say it, but now is the right time:

"I love you."

She says it back. It's official. We are in love.

I take Ramona as my date to the *Vanity Fair* Oscars party. We hold hands in front of all of Hollywood. It is a big deal in a way, but it's also not. I feel like I have nothing to hide—except the pain from wearing a forty-pound metallic dress that night. I look around the party and see the young stars of HBO's teen drama series *Euphoria*, and similar shows, and they couldn't be more fluid or comfortable just being themselves. It seems that with Young Hollywood, most of them don't define themselves as "straight." They're all somewhere on the spectrum and it's not a big deal. Gone are those days where journalists would "out" celebrities. It just isn't done now. No journalist from the *VF* press line writes anything. Perhaps this memo hasn't crossed the desk of this sad Australian journalist? Or he just doesn't care. This guy doesn't know our family situation. Also, I know that in Latvia, where Ramona was born, there have been serious crimes against LGBTQ+ people. In my opinion, he could've put us in real danger.

Now this guy is forcing us to make our relationship public before we're ready. We've been slowly doing things on our own timeline. I told my sisters when they came out for the Super Bowl (go Rams!)—they were both amazingly supportive, but it took courage for me to have that conversation. It's a process. I told all my close friends, but some people, including a few family members, still don't know.

I hold Ramona's soft hand as we both stare out the front windshield. What are we going to do?

Earlier this month I took Ramona to my last appearance on the final season of *Ellen*. Over the past decade, every time I appeared on *Ellen*—almost like clockwork—a girl from my high school would email me to tell me that she was a lesbian. It started to get funny. After each episode aired, bang, the next day, there was an email in my inbox from yet another girl from Tara coming out. I don't know why this was. Maybe because Ellen was such a gay icon, or they saw me laughing with her so they figured I must be cool with gays. I loved their emails, though— so warm and honest. I respected it and was so happy for them. Some didn't tell me until after it became public that I was dating Ramona . . . it was like it gave them permission to tell me that they were also not 100 percent straight.

During my final appearance on *Ellen*, it was my turn to start spreading my love-life news. As we went to commercial break, I pointed into the crowd at Ramona and told Ellen, "That's my girlfriend." I think Ellen knew what I was saying—but sometimes when I'd introduce Ramona that way, people would just think I was referring to my friend who is a girl. I felt proud telling Ellen. Like it was a full-circle moment. Ramona was sitting in the front row smiling and waving. She loves Ellen. I hugged Ramona tenderly in the crowd after my appearance. A woman in the row behind said to Ramona, "You must be so proud of your daughter!" Ramona was horrified, as I'm actually a few years older—but I thought it was hilarious. The woman assumed we must have been close but never suspected that we were girlfriends. Was it all the jokes I'd made in my career about ogling male celebrities? Was it because we both had long blond hair? Or because we didn't really look stereotypically lesbian?

I remember very clearly when Ellen came out in the nineties, and for a time it had disastrous consequences for her career. I think she once told me that she didn't work for two years after coming out. Things like that stick with you. This was probably part of the reason I was too scared to explore my sexuality before . . . along with so many other things. Growing up in a Christian environment was obviously a biggie. It was only a few years earlier that Australia had passed the Marriage Act with the help of some amazing people, like my friend the beloved Australian actress Magda Szubanski.

I'd seen plays like *Angels in America* and *The Inheritance* and movies like *Boys Don't Cry, Portrait of a Lady on Fire* and *Ammonite.* While these are brilliant, masterful pieces of art, so moving, the message for me was clear: hey, it can be brutal being gay. I guess I didn't want my life to be harder than it had to be. And I was attracted to men. So, I just went with that. But now, in 2022, things were very different. There were so many positive examples of people who didn't identify as straight. There has been so much progress—almost as if it's "boring" now to be straight. Unlike my coffin fall in *Fiddler on the Roof,* the timing seemed good now to bust out of confinement. I knew I wasn't going to get seriously hurt, and I now knew I was ready to explore other sides of my sexuality.

Now, I know what some of you readers might be thinking: "Lezbi-honest, Rebel! Maybe you waited so long to lose your virginity because you were just hiding the fact that you were gay all along!" But I have to tell you, my intimacy issues were far more about my emotional issues and hang-ups about my weight rather than sexuality. My handful of relationships with men were very genuine. And still, today, I don't think of myself as "gay." I don't really want to define myself. I know that can be confusing to some people because I am a woman in a relationship with another woman. I just believe that sexuality is much more nuanced and complicated than what society makes it out to be. I think your attractions can also change like the tides. I think you shouldn't have to label your sexuality, and even now, I still don't wish to label mine. Labels are for packages, not sexuality. (Which is why my friends and I created a free dating app in 2023 called Fluid where you don't have to define yourself or your sexuality. You can just click on whomever you are attracted to.)

Before I met Ramona, she had been on the hunt for a Turkish husband. (Fun fact about Ramona: She LOVES all things Turkish. Just leave her in a room with plenty of lahmacun and she'll be ecstatic!) She wasn't looking to have a serious relationship with a woman, she doesn't consider herself technically gay either, but then I came along, and it just worked. Love is love.

A few months into our relationship I need to bring up something super serious over dinner. I pause *Entertainment Tonight* on the TV, because Leo's latest young girlfriend does not matter at this point. "Um, babe, I have to tell you something."

"Okayyyyy . . . ," Ramona says hesitantly, not knowing what is about to come out of my mouth.

"I'm going to have a baby."

Pause. "You are?"

"Yeah. Well, my surrogate just got pregnant with my baby and it looks to be sticking."

I haven't told anyone about this. The miraculous male embryo was implanted in a surrogate, but sadly, at seven weeks, there was a miscarriage. That little soul looked to be defying all odds, but then it wasn't strong enough. I'd gotten so excited when the implantation worked that I'd told family and a few friends—only to have to tell them a few weeks later it hadn't panned out. Telling people is often worse than being told the news yourself. It's a repetition of the sadness, and it hurts more and more.

My darling sister Anna bought me a candle to light in remembrance. I put it on my outdoor table and would light it every day whilst I sat and sent prayers out. After the first day, a tiny hummingbird started to fly above the table. It would come down to eye level with me as I'd sit on my outdoor couch. It came so close I thought at first it wasn't real. It wasn't scared. It came almost face-to-face with me . . . this tiny little thing, telling me with its sweet little flutter that it was all right. (Every day since then I've seen it in my backyard, and Ramona created a special feeder that attracts multiple hummingbirds.)

This time, my second and last embryo, the female one, was implanted into a different surrogate, and I haven't told anybody. I've been praying that this embryo will continue to grow into a baby. It has the classic 70 percent chance that a genetically normal embryo has, but I've had so many ups and downs on my fertility journey that I'm almost expecting the worst. This time, I don't want to have to repeatedly share the bad news if something happens. But I feel like I have to tell Ramona. Our relationship is developing so quickly that I can't keep this secret from her. This is something I planned by myself, so I tell her that if this is not what she wants, she should just run from me now.

But it's like she doesn't even blink. She doesn't waver.

"Well, I'll love your child as much as I love you," she says emotionally.

I hug her. She so genuinely means it. And whenever we hug it's like my anxieties instantly disappear. I don't know why this is, it's just Ramona's superpower over me.

But now we're both anxious as this Australian journalist threatens to rob us of our personal narrative. We knew at some point this would happen because so many people know. Again, we aren't hiding it. But we don't want it to become public right at this second. We have been slowly talking to people at our own pace, and it feels good. It's led to good conversations. But it's confronting.

I only just told my own dear mum a few weeks earlier. I really didn't know how my mother would react even though I knew she had a lot of gay friends in the dog-showing world. Two places where you're guaranteed to find gay people: dog shows and theaters. But I truly didn't know. No one else in my family had ever been openly gay, so this was new territory. (After my announcement, one of my cousins came out as being in a same-sex relationship.) I was very nervous to tell Mum. I tried to tell her in person when I was in Australia for the opening of the Rebel Theatre in Sydney. I tried to tell her when we were both in my plunge pool, but then my ninety-five-year-old grandfather had a car accident and Mum had to run off to help him (PS: Ninety-five-year-olds really shouldn't be driving). I tried to tell her the next day on a walk to the nail salon and then three paparazzi were chasing us. There really wasn't a right time—a perfect moment.

But I had to tell her—she's my mother. I wanted her to know. It's just that for some reason, my chat with her was the hardest. Like opening a stubborn jam jar that just won't open. There was no easy twist. The only other time we'd talked about the "sexuality" subject was when she was at the oven pulling out the fish fingers when I was nineteen. "You're not gay, are you?" "No," I'd answered at record speed. End of conversation. Fish fingers and potato gems were then eaten in awkward silence.

Mum was coming to Los Angeles to visit me and she was going to clearly see that I was in a relationship with Ramona. I didn't want to blindside her when she arrived jet-lagged, so I ended up telling her over the phone two days before she was about to fly to LA. I thought then she'd have some time to digest it and that hopefully she'd be willing to meet Ramona in person when she arrived. (Again, I wasn't exactly sure how the chat would go.)

Mum was sitting in her car on the side of the road when I called her. My heart was racing as I sat on my couch in Los Angeles. It was now or never. I had to tell her because NOT telling her was causing me so much anxiety. Ramona had told her mother, who lives in Latvia, and that didn't go over well. Her mother responded with, "Are you trying to kill me?"

"I have something I need to tell you, Mum."

"What? What's happened?!" she said kind of accusatorially. I love how my mum always assumes I've done something wrong when I try to talk to her seriously . . . and by that, I mean I HATE when she does that. "Oh, hang on. Anna's walking by. Anna! Hi, Anna!" (My family lives within walking distance of each other in Sydney.)

"Oh good. Okay, yeah," I said. "Get Anna in the car so she can hear this too."

Anna got in the car. She already knew, so I was thinking she could be helpful in this situation if things started to go awry. Anna also has a very calming energy. Even though she's the youngest, she's like the rock.

"Mum, you know my friend Ramona, who you heard on the phone that day?"

"Yes."

"Well, she's not just my friend," I said. "We're dating."

"So Ramona's a woman?"

"Yes."

"So you're dating a woman?"

"Yes."

Pause. Silence. It was only a five-second pause, but it felt like an eternity. Here I was, forty-two years old, coming out to my mother. Was the rainbow flag going to fly or be shoved back onto the highest shelf in the cupboard with her old wedding photo album? What was she going to say??

"Well, that's great, darling. You know I love you no matter what."

Oh my God!!! What a relief. After all the buildup, Mum was totally fine.

She was more upset about the fact that my sisters knew before she did than the fact that I was dating a woman. "Well, why didn't you tell me FIRST!?" she blurted out.

"I don't know. I wanted to wait until it was something really serious before telling you."

"I love you, darling," Mum said to me.

"I love you too, Mum."

"Now, what color do you think I should paint the side fence? I'll text you some photos."

Mum met Ramona soon after landing in LA and we went for dinner at Sunset Tower. Ramona was a bit nervous. She was vaping more than usual. My mum was acting a bit funny too; even though she was clearly cool with it, this was the first time she was meeting Ramona and I guess she didn't quite know how to react. She'd seen me around only three male love interests before, so it's not like she was used to meeting one of my lovers—and now it was a woman.

Ramona was ready, once she'd had a glass of rosé, to answer any of Mum's hard-hitting questions. She said to Mum kindly, "Look, Sue, if there's any questions you want to ask me, please, I want you to know you can ask me anything."

Mum leaned in and said: "Yes . . . Is that your natural hair color?!"

Oh my God, Mum, you are so embarrassing! That was the first question she asked. I guess she wasn't quite prepared to talk about heavy stuff—and it would've been more embarrassing if she'd said something like, "Soooo, what's scissoring?"

Mum, a.k.a. Mumarazzi, then got in trouble for taking pictures in the restaurant, which was "against their policy." But Mum waited with her innocent face 'til the maître d' was out of sight and then continued to take photos of me and Ramona. She takes photos of her family as if it's our last day on earth, and half of these photos end up on her Facebook page, where the larger dog show community can see them. It's annoying at times, but then it's also sweet . . . and the fact that she was taking photos of Ramona was a very positive sign.

That weekend, we all went up to Santa Barbara to watch Prince Harry and Nacho Figueras play polo (and yes, I know how bougie that sentence sounds). As we arrived at the polo field, almost immediately we saw Prince Harry with Nacho. Prince Harry gave Mum a huge hug and took a photo with her and all of us. Without knowing it, he really did me a solid. Mum was in such a great mood after that! She started to relax . . . but first she IMMEDIATELY posted her photo with Harry on Facebook for her five thousand dog-showing friends!

That night at dinner, Mum and Ramona started having deep chats. They started to bond, and it was brilliant to see, particularly because Ramona's mother had not been at all supportive and was currently denying that I existed. Mum could see that Ramona was a genuine, lovely person. They exchanged phone numbers. Mumarazzi took heaps more photos of us and AirDropped them to both of us.

When we got back to Los Angeles, Ramona offered to drive Mum back to my office house. I was so happy that Mum and Ramona were getting on so well that I forgot to warn her that my sweet kindergarten-teacher, dog-showing mother has another side to her. We in the family call it "the CIA agent." She will extract the information she needs out of her captive expertly, using her clever disguise as a sweet older Australian woman.

As Ramona was driving Mum down the hill to my second house, Mum craftily turned down the radio so it was barely audible.

"So," she said, "when did you and Rebel first meet?" I guess she was trying to ascertain the exact timeline, because I had told Mum we'd only been dating for a few months when in fact, at this point, it was actually over six months. Ramona easily gave up the full information, including dates. She got me on this!

"And so, when was your first experience with a woman?" Mum asked. Ramona told me she started blushing, but she didn't know what to do—so she told my mum everything. Just like how she'd told me on the phone on our first cheeky chat.

Ramona had been fully cross-examined, but she'd obviously passed the test.

Before she left LA, Mum wanted Ramona to know that even if her own family was not accepting, she had a new Australian family who were ready to welcome her with loving arms. (And PS: Now Mum texts Ramona probably as much as, if not more than, she texts me!) I felt bad for ever doubting my mum's reaction to the news that I was in a same-sex relationship. I felt like I'd unfairly underestimated her. The truth is she was a total champion. So accepting and so loving.

And most important, Mum was able to hear the news from me first. This wasn't some snarky journalist's news to tell. This was ours to share.

Ramona and I are now hashing it out with Marcy over the phone. Her voice is coming through the car's speakers. We're supposed to be going to this dinner party. Melanie Griffith is inside, for God's sake. High-priced Indian takeout is awaiting us. What are we going to do?

"Yeah, this asshole's going to publish a story," Marcy says.

Who knows what he's going to write?

"Well, let's just announce it ourselves on social media," I say.

I'm sure Ramona is feeling huge anxiety at this point . . . because she's vaping like that's the only way she can get air. Her own father doesn't know, and she doesn't want to call him, so she's resigned to the fact that he is now going to find out via the press. (Which he did, and he has not spoken to her since.) Yet Ramona and I decide to post a picture of us together on Instagram with a nice comment confirming that, yes, we are in a relationship. I am proud of Ramona for wanting to take this huge step knowing that culturally she's in danger of being rejected.

I call my family to tell them that the news is coming out publicly. And my mum, like a brave soldier, says, "Right, well, I have to get over straightaway to your grandparents' to tell them." She immediately drives an hour to my grandparents' house so they won't find out about it on the news. My grandma Gar is ninety-two, but one of her caretakers taught her how to use an iPhone, so she gets Google alerts on me every day. Mum also calls my brother, so he knows too. I haven't had the chance to talk to him yet, although I'm sure he'll be cool with it. He's a vegan—aren't they cool with shit like that? Everyone is being so amazing, but I just wish I'd had the time to tell them myself. My grandparents Gar and Poppy think it's brilliant news. I imagine them waving their walkers in solidarity, they're that positive about it.

Ramona and I are like, "Geez, what photo are we going to put up?" We have tons of cute photos together . . . partly thanks to Mumarazzi. We select a photo from one of our first dates at the Polo Lounge in Beverly Hills, the second night we met in person. We both look so happy.

My caption on Instagram is: "I thought I was searching for a Disney Prince. But maybe what I really needed all this time was a Disney Princess? #loveislove"

Ramona is my Disney princess. She's beautiful. She's heroic. She's smart. She's kind.

At around eight a.m. on Friday, June 10, 2022, I hit send. The post receives almost two million likes and, according to Instagram, over fifteen million impressions.

Then imagine everyone you've ever met plus pesky journalists contacting you over a few days, via every form of communication possible. That's what happened to Ramona. It's a tsunami of interest. While a lot of the comments were positive, there were also negative ones, and that's hard for someone who's not in the public eye and isn't used to it. I'm used to people writing mean things about me and it still stings. I was so impressed with how Ramona handled all the attention that week. We declined all interviews and instead just left town and went to Europe.

The *Sydney Morning Herald* journalist, Andrew Hornery, subsequently got a lot of backlash for trying to out me. I think he was pissed that I had hijacked his "exclusive story" and wrote about it, which only shone a light on his own grubby behavior. It's mind-boggling that he didn't think this would backfire on him. He deserves the karma . . . but I don't hold anything against him. To me, this is a story of Ramona and me falling in love and then subsequently making that love visible. And that's such a hugely positive story.

Ramona and I went to see the touring version of the stage musical *The Prom* and a fourteen-year-old girl came up to us at the interval. "I just want to say, you two are my inspiration." She was almost crying and was shaking a bit when she spoke to us. In this moment all the negative comments and repercussions melted away. All we'd done is be ourselves. It's hard to grasp how that can be so meaningful to other people, but it can.

Even though I still don't know whether being in a same-sex relationship will affect my career in any way (it shouldn't), and I still don't know whether I will face any huge homophobia or discrimination (I hope that I don't), I'm so proud of my relationship with Ramona. She's such an amazing partner.

It's the truly intimate connection we have that is so special. The way every night in bed the soles of our feet touch tenderly before we go to sleep. Ramona sticks her foot out to feel that I'm next to her. We say "I love you" and fall peacefully asleep.

Valentine's Day 2023 was coming up, and seeing as Ramona had gone all out the year before, I was taking it upon myself to make this one very special. We had planned a VIP day at Disneyland for just the two of us, and a little voice inside me started piping up with, "That'd be a great day to propose! She won't see it coming!" I was going to wait until the summer to do it—when we'd be on some beach in Europe somewhere—but my heart was saying to do it now. I messaged Disney CEO Bob Iger and asked if it was possible to do a cool proposal in the park. He instantly said yes and connected me with the right people at the park, who sprang into action.

I always thought I'd be the one getting proposed to—but now I'm the one making the proposal. I call Tiffany and they arrange for me to come into their Rodeo Drive store, where they have a special VIP section on the top floor. They bring me eight rings to choose from that they'd like to generously gift to us. I don't know much about jewelry but Ramona is a skilled master jeweler, so I'm feeling the pressure like a little lump of coal. I FaceTime Ramona's bestie whilst I'm at Tiffany to get her advice. "Yes, she likes classic shapes! I like the round one," Natalia says. They all look beautiful; it's so hard to choose. When the saleswoman leaves to get me some macaroons, I look closely at all the carat sizes on the price tags, and the bogan in me, considering this is free, chooses the one with the biggest stone. It's a round diamond in a signature Tiffany setting. It's stunning. Tiffany makes me a special "R & R" box for it, which they'll deliver to the office house a few days later. Ramona has no idea all this is happening and calls me whilst I'm in Tiffany, wondering where I am and when I'm coming home.

At Disneyland, a special area outside the castle will be cordoned off for half an hour—from five to five thirty p.m. The team will place topiary trees around the area so that even though we'll be in the middle of Disneyland on a hugely busy day in the park, no one will be able to see in. I've organized a photographer and videographer, flowers and a violin player. All I have to do is get Ramona to the spot at five p.m.

I try to keep calm as Ramona and I go on some of our favorite rides in California Adventure Park: Soarin', the *Cars* ride. We stop in at the Club 33 members' club 1901 and I wire myself with a microphone in the bathroom. The whole time Ramona has no idea what's about to happen. But I do. And suddenly I'm so nervous. I'm not worried she'll say no. I'm just nervous something won't go right. I want this to be so special for my princess.

Our VIP guide Barbra knows a special surprise is coming but doesn't exactly know what. I tell Ramona a ruse that we've got to go over to Disneyland to try the new Mickey and Minnie ride. Instead of walking through the castle, I pull her slightly to the left into our special area. Ramona sees the pastel rose petals all over the ground and the roses in vases. She hears the violinist playing "Can You Feel the Love Tonight" from *The Lion King*. I pull out the turquoise Tiffany box and a speech I wrote—I was worried I'd get too choked up in the moment, so I wrote down my thoughts the day before. But this whole thing is moving so fast, and I have so many emotions, it's a blur. It takes Ramona all of about three seconds to realize that this is a proposal, and she instantly starts crying with happiness. I hug her—she's being so adorable right now—and I start my speech. Like a true performer, I have to get my lines out. I tell her how special she is to me. How I never thought real, deep, meaningful love would come to me and then I suddenly found it in her. I tell her all the things I love about her—but I think I forget to add that she's the world's best karaoke singer and should've represented Latvia in Eurovision as a teenager (which she almost did)—and then I get down on one knee and open the ring box. I end with "So in this cliché way, on this cliché day, Ramona Agruma, will you marry me?"

Ramona gets down on her knees and joins me. "Yes," she says through the tears streaming down her face.

After lots of hugs and kisses and loving photos, we do end up going on the new Mickey & Minnie's Runaway Railway ride. I end up collapsing on the ground in the "pre-ride" area where they show the video. I've had so many emotions pumping through my body for days that once I know it's gone well, I just collapse. I'm now an engaged woman. It feels fucking amazing to know that someone (quoting Savage Garden here) "truly, madly, deeply" loves me too.

I hope Ramona will be my Disney princess forever! And we'll sing romantic duets together like Aladdin and Jasmine whilst having a "magic carpet ride." Wait . . . too cheeky?

THIRTY-THREE

Roycie

Despite the emotional roller coaster of the fertility treatments, something inside me said, "Keep going! Keep trying!" My last viable embryo in the bank, the female one, was implanted into a surrogate in Los Angeles. Technically I could've carried the baby myself, but because of my age (I was now almost forty-two) and my PCOS, my doctor told me that I'd have a much better chance of a successful pregnancy with a younger surrogate. So that's what I did. I only had this one chance now, so I wanted the best odds possible.

I found it quite easy contracting a surrogate. There were plenty of lovely women who wanted to do it, and again, in LA it's now quite common. In true celebrity style, I had a "surrogate concierge" who managed all the surrogate's appointments and visited her at home to check on her. My surrogate already had four children of her own and found the labor process relatively easy, so she thought being a surrogate was a good way to earn money for her family whilst she stayed at home with her kids.

My surrogate concierge didn't recommend direct contact with the surrogate until the pregnancy was through the first trimester. I think this is because there is always a chance of miscarriage during the first three months, so they don't encourage early contact. But once the first trimester was done, we would meet once a month at the surrogate's medical appointments. It's strange meeting the kind woman who is carrying your baby for the first time, because on the one hand, this is something that is deeply personal, but on the other, it's a business transaction.

The surrogate seems a bit shy when I first meet her at the gynecologist's office but very conscientious and loving. I can tell that she's a great mum to her children. Each time we meet I bring her gifts—a handbag, an iPad for her kids. I can't help myself. She's giving me the greatest gift of all, so I feel silly bringing her these things—but it's my way of trying to show my gratitude. (After the birth I do give her and her family a VIP weekend at Disneyland, which they LOVE!)

At the six-month mark, I receive the horrifying news that the baby has stopped growing. Everything else seemed fine up until this point. Ramona is planning a baby shower and everybody in my close circle knows at this point. And now—a sudden complication. "Why isn't the baby growing?" I ask. Is something wrong? My doctor explains that it could be because of poor blood flow to the placenta, but they're not really sure. And then a few days later my gynecologist calls—her voice has an alarming tone, like a smoke detector going off in your bedroom at three in the morning. "She's tested positive for alcohol!" the gynecologist says.

"What?! What do you mean?"

"This is it! This is why the baby's not growing. She's drinking! This is a criminal offense. She's still here in the clinic—hang on, I'm going to go and interrogate her and I'll call you back."

Every part of me wants to scream. "No, no, no. This can NOT be happening." My only stipulation when I was hiring surrogates was that they didn't drink, smoke or do drugs. For obvious reasons. And isn't she regularly tested for these substances? How could this happen? I absolutely freak out.

The gynecologist speaks to the surrogate, who swears she didn't drink any alcohol. I call my fertility lawyer asking for advice, and I send my doctor and the surrogate concierge to be with the surrogate (after the baby's normal growth stopped, we got her an apartment near Cedars-Sinai hospital in Beverly Hills in case of an emergency). The surrogate swears she would never do anything to harm the unborn baby. I'm in New York for work and just stressing out of my mind. Fetal alcohol syndrome can do terrible things to a baby. I blame myself for being away, for not carrying my own child. "Why is this happening!?"

There's an agonizing day waiting. A day of absolute despair. I don't know what to believe. And then we find out that the lab equipment has malfunctioned, and the test results were wrong. The surrogate was never positive for alcohol. She was telling the truth the whole time.

Phew. It's a massive relief, but now I feel terrible that this poor woman has been interrogated. She was in the right the entire time but for a day had been treated like a criminal. I go from almost having to order an emergency C-section to save my baby to suddenly everything being fine again.

We still don't know why my precious baby girl stopped growing for a month, but after some steroid shots she grew to over five pounds, which is what the doctors were hoping for before birth. This meant that even though she'd be on the small side, she wouldn't need to be in intensive care when she was born.

The cool thing about a surrogate birth is that you can choose the day and time of the birth. Ramona looks up star charts to try to work out what birthday would be the best. We decide on 11/2/22 midmorning.

Ramona and I drive in my G-wagon to Cedars hospital around midnight. We pull into the VIP parking lot, where we've been told to park (they have a lot of surrogate births at this hospital, so they have the system down pat), but the G-wagon is too tall for the parking structure and I hear the height bar scrape across the top of my car on entry. Whoops. Too late to turn back now. I'm about to have a baby. It feels surreal. This has been years in the making. I have wanted this so badly. But I feel a little disconnected from it all because the baby hasn't been growing inside me. It's exciting but it's scary. I'm glad Ramona is here to hold my hand.

We get our own room, down the hall from the surrogate. I visit her after she's been induced into labor. She's calm and feels good. Her husband is with her for support. They're good people, that's crystal clear. She's crafted a present for the baby's room using some of the first ultrasound photos. Her mother has stitched the baby a pink and white blanket. I am beyond moved by these gifts.

I go back to my room and wait with Ramona. Neither of us can sleep.

It wasn't planned for Ramona to be in the room for the actual birth, but when it gets close to go-time the surrogate feels comfortable having her there as well and wants her to join. So, after ten hours of anxious waiting, Ramona and I race down the hallway together into the surrogate's room and my gynecologist is called. Then, in only a few minutes, out she pops—like she's hurtling out of a fun waterslide—weighing just under six pounds. Welcome to the world, Royce Lillian Elizabeth Wilson.

I cut the umbilical cord, and then, as she's being weighed and measured, she grabs one of my fingers with her tiny left hand and one of Ramona's fingers with her tiny right hand. She opens her eyes, and she looks at us. We're a family now.

All I care about is that she's healthy. And she is. And despite the next forty-eight hours of no sleep, I'm so thrilled and excited. It has taken a lot to bring little Roycie into the world—over three years of trying, five egg-harvesting cycles—but now she's here, and she is absolutely perfect. I can't stop staring at her and checking constantly to see if she's breathing.

The next day we drive her home up Laurel Canyon and onto Mulholland Drive. I'm going slowly because now it's not just me in the car. Now I'm carrying the most precious cargo with me: my love and my baby girl. There's no radio playing . . . there's just the quiet sound of . . . love.

We get to our home in the Hollywood Hills, wiping off our shoes on the welcoming doormat. The hummingbirds are at the feeder outside. Bunnies and squirrels are on the grass. I blow a kiss toward the

Hollywood sign. Roycie's room (my former office) has the best view of the sign. She's so tiny, like a little spider monkey, and so gorgeous. I want to be an amazing mother to her. I have no idea how. But I just know I'm going to try my best.

All of this was worth it. The weight loss, the fertility struggles.

I've chucked a lot of personal baggage out the window throughout my journey. I've lost the excess pounds. I've lost the idea that I'm unlovable. I've quieted a lot of that inner voice that tells me I'm not good enough. (Although it's still been rather active during the process of writing this book, let me tell you! Digging up my entire life's memories hasn't been easy, reader! Like a Method actor, I've had to relive these often yucky, ewwww-y emotions in order to write them down . . . I was on my friend Lisa's yacht—bougie, I know!—hiding away from everyone, writing the chapter about my dad's death late at night, tears streaming down my face. Lisa walks into the room and sees me. "Is everything okay?" she says kindly. "Yeah, I'm just writing my book," I say softly. My laptop is surrounded by a mound of wet tissues. She leaves me alone. I get up from the desk that night only to get a "free" water from the mini fridge.)

We take Roycie up the stairs to her nursery. We used plush wallpaper that's reminiscent of the Beverly Hills Hotel color palette—there are pink animals among green foliage. Are the custom crib, matching custom poufs and $25,000 lamps too expensive for a baby's room? Ramona definitely thinks so. But I wanted everything to be right for Roycie. I've hardly slept. My skin is definitely a little less plump. My hair is definitely feral. But I've somehow managed to strengthen myself. Now, as I look into the eyes of my daughter, have I finally "made it"?

I'm forty-two years old and I have a baby. I'm a mother. It's a bloody miracle.

I instantly have a new respect for my mother. How the hell did she have four children on top of everything else she had to deal with? I have a new respect for all the mothers out there. This next chapter isn't going to be easy. Even though James Corden recommended the world's best baby nanny, Patty—a six-foot-three Trinidadian version of Mary Poppins.

Ramona unpacks a small green suitcase that's full of Roycie's new-born possessions. Little hand mittens so she doesn't scratch her face, diapers, some premature onesies, a spare blanket and socks. It re-minds me of the one suitcase I had when I arrived in America. Roycie has arrived in America with one suitcase too. Hers is just baby-size.

I don't quite know how to feed her. I just know that I'm definitely not going to introduce her to sugar too early. For now, it'll just be the best-quality baby formula. I'm going to try not to pass on my emotional eating to her in future years. I hope I pass on my strong work ethic, though. I hope she gets some of my academic talents. I hope I pass on my confidence—the sense of self-belief I must have had to start a risky career in a foreign country by myself at age thirty. The confidence I had to go to Africa as an eighteen-year-old and then follow my crazy malaria-induced dream. The confidence to constantly defy expecta-tions and to follow my heart and find love. I hope she's brave like me. Ambitious like me. Unique like . . . herself.

What's that old saying—"The cream always rises to the top"? And at the top of the hill right now, with my new family, I feel like the fullest-fat cream that there is.

Acknowledgments

Hi, reader, you've gotten to the end. Yay!! And thank you!! If this were a comedy movie there'd now be fun blooper credits—but I won't show you the bloopers of writing this book, because it's basically just been me in free airplane pajamas sitting at a laptop with no makeup and feral hair, getting certain things grammatically wrong. Occasionally whilst writing, I'd stop to eat (favorite writing snacks have included Cadbury chocolate, KitKats, jelly snakes, chips and Coca-Cola—both full-strength and Diet—and yes I've naturally gained some pounds back!), to go for a walk or watch reality TV on the couch (*Survivor*, *Real Housewives*, *The Block*, to name a few). Whilst writing some chapters, I'd have to stop because I was crying too much remembering certain things. Other times I've just laughed to myself, and anyone observing me would think I'm completely mental. But luckily no one was watching, because I have to write in complete solitude and silence.

Thank you to Ramona for hugging me after I would come home mentally drained. You are my WDPF. Your hugs are like comfy Ugg boots for my whole body. You're just an exceptional partner and have been so supportive . . . except for when you said constantly not to mention the bit about Adele, like you're afraid you're going to get barred from her concerts or something? I don't think that'll happen, babe. Although, to anyone I've name-dropped in this book, please know that I've done it purely to sell copies of the book by adding some celebrity spice (just joking)—I don't mean to tarnish any of your reputations—I actually feel lucky that I've met you all in real life and had interactions

with you, either good or bad. Brad Pitt—feel free to contact me any-
time about anything.

Thank you to my darling Roycie, who cracks the biggest smiles
whenever she sees me, which helps ease the guilt I have about taking
so much time away to write this. I promise to make it up to you, my
baby. You are so gorgeous and perfect and I love you forever. I can't
wait to see what your life journey holds. With each generation of our
family, it seems to get better for women. Gar was a "rebel" back in her
day, being one of the rare women to own her own business. Mum had
four kids and still managed to help thousands of others as a teacher,
including hundreds of refugees who needed special help with English.
And I could choose whatever career I wanted. I had a baby my own
way and now I get to make often really positive content to put into
the world that's empowering for women. My latest is a feature film
I'm also directing called *The Deb* about a "fugly" girl trying to go to
her debutante ball in a small country town. The message of the film is
that you don't have to be "pretty" to succeed in life, you just have to be
"pretty strong." I am so proud of all the women in my life, in my family,
who are "pretty strong."

Thank you to Snickers, my dear friend who was the only person I
let read this manuscript outside of those from S&S actually working
on it. Nic, over the years, you've always given me the BEST advice,
whether it's about a joke I'm preparing to say in front of royals or a
matter of the heart. I can always rely on your opinion. You are an amazing friend. And truly, you are the ONLY person who back in the day
thought I could be successful as an actress. It was so scary, emailing
you the full manuscript, knowing my most secret thoughts were contained within, but I knew I could trust you and I love that you were
Reader Number One. Here's to us former Youth Ambassadors going
out into the world and absolutely crushing it!

This book has been a bit of a bitch to write. Some weeks A LOT
of a bitch. In the beginning I was pretending to be all "lofty novelist"
and it sounded weird, so thank you to my editor, Mindy Marqués, for

all your support, encouragement and wisdom throughout the writing process and helping me find my "memoir" voice. I'd like to thank my literary agents, Erin Malone and Matilda Forbes Watson at WME, for getting me a great deal and allowing me to buy a newer model G-wagon (joking). Seriously though, you gave me an opportunity to tell my story, my way, and I am very grateful for that—especially in a time period that was marred by COVID restrictions and industry strikes. At first I thought I was too young to write a memoir, because I feel like now that I'm in my forties, I'm only just hitting my prime as an artist and a performer, but I am really glad I've done this now.

I'd also like to thank my fabulous publicist, Marcy Engelman, who no doubt is right now trying to make this book a bestseller! Thank you for your constant support, Marcy, you're amazing! And to all my family and friends, who have put up with me retreating for sometimes weeks on end to get drafts of this book completed. Sorry I've been a bit MIA this past year. I look forward to being on the beach or sitting at a café with you sometime soon, catching up. My relationships with you all are what I hold most dear. See you soon!

And finally, I have to give a shout-out to Mum, who is very worried about what I've written in this book and has told me so every single week since I told her about it. She thinks that anything I write or say that is remotely negative will cast a bad shadow over her and ruin her reputation in the dog-showing world—so just to emphasize that, my mother is WONDERFUL! She did an incredible job raising me and my siblings. Please hire her for all your international-dog-show-judging needs! Mum gave me so much and I will be forever grateful to her. She is the BEST!

Lots of love,
Rebel xoxo